Space Science

comet

UNIVERSE

electromagnetic
radiation

telescope

EARTH SCIENCE

A ▶ Earth's Surface
B ▶ The Changing Earth
C ▶ Earth's Waters
D ▶ Earth's Atmosphere
E ▶ Space Science

PHYSICAL SCIENCE

A ▶ Matter and Energy
B ▶ Chemical Interactions
C ▶ Motion and Forces
D ▶ Waves, Sound, and Light
E ▶ Electricity and Magnetism

LIFE SCIENCE

A ▶ Cells and Heredity
B ▶ Life Over Time
C ▶ Diversity of Living Things
D ▶ Ecology
E ▶ Human Biology

Acknowledgments: Excerpts and adaptations from *National Science Education Standards* by the National Academy of Sciences. Copyright © 1996 by the National Academy of Sciences. Reprinted with permission from the National Academies Press, Washington, D.C.

Excerpts and adaptations from *Benchmarks for Science Literacy: Project 2061.* Copyright © 1993 by the American Association for the Advancement of Science. Reprinted with permission.

ISBN: 0-618-33421-1   4 5 6 7 8 VJM 08 07 06 05

Internet Web Site: http://www.mcdougallittell.com

Science Consultants

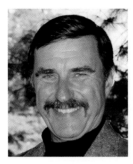

Chief Science Consultant
James Trefil, Ph.D. is the Clarence J. Robinson Professor of Physics at George Mason University. He is the author or co-author of more than 25 books, including *Science Matters* and *The Nature of Science*. Dr. Trefil is a member of the American Association for the Advancement of Science's Committee on the Public Understanding of Science and Technology. He is also a fellow of the World Economic Forum and a frequent contributor to *Smithsonian* magazine.

Rita Ann Calvo, Ph.D. is Senior Lecturer in Molecular Biology and Genetics at Cornell University, where for 12 years she also directed the Cornell Institute for Biology Teachers. Dr. Calvo is the 1999 recipient of the College and University Teaching Award from the National Association of Biology Teachers.

Kenneth Cutler, M.S. is the Education Coordinator for the Julius L. Chambers Biomedical Biotechnology Research Institute at North Carolina Central University. A former middle school and high school science teacher, he received a 1999 Presidential Award for Excellence in Science Teaching.

Instructional Design Consultants

Douglas Carnine, Ph.D. is Professor of Education and Director of the National Center for Improving the Tools of Educators at the University of Oregon. He is the author of seven books and over 100 other scholarly publications, primarily in the areas of instructional design and effective instructional strategies and tools for diverse learners. Dr. Carnine also serves as a member of the National Institute for Literacy Advisory Board.

Linda Carnine, Ph.D. consults with school districts on curriculum development and effective instruction for students struggling academically. A former teacher and school administrator, Dr. Carnine also co-authored a popular remedial reading program.

Donald Steely, Ph.D. serves as principal investigator at the Oregon Center for Applied Science (ORCAS) on federal grants for science and language arts programs. His background also includes teaching and authoring of print and multimedia programs in science, mathematics, history, and spelling.

Sam Miller, Ph.D. is a middle school science teacher and the Teacher Development Liaison for the Eugene, Oregon, Public Schools. He is the author of curricula for teaching science, mathematics, computer skills, and language arts.

Vicky Vachon, Ph.D. consults with school districts throughout the United States and Canada on improving overall academic achievement with a focus on literacy. She is also co-author of a widely used program for remedial readers.

Content Reviewers

John Beaver, Ph.D.
Ecology
Professor, Director of Science Education Center
College of Education and Human Services
Western Illinois University
Macomb, IL

Donald J. DeCoste, Ph.D.
Matter and Energy, Chemical Interactions
Chemistry Instructor
University of Illinois
Urbana-Champaign, IL

Dorothy Ann Fallows, Ph.D., MSc
Diversity of Living Things, Microbiology
Partners in Health
Boston, MA

Michael Foote, Ph.D.
The Changing Earth, Life Over Time
Associate Professor
Department of the Geophysical Sciences
The University of Chicago
Chicago, IL

Lucy Fortson, Ph.D.
Space Science
Director of Astronomy
Adler Planetarium and Astronomy Museum
Chicago, IL

Elizabeth Godrick, Ph.D.
Human Biology
Professor, CAS Biology
Boston University
Boston, MA

Isabelle Sacramento Grilo, M.S.
The Changing Earth
Lecturer, Department of the Geological Sciences
San Diego State University
San Diego, CA

David Harbster, MSc
Diversity of Living Things
Professor of Biology
Paradise Valley Community College
Phoenix, AZ

Richard D. Norris, Ph.D.
Earth's Waters
Professor of Paleobiology
Scripps Institution of Oceanography
University of California, San Diego
La Jolla, CA

Donald B. Peck, M.S.
*Motion and Forces; Waves, Sound, and Light;
Electricity and Magnetism*
Director of the Center for Science Education (retired)
Fairleigh Dickinson University
Madison, NJ

Javier Penalosa, Ph.D.
Diversity of Living Things, Plants
Associate Professor, Biology Department
Buffalo State College
Buffalo, NY

Raymond T. Pierrehumbert, Ph.D.
Earth's Atmosphere
Professor in Geophysical Sciences (Atmospheric Science)
The University of Chicago
Chicago, IL

Brian J. Skinner, Ph.D.
Earth's Surface
Eugene Higgins Professor of Geology and Geophysics
Yale University
New Haven, CT

Nancy E. Spaulding, M.S.
Earth's Surface, The Changing Earth, Earth's Waters
Earth Science Teacher (retired)
Elmira Free Academy
Elmira, NY

Steven S. Zumdahl, Ph.D.
Matter and Energy, Chemical Interactions
Professor Emeritus of Chemistry
University of Illinois
Urbana-Champaign, IL

Susan L. Zumdahl, M.S.
Matter and Energy, Chemical Interactions
Chemistry Education Specialist
University of Illinois
Urbana-Champaign, IL

Safety Consultant

Juliana Texley, Ph.D.
Former K–12 Science Teacher and School Superintendent
Boca Raton, FL

English Language Advisor

Judy Lewis, M.A.
Director, State and Federal Programs for reading proficiency
and high risk populations
Rancho Cordova, CA

Teacher Panel Members

Carol Arbour
Tallmadge Middle School,
Tallmadge, OH

Patty Belcher
Goodrich Middle School,
Akron, OH

Gwen Broestl
Luis Munoz Marin Middle School,
Cleveland, OH

Al Brofman
Tehipite Middle School,
Fresno, CA

John Cockrell
Clinton Middle School,
Columbus, OH

Jenifer Cox
Sylvan Middle School,
Citrus Heights, CA

Linda Culpepper
Martin Middle School,
Charlotte, NC

Kathleen Ann DeMatteo
Margate Middle School,
Margate, FL

Melvin Figueroa
New River Middle School,
Ft. Lauderdale, FL

Doretha Grier
Kannapolis Middle School,
Kannapolis, NC

Robert Hood
Alexander Hamilton Middle School,
Cleveland, OH

Scott Hudson
Covedale Elementary School,
Cincinnati, OH

Loretta Langdon
Princeton Middle School,
Princeton, NC

Carlyn Little
Glades Middle School,
Miami, FL

Ann Marie Lynn
Amelia Earhart Middle School,
Riverside, CA

James Minogue
Lowe's Grove Middle School,
Durham, NC

Joann Myers
Buchanan Middle School,
Tampa, FL

Barbara Newell
Charles Evans Hughes Middle School,
Long Beach, CA

Anita Parker
Kannapolis Middle School,
Kannapolis, NC

Greg Pirolo
Golden Valley Middle School,
San Bernardino, CA

Laura Pottmyer
Apex Middle School,
Apex, NC

Lynn Prichard
Booker T. Washington Middle Magnet
School, Tampa, FL

Jacque Quick
Walter Williams High School,
Burlington, NC

Robert Glenn Reynolds
Hillman Middle School,
Youngstown, OH

Stacy Rinehart
Lufkin Road Middle School,
Apex, NC

Theresa Short
Abbott Middle School,
Fayetteville, NC

Rita Slivka
Alexander Hamilton Middle School,
Cleveland, OH

Marie Sofsak
B F Stanton Middle School,
Alliance, OH

Nancy Stubbs
Sweetwater Union Unified School District,
Chula Vista, CA

Sharon Stull
Quail Hollow Middle School,
Charlotte, NC

Donna Taylor
Okeeheelee Middle School,
West Palm Beach, FL

Sandi Thompson
Harding Middle School,
Lakewood, OH

Lori Walker
Audubon Middle School & Magnet Center,
Los Angeles, CA

Teacher Lab Evaluators

Andrew Boy
W.E.B. DuBois Academy,
Cincinnati, OH

Jill Brimm-Byrne
Albany Park Academy,
Chicago, IL

Gwen Broestl
Luis Munoz Marin Middle School,
Cleveland, OH

Al Brofman
Tehipite Middle School,
Fresno, CA

Michael A. Burstein
The Rashi School,
Newton, MA

Trudi Coutts
Madison Middle School,
Naperville, IL

Jenifer Cox
Sylvan Middle School,
Citrus Heights, CA

Larry Cwik
Madison Middle School,
Naperville, IL

Jennifer Donatelli
Kennedy Junior High School,
Lisle, IL

Melissa Dupree
Lakeside Middle School,
Evans, GA

Carl Fechko
Luis Munoz Marin Middle School,
Cleveland, OH

Paige Fullhart
Highland Middle School,
Libertyville, IL

Sue Hood
Glen Crest Middle School,
Glen Ellyn, IL

William Luzader
Plymouth Community Intermediate School,
Plymouth, MA

Ann Min
Beardsley Middle School,
Crystal Lake, IL

Aileen Mueller
Kennedy Junior High School,
Lisle, IL

Nancy Nega
Churchville Middle School,
Elmhurst, IL

Oscar Newman
Sumner Math and Science Academy,
Chicago, IL

Lynn Prichard
Booker T. Washington Middle Magnet
School, Tampa, FL

Jacque Quick
Walter Williams High School,
Burlington, NC

Stacy Rinehart
Lufkin Road Middle School,
Apex, NC

Seth Robey
Gwendolyn Brooks Middle School,
Oak Park, IL

Kevin Steele
Grissom Middle School,
Tinley Park, IL

eEdition

Space Science

Unit Features

SCIENTIFIC AMERICAN

1 Exploring Space   6

the BIG idea

People develop and use technology to explore and study space.

2 Earth, Moon, and Sun   40

the BIG idea

Earth and the Moon move in predictable ways as they orbit the Sun.

What would you see if you looked at the Moon with a telescope? page 40

This image shows Jupiter with one of its large moons. How big are these objects compared with Earth? page 76

3 Our Solar System

76

4 Stars, Galaxies, and the Universe

112

Handbooks and Resources

R1

Features

Visual Highlights

Internet Resources @ ClassZone.com

INVESTIGATIONS AND ACTIVITIES

Standards and Benchmarks

Each chapter in **Space Science** covers some of the learning goals that are described in the *National Science Education Standards* (NSES) and the Project 2061 Benchmarks for Science Literacy. Selected content and skill standards are shown below in shortened form. The following National Science Education Standards are covered on pages xii-xxvii, in Frontiers in Science, and in Timelines in Science, as well as in chapter features and laboratory investigations: Understandings About Scientific Inquiry (A.9), Understandings About Science and Technology (E.6), Science and Technology in Society (F.5), Science as a Human Endeavor (G.1), Nature of Science (G.2), and History of Science (G.3).

Content Standards

1 Exploring Space

National Science Education Standards

A.9.d	Technology allows scientists to be more accurate and to use data.
B.3.f	Energy from the Sun has a range of wavelengths, including visible light, infrared radiation, and ultraviolet radiation.
F.5.c	Technology influences society through its products and processes. Technology influences the quality of life and the ways people act.

Project 2061 Benchmarks

3.A.2	Technology is essential in order to access outer space and other remote locations, to collect, use, and share data, and to communicate.
4.A.1	• The Sun is a star in a disk-shaped galaxy. • Galaxies contain many billions of stars. • The universe contains many billions of galaxies.
10.A.2	Telescopes reveal that • there are many more stars than are evident to the unaided eye • the surface of the Moon has many craters and mountains • the Sun has dark spots • Jupiter and some other planets have their own moons

2 Earth, Moon, and Sun

National Science Education Standards

D.3.b	The regular and predictable motions of objects in the solar system explain such phenomena as the day, the year, phases of the Moon, and eclipses.
D.3.c	Gravity holds us to Earth's surface and explains the phenomena of the tides.
D.3.d	Seasons result from varying amounts of the Sun's energy hitting the surface due to the tilt of Earth's axis and the length of the day.

Project 2061 Benchmarks

4.B.4	Seasons occur due to the intensity of sunlight on different parts of Earth, which changes over the year because • Earth turns daily on its axis • Earth orbits the Sun yearly • Earth's axis is tilted with respect to Earth's orbit
4.B.5	Phases of the Moon occur because the Moon's orbit changes the amount of the sunlit part of the Moon that can be seen from Earth.
4.G.2	The Sun's gravitational pull holds Earth in its orbit, just as Earth's gravitational pull holds the Moon in orbit.

③ Our Solar System

National Science Education Standards

D.1.a | Landforms are the result of a combination of forces, including crustal deformation, volcanic eruption, weathering, and erosion.

D.2.a | Earth processes include changes in atmospheric conditions and occasional events such as the impact of a comet or asteroid.

D.3.a | The Sun is the central and largest body in a system that includes nine planets and their moons and smaller objects, such as asteroids and comets.

Project 2061 Benchmarks

4.A.3 | Nine planets that vary in size, composition, and surface features orbit the Sun in nearly circular orbits. Some planets have rings and a variety of moons. Some planets and moons show signs of geological activity.

4.A.4 | Chunks of rock that orbit the Sun sometimes impact Earth's atmosphere and sometimes reach Earth's surface. Other chunks of rock and ice produce long, illuminated tails when they pass close to the Sun.

④ Stars, Galaxies, and the Universe

National Science Education Standards

B.3.a | Energy is associated with heat, light, electricity, motion, sound, nuclei, and the nature of a chemical. Energy is transferred in many ways.

G.2.a | Scientists use observations, experiments, and models to test their explanations.

G.2.b | All scientific ideas are subject to change. Scientists change their ideas when they find evidence that does not match their existing explanations. However, most major ideas in science have a lot of experimental and observational confirmation and are not likely to change much in the future.

Project 2061 Benchmarks

4.A.2 | Light takes time to travel, so distant objects seen from Earth appear as they were long ago. It takes light
• a few minutes to reach Earth from the Sun, the closest star
• a few years to reach Earth from the next-nearest stars
• several billion years to reach Earth from very distant galaxies
A fast rocket would take thousands of years to reach the star nearest the Sun.

11.B.1 | Models are often used to think about processes that cannot be observed directly, changed deliberately, or examined safely.

Process and Skill Standards

National Science Education Standards

A.2 | Design and conduct a scientific investigation.

A.3 | Use appropriate tools and techniques to gather and interpret data.

A.4 | Use evidence to describe, predict, explain, and model.

A.5 | Use critical thinking to find relationships between results and interpretations.

A.7 | Communicate procedures, results, and conclusions.

A.8 | Use mathematics in scientific inquiry.

F.4.b | Understand the risks associated with natural hazards.

Project 2061 Benchmarks

1.B.1 | Design an investigation in which you
• collect relevant evidence
• reason logically
• use imagination to devise hypotheses

11.A.2 | Think about things as systems by looking for the ways each part relates to others.

12.B.2 | Use and compare numbers in equivalent forms such as decimals and percents.

12.B.9 | Express numbers like 100, 1,000, and 1,000,000 as powers of 10.

12.D.1 | Use tables and graphs to organize information and identify relationships.

12.E.4 | Recognize more than one way to interpret a given set of findings.

Introducing Earth Science

Scientists are curious. Since ancient times, they have been asking and answering questions about the world around them. Scientists are also very suspicious of the answers they get. They carefully collect evidence and test their answers many times before accepting an idea as correct.

In this book you will see how scientific knowledge keeps growing and changing as scientists ask new questions and rethink what was known before. The following sections will help get you started.

What Is Earth Science?

Earth science is the study of Earth's interior, its rocks and soil, its atmosphere, its oceans, and outer space. For many years, scientists studied each of these topics separately. They learned many important things. More recently, however, scientists have looked more and more at the connections among the different parts of Earth—its oceans, atmosphere, living things, and rocks and soil. Scientists have also been learning more about other planets in our solar system, as well as stars and galaxies far away. Through these studies they have learned much about Earth and its place in the universe.

The text and pictures in this book will help you learn key concepts and important facts about earth science. A variety of activities will help you investigate these concepts. As you learn, it helps to have a big picture of earth science as a framework for this new information. The four unifying principles listed below will give you this big picture. Read the next few pages to get an overview of each of these principles and a sense of why they are so important.

- **Heat energy inside Earth and radiation from the Sun provide energy for Earth's processes.**

- **Physical forces, such as gravity, affect the movement of all matter on Earth and throughout the universe.**

- **Matter and energy move among Earth's rocks and soil, atmosphere, waters, and living things.**

- **Earth has changed over time and continues to change.**

Each chapter begins with a big idea. Keep in mind that each big idea relates to one or more of the unifying principles.

Heat energy inside Earth and radiation from the Sun provide energy for Earth's processes.

The lava pouring out of this volcano in Hawaii is liquid rock that was melted by heat energy under Earth's surface. Another, much more powerful energy source constantly bombards Earth's surface with energy, heating the air around you, and keeping the oceans from freezing over. This energy source is the Sun. Everything that moves or changes on Earth gets its energy either from the Sun or from the inside of our planet.

What It Means

You are always surrounded by different forms of energy, such as heat energy or light. **Energy** is the ability to cause change. All of Earth's processes need energy to occur. A process is a set of changes that leads to a particular result. For example, **evaporation** is the process by which liquid changes into gas. A puddle on a sidewalk dries up through the process of evaporation. The energy needed for the puddle to dry up comes from the Sun.

Heat Energy Inside Earth

Underneath the cool surface layer of rock, Earth's interior is so hot that the solid rock there is able to flow very slowly—a few centimeters each year. In a process called **convection,** hot material rises, cools, then sinks until it is heated enough to rise again. Convection of hot rock carries heat energy up to Earth's surface, where it provides the energy to build mountains, cause earthquakes, and make volcanoes erupt.

Radiation from the Sun

Earth receives energy from the Sun as **radiation**—energy that travels across distances in the form of certain types of waves. Visible light is one type of radiation. Radiation from the Sun heats Earth's surface, making bright summer days hot. Different parts of Earth receive different amounts of radiation at different times of the year, causing seasons. Energy from the Sun also causes winds to blow, ocean currents to flow, and water to move from the ground to the atmosphere and back again.

Why It's Important

Understanding Earth's processes makes it possible to

- know what types of crops to plant and when to plant them
- know when to watch for dangerous weather, such as tornadoes and hurricanes
- predict a volcano's eruption in time for people to leave the area

Physical forces, such as gravity, affect the movement of all matter on Earth and throughout the universe.

The universe is everything that exists, and everything in the universe is governed by the same physical laws. The same laws govern the stars shown in this picture and the page on which the picture is printed.

What It Means

What do the stars in a galaxy, the planet Earth, and your body have in common? For one thing, they are all made of matter. **Matter** is anything that has mass and takes up space. Rocks are matter. You are matter. Even the air around you is matter. Matter is made of tiny particles called **atoms** that are too small to see through an ordinary microscope.

Everything in the universe is also affected by the same physical forces. A **force** is a push or a pull. Forces affect how matter moves everywhere in the universe.

- One force you experience every moment is **gravity,** which is the attraction, or pull, between two objects. Gravity is pulling you to Earth and Earth to you. Gravity is the force that causes objects to fall downward toward the center of Earth. Gravity is also the force that keeps objects in orbit around planets and stars.

- **Friction** is the force that resists motion between two surfaces that are pressed together. Friction can keep a rock on a hillside from sliding down to the bottom of the hill. If you lightly rub your finger across a smooth page in a book and then across a piece of sandpaper, you can feel how the different surfaces produce different frictional forces. Which is easier to do?

- There are many other forces at work on Earth and throughout the universe. For example, Earth has a magnetic field. A compass needle responds to the force exerted by Earth's magnetic field. Another example is the contact force between a rock and the ground beneath it. A contact force occurs when one object pushes or pulls on another object by touching it.

Why It's Important

Physical forces influence the movement of all matter, from the tiniest particle to you to the largest galaxy. Understanding forces allows people to

- predict how objects and materials move on Earth
- send spacecraft and equipment into space
- explain and predict the movements of Earth, the Moon, planets, and stars

Matter and energy move among Earth's rocks and soil, atmosphere, waters, and living things.

When a wolf eats a rabbit, matter and energy move from one living thing into another. When a wolf drinks water warmed by the Sun, matter and energy move from Earth's waters into one of its living things. These are just two examples of how energy and matter move among different parts of the Earth system.

What It Means

Think of Earth as a huge system, or an organized group of parts that work together. Within this system, matter and energy move among the different parts. The four major parts of Earth's system are the

- **atmosphere,** which includes all the air surrounding the solid planet
- **geosphere,** which includes all of Earth's rocks and minerals, as well as Earth's interior
- **hydrosphere,** which includes oceans, rivers, lakes, and every drop of water on or under Earth's surface
- **biosphere,** which includes all the living things on Earth

Matter in the Earth System

It's easy to see how matter moves within the Earth system. When water in the atmosphere falls as rain, it becomes part of the hydrosphere. When an animal drinks water from a puddle, the water becomes part of the biosphere. When rainwater soaks into the ground, it moves through the geosphere. As the puddle dries up, the water becomes part of the atmosphere again.

Energy in the Earth System

Most of the energy you depend on comes from the Sun and moves among the four major parts of the Earth system. Think again about the puddle that is drying up. Sunlight shines through the water and heats the soil, or geosphere, beneath the puddle. Some of this heat energy goes into the puddle, moving into the hydrosphere. As the water evaporates and becomes part of the atmosphere, it takes the energy that came from the Sun with it. The Sun provides energy for all weather and ocean currents. Without the Sun, life could not exist on Earth's surface.

Why It's Important

Understanding how matter and energy move through the Earth system makes it possible to

- predict how a temperature change in ocean water might affect the weather
- determine how clearing forests might affect rainfall
- explain where organisms on the ocean floor get energy to carry out life processes

Earth has changed over time and continues to change.

You see Earth changing all of the time. Rain turns dirt to mud, and a dry wind turns the mud to dust. Many changes are small and can take hundreds, thousands, or even millions of years to add up to much. Other changes are sudden and can destroy in minutes a house that had stood for many years.

What It Means

Events are always changing Earth's surface. Some events, such as the building or wearing away of mountains, occur over millions of years. Others, such as earthquakes, occur within seconds. A change can affect a small area or even the entire planet.

Records of Change

What was the distant past like? Think about how scientists learn about ancient people. They study what the people left behind and draw conclusions based on the evidence. In a similar way, scientists learn about Earth's past by examining the evidence they find in rock layers and by observing processes now occurring.

By observing that water breaks down rocks and carries the material away to other places, people learned that rivers can slowly carve deep valleys. Evidence from rocks and fossils along the edges of continents shows that all continents were once joined and then moved apart over time. A **fossil** is the trace of a once-living organism. Fossils also show that new types of plants and animals develop, and others, such as dinosaurs, die out.

Change Continues Today

Every year, earthquakes occur, volcanoes erupt, and rivers flood. Continents continue to move slowly. The Himalayan Mountains of Asia push a few millimeters higher. **Climate**—the long-term weather patterns of an area— may also change. Scientists are studying how changes in climates around the world might affect Earth even within this century.

Why It's Important

Understanding the changing Earth makes it possible to

- predict and prepare for events such as volcanic eruptions, landslides, floods, and climate changes
- design buildings to withstand shaking during earthquakes
- protect important environments for plants and animals

The Nature of Science

You may think of science as a body of knowledge or a collection of facts. More important, however, science is an active process that involves certain ways of looking at the world.

Scientific Habits of Mind

Scientists are curious. They ask questions. A scientist who finds an unusual rock by the side of a river would ask questions such as, "Did this rock form in this area?" or "Did this rock form elsewhere and get moved here?" Questions like these make a scientist want to investigate.

Scientists are observant. They look closely at the world around them. A scientist who studies rocks can learn a lot about a rock just by picking it up, looking at its color, and feeling how heavy it is.

Scientists are creative. They draw on what they know to form possible explanations for a pattern, an event, or an interesting phenomenon that they have observed. Then scientists put together a plan for testing their ideas.

Scientists are skeptical. Scientists don't accept an explanation or answer unless it is based on evidence and logical reasoning. They continually question their own conclusions as well as the conclusions suggested by other scientists. Scientists only trust evidence that can be confirmed by other people or other methods.

Scientists use seismographs to observe and measure vibrations that move through the ground.

This scientist is collecting a sample of melted rock from a hot lava flow in Hawaii.

Science Processes at Work

You can think of science as a continuous cycle of asking and seeking answers to questions about the world. Although there are many processes that scientists use, all scientists typically do the following:

- Observe and ask a question
- Determine what is known
- Investigate
- Interpret results
- Share results

Observe and Ask a Question

It may surprise you that asking questions is an important skill. A scientific investigation may start when a scientist asks a question. Perhaps scientists observe an event or a process that they don't understand, or perhaps answering one question leads to another.

Determine What Is Known

When beginning an inquiry, scientists find out what is already known about a question. They study results from other scientific investigations, read journals, and talk with other scientists. The scientist who is trying to figure out where an unusual rock came from will study maps that show what types of rocks are already known to be in the area where the rock was found.

Investigate

Investigating is the process of collecting evidence. Two important ways of doing this are experimenting and observing.

An **experiment** is an organized procedure to study something under controlled conditions. For example, the scientist who found the rock by the river might notice that it is lighter in color where it is chipped. The scientist might design an experiment to determine why the rock is a different color on the inside. The scientist could break off a small piece of the inside of the rock and heat it up to see if it becomes the same color as the outside. The scientist would need to use a piece of the same rock that is being studied. A different rock might react differently to heat.

A scientist may use photography to study fast events, such as multiple flashes of lightning.

Rocks, such as this one from the Moon, can be subjected to different conditions in a laboratory.

Observing is the act of noting and recording an event, characteristic, or anything else detected with an instrument or with the senses. A scientist makes observations while performing an experiment. However, some things cannot be studied using experiments. For example, streaks of light called meteors occur when small rocks from outer space hit Earth's atmosphere. A scientist might study meteors by taking pictures of the sky at a time when meteors are likely to occur.

Forming hypotheses and making predictions are two other skills involved in scientific investigations. A **hypothesis** is a tentative explanation for an observation or a scientific problem that can be tested by further investigation. For example, the scientist might make the following hypothesis about the rock from the beach:

The rock is a meteorite, which is a rock that fell to the ground from outer space. The outside of the rock changed color because it was heated up from passing through Earth's atmosphere.

A **prediction** is an expectation of what will be observed or what will happen. To test the hypothesis that the rock's outside is black because it is a meteorite, the scientist might predict that a close examination of the rock will show that it has many characteristics in common with rocks that are already known to be meteorites.

Interpret Results

As scientists investigate, they analyze their evidence, or data, and begin to draw conclusions. **Analyzing data** involves looking at the evidence gathered through observations or experiments and trying to identify any patterns that might exist in the data. Scientists often need to make additional observations or perform more experiments before they are sure of their conclusions. Many times scientists make new predictions or revise their hypotheses.

Scientists use computers to gather and interpret data.

Scientists make images such as this computer drawing of a landscape to help share their results with others.

Share Results

An important part of scientific investigation is sharing results of experiments. Scientists read and publish in journals and attend conferences to communicate with other scientists around the world. Sharing data and procedures gives scientists a way to test each others' results. They also share results with the public through newspapers, television, and other media.

The Nature of Technology

When you think of technology, you may think of cars, computers, and cell phones. Imagine having no refrigerator or radio. It's difficult to think of a world without the products of what we call technology. Technology, however, is more than just devices that make our daily activities easier. Technology is the process of using scientific knowledge to design solutions to real-world problems.

Science and Technology

Science and technology go hand in hand. Each depends upon the other. Even a device as simple as a thermometer is designed using knowledge of the ways different materials respond to changes in temperature. In turn, thermometers have allowed scientists to learn more about the world. Greater knowledge of how materials respond to changes in temperature helped engineers to build items such as refrigerators. They have also built thermometers that could be read automatically by computers. New technologies lead to new scientific knowledge and new scientific knowledge leads to even better technologies.

The Process of Technological Design

The process of technological design involves many choices. What, for example, should be done to protect the residents of an area prone to severe storms such as tornadoes and hurricanes? Build stronger homes that can withstand the winds? Try to develop a way to detect the storms long before they occur? Or learn more about hurricanes in order to find new ways to protect people from the dangers? The steps people take to solve the problem depend a great deal on what they already know about the problem as well as what can reasonably be done. As you learn about the steps in the process of technological design, think about the different choices that could be made at each step.

Identify a Need

To study hurricanes, scientists needed to know what happens inside the most dangerous parts of the storm. However, it was not safe for scientists to go near the centers of hurricanes because the winds were too strong and changed direction too fast. Scientists needed a way to measure conditions deep inside the storm without putting themselves in danger.

Design and Develop

One approach was to design a robotic probe to take the measurements. The probe and instruments needed to be strong enough to withstand the fast winds near the center of a hurricane. The scientists also needed a way to send the probe into the storm and to get the data from the instruments quickly.

Scientists designed a device called a dropsonde, which could be dropped from an airplane flying over the hurricane. A dropsonde takes measurements from deep inside the storm and radios data back to the scientists.

Test and Improve

Even good technology can usually be improved. When scientists first used dropsondes, they learned about hurricanes. They also learned what things about the dropsondes worked well and what did not. For example, the scientists wanted better ways to keep track of where the probe moved. Newer dropsondes make use of the Global Positioning System, which is a way of pinpointing any position on Earth by using satellite signals.

Using McDougal Littell Science

Reading Text and Visuals

This book is organized to help you learn. Use these boxed pointers as a path to help you learn and remember the **Big Ideas** and **Key Concepts.**

Take notes.

Use the strategies on the **Getting Ready to Learn** page.

Read the Big Idea.

As you read **Key Concepts** for the chapter, relate them to **the Big Idea.**

CHAPTER 2

Getting Ready to Learn

◀ **CONCEPT REVIEW**

- The sky seems to turn as Earth rotates.
- The motions of nearby space objects are visible from Earth.
- Light and other radiation carry information about space.

◀ **VOCABULARY REVIEW**

orbit p. 10
electromagnetic radiation p. 15
satellite p. 23
See Glossary for definitions.
force, gravity, mass

CONTENT REVIEW
CLASSZONE.COM
Review concepts and vocabulary.

▶ **TAKING NOTES**

COMBINATION NOTES

To take notes about a new concept, first make an informal outline of the information. Then make a sketch of the concept and label it so you can study it later.

VOCABULARY STRATEGY

Write each new vocabulary term in the center of a **frame game** diagram. Decide what information to frame the term with. Use examples, descriptions, pictures, or sentences in which the term is used in context. You can change the frame to fit each term.

See the Note-Taking Handbook on pages R45–R51.

SCIENCE NOTEBOOK

NOTES

Earth turns.
- It turns on an imaginary axis.
  - Poles are ends of axis.
  - Equator is halfway.
- Rotation takes 24 hours.
- Sun shines on one side only.
  - Light side is daytime.
  - Dark side is night.

north
night | day
equator
sun
south

includes north and south poles

AXIS OF ROTATION

Earth turns on its axis of rotation.

CHAPTER

2 Eart
and

the **BIG** idea

Earth and the Moon move in predictable ways as they orbit the Sun.

Key Concepts

SECTION
2.1 **Earth rotates on a tilted axis and orbits the Sun**
Learn what causes day and night and why there are seasons.

SECTION
2.2 **The Moon is Earth's natural satellite.**
Learn about the structure a motion of Earth's Moon.

SECTION
2.3 **Positions of the Sun and Moon affect Ea**
Learn about phases of th Moon, eclipses, and tides.

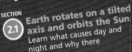
Internet Preview
CLASSZONE.COM
Chapter 2 online resources: Content Review, two Visualizations, two Resource Centers, Math Tutorial, Test Practice

Read each heading.

See how it fits into the outline of the chapter.

KEY CONCEPT

2.1 Earth rotates on a tilted axis and orbits the Sun.

Remember what you know.

Think about concepts you learned earlier and preview what you'll learn now.

◄ **BEFORE, you learned**

- Stars seem to rise, cross the sky, and set because Earth turns
- The Sun is very large and far from Earth
- Earth orbits the Sun

▶ **NOW, you will learn**

- Why Earth has day and night
- How the changing angles of sunlight produce seasons

Try the activities.

They will introduce you to science concepts.

VOCABULARY

axis of rotation p. 44
revolution p. 45
season p. 46
equinox p. 46
solstice p. 46

EXPLORE Time Zones

What time is it in Iceland right now?

PROCEDURE

① Find your location and Iceland on the map. Identify the time zone of each.

② Count the number of hours between your location and Iceland. Add or subtract that number of hours from the time on your clock.

MATERIAL
time zone map

WHAT DO YOU THINK?

- By how much is Iceland's time earlier or later than yours?
- Why are clocks set to different times?

Earth's rotation causes day and night.

When astronauts explored the Moon, they felt the Moon's gravity pulling them down. Their usual "down"—Earth—was up in the Moon's sky.

As you read this book, it is easy to tell which way is down. But is down in the same direction for a person on the other side of Earth? If you both pointed down, you would be pointing toward each other. Earth's gravity pulls objects toward the center of Earth. No matter where you stand on Earth, the direction of down will be toward Earth's center. There is no bottom or top. Up is out toward space, and down is toward the center of the planet.

As Earth turns, so do you. You keep the same position with respect to what is below your feet, but the view above your head changes.

Learn the vocabulary.

Take notes on each term.

CHECK YOUR READING In what direction does gravity pull objects near Earth?

Answer the questions.

Check Your Reading questions will help you remember what you read.

Chapter 2: **Earth, Moon, and Sun** 43 **E**

Reading Text and Visuals

Study the visuals.

- Read the title.
- Read all labels and captions.
- Figure out what the picture is showing. Notice colors, arrows, and lines.

The Electromagnetic Spectrum

The different forms of electromagnetic radiation vary in their wavelengths.

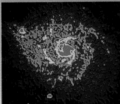

visible light

wavelength

| radio waves | microwaves | infrared | ultraviolet | x-rays | gamma rays |

Radio Waves

This image of a galaxy shows where radio waves are emitted.

Visible Light

Visible light is the only form of radiation our eyes can detect.

X-Rays

This image shows where the same galaxy emits x-rays.

READING TiP

A prism is a transparent object that is used to separate the wavelengths of light.

If you shine a flashlight through a prism, the beam of white light will separate into a range of colors called a **spectrum** (SPEHK-truhm). The colors that make up visible light are red, orange, yellow, green, blue, indigo, and violet. These are the colors in a rainbow, which appears when light spreads out as it passes through raindrops.

In a spectrum, the colors of visible light appear in the order of their wavelengths. **Wavelength** is the distance between one wave peak and the next wave peak. Red light has the longest wavelength. Violet light has the shortest.

As you can see in the illustration above, visible light is just a tiny part of a larger spectrum called the electromagnetic spectrum. The electromagnetic spectrum includes all the forms of electromagnetic radiation. Notice that the wavelength of infrared radiation is longer than the wavelength of visible light but not as long as the wavelength of microwaves or radio waves. The wavelength of ultraviolet radiation is shorter than the wavelength of visible light but not as short as the wavelength of x-rays or gamma rays.

CHECK YOUR READING How is visible light different from other forms of electromagnetic radiation?

Read one paragraph at a time.

Look for a topic sentence that explains the main idea of the paragraph. Figure out how the details relate to that idea. One paragraph might have several important ideas; you may have to reread to understand.

Answer the questions.

Check Your Reading questions will help you remember what you read.

16 Unit: **Space Science**

Doing Labs

To understand science, you have to see it in action. Doing labs helps you understand how things really work.

① Read the entire lab first.

② Form a hypothesis.

③ Follow the procedure.

④ Record the data.

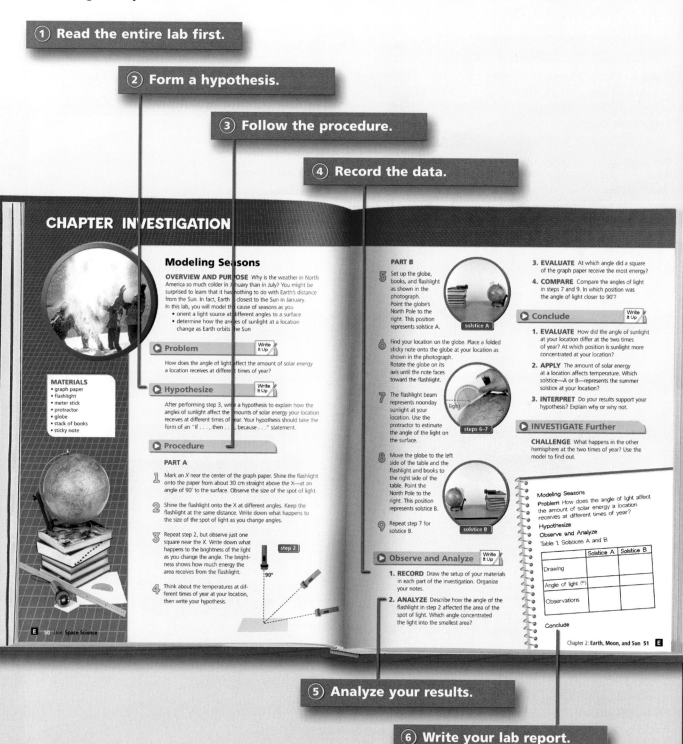

CHAPTER INVESTIGATION

Modeling Seasons

OVERVIEW AND PURPOSE Why is the weather in North America so much colder in January than in July? You might be surprised to learn that it has nothing to do with Earth's distance from the Sun. In fact, Earth is closest to the Sun in January. In this lab, you will model the cause of seasons as you
• orient a light source at different angles to a surface
• determine how the angles of sunlight at a location change as Earth orbits the Sun

▶ **Problem** — Write It Up

How does the angle of light affect the amount of solar energy a location receives at different times of year?

▶ **Hypothesize** — Write It Up

After performing step 3, write a hypothesis to explain how the angles of sunlight affect the amounts of solar energy your location receives at different times of year. Your hypothesis should take the form of an "If . . . , then . . . , because . . ." statement.

▶ **Procedure**

PART A

1. Mark an X near the center of the graph paper. Shine the flashlight onto the paper from about 30 cm straight above the X—at an angle of 90° to the surface. Observe the size of the spot of light.

2. Shine the flashlight onto the X at different angles. Keep the flashlight at the same distance. Write down what happens to the size of the spot of light as you change angles.

3. Repeat step 2, but observe just one square near the X. Write down what happens to the brightness of the light as you change the angle. The brightness shows how much energy the area receives from the flashlight.

4. Think about the temperatures at different times of year at your location, then write your hypothesis.

MATERIALS
• graph paper
• flashlight
• meter stick
• protractor
• globe
• stack of books
• sticky note

step 2 90°

E 50 Unit: Space Science

PART B

5. Set up the globe, books, and flashlight as shown in the photograph. Point the globe's North Pole to the right. This position represents solstice A. *solstice A*

6. Find your location on the globe. Place a folded sticky note onto the globe at your location as shown in the photograph. Rotate the globe on its axis until the note faces toward the flashlight.

7. The flashlight beam represents noonday sunlight at your location. Use the protractor to estimate the angle of the light on the surface. *light, steps 6–7*

8. Move the globe to the left side of the table and the flashlight and books to the right side of the table. Point the North Pole to the right. This position represents solstice B. *solstice B*

9. Repeat step 7 for solstice B.

▶ **Observe and Analyze** — Write It Up

1. **RECORD** Draw the setup of your materials in each part of the investigation. Organize your notes.

2. **ANALYZE** Describe how the angle of the flashlight in step 2 affected the area of the spot of light. Which angle concentrated the light into the smallest area?

3. **EVALUATE** At which angle did a square of the graph paper receive the most energy?

4. **COMPARE** Compare the angles of light in steps 7 and 9. In which position was the angle of light closer to 90°?

▶ **Conclude** — Write It Up

1. **EVALUATE** How did the angle of sunlight at your location differ at the two times of year? At which position is sunlight more concentrated at your location?

2. **APPLY** The amount of solar energy at a location affects temperature. Which solstice—A or B—represents the summer solstice at your location?

3. **INTERPRET** Do your results support your hypothesis? Explain why or why not.

▶ **INVESTIGATE Further**

CHALLENGE What happens in the other hemisphere at the two times of year? Use the model to find out.

Modeling Seasons
Problem How does the angle of light affect the amount of solar energy a location receives at different times of year?
Hypothesize
Observe and Analyze
Table 1. Solstices A and B

	Solstice A	Solstice B
Drawing		
Angle of light (°)		
Observations		

Conclude

Chapter 2: Earth, Moon, and Sun 51 E

⑤ Analyze your results.

⑥ Write your lab report.

Using Technology

The Internet is a great source of information about up-to-date science.
The ClassZone Website and SciLinks have exciting sites for you to
explore. Video clips and simulations can make science come alive.

Look for red banners.

Go to **ClassZone.com** to see
simulations, visualizations,
resources centers, and
content review.

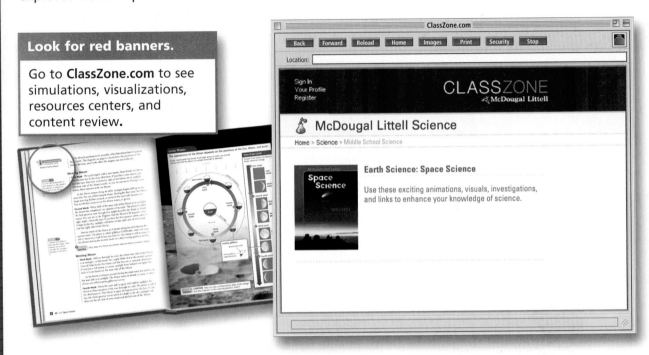

Watch the videos.

See science at work in
the **Scientific American
Frontiers** video.

Look up SciLinks.

Go to **scilinks.org** to explore
the topic.

Space Probes **Code: MDL057**

Space Science
Contents Overview

Unit Features

1 Exploring Space   6

the **BIG** idea

People develop and use technology
to explore and study space.

2 Earth, Moon, and Sun   40

the **BIG** idea

Earth and the Moon move in predictable
ways as they orbit the Sun.

3 Our Solar System   76

the **BIG** idea

Planets and other objects form a
system around our Sun.

4 Stars, Galaxies, and the Universe   112

the **BIG** idea

Our Sun is one of billions of stars
in one of billions of galaxies in the
universe.

DANGER
from the Sky

How can astronomers find out whether a large object from space is going to strike our planet?

SCIENTIFIC AMERICAN FRONTIERS

View the video segment "Big Dish" to learn how astronomers use the largest radio telescope on Earth.

The streak of light in the photograph above was produced by a tiny particle from space burning up in Earth's atmosphere. Shown to the left is Barringer Crater in Arizona.

Collisions in Space

In the summer of 1994, telescopes all over the world were aimed at Jupiter. For the first time in history, astronomers had warning of a collision in space. Jupiter's gravity had split a comet named Shoemaker-Levy 9 into more than 20 large pieces. As the rocky objects collided with Jupiter's atmosphere, they exploded spectacularly.

Astronomers have found evidence of impacts closer to home. The craters that cover much of the Moon's surface were caused by collisions with space objects billions of years ago. In 1953 an astronomer even caught on film the bright flash of an object hitting the Moon. Other solid bodies in space also have impact craters. Little evidence of impacts remains on Earth because its surface is always changing. Fewer than 200 craters are still visible.

Earth's atmosphere protects us from collisions with small objects, which burn up in the air. However, when a large object strikes Earth, the atmosphere can spread the effects of the impact far beyond the crater. A large collision may throw dust high into the air, where it can be carried around the globe. The dust can block sunlight for months and sharply lower global temperatures.

About 65 million years ago, a large space object struck Earth. The dust from this collision can be found around the world in a layer of rock that was forming at the time. At about the same time, most species of organisms died out, including the dinosaurs. Many scientists think that the collision caused this global devastation.

The Risk of a Major Collision

When will the next space object hit Earth? A collision is probably occurring as you read this sentence. Tiny particles hit Earth's atmosphere all the time. Some of these particles have enough mass to make it through the atmosphere. Objects that reach Earth's surface are called meteorites. Most meteorites splash harmlessly into the ocean or hit unpopulated areas. Every few years a meteorite damages a home or other property. However, there is no known case of a meteorite's killing a person.

Collisions that cause widespread damage happen less often because the solar system contains fewer large objects. In 1908 a large object from space exploded above a remote region of Russia. The explosion knocked down trees across an area more than half the size of Rhode Island. Even this impact was small in comparison with major collisions that affect the entire world. Such collisions happen on average about twice every million years. Events that kill off many species occur even less often.

Tracking Asteroids

Although Earth is unlikely to have a major collision with a space object anytime soon, the danger is too great to ignore. Scientists are using telescopes to find large, rocky space objects called asteroids. After locating an asteroid, they use computer models to predict its path centuries into the future. Scientists expect that by 2008 they will have found almost all of the asteroids that could cause global devastation on Earth.

Locating objects that may threaten life on Earth is just the first step. Scientists also want to

SCIENTIFIC AMERICAN FRONTIERS

View the "Big Dish" segment of your *Scientific American Frontiers* video to learn how astronomers are using the giant Arecibo radio telescope to explore the universe.

IN THIS SCENE FROM THE VIDEO ▶

You see a close-up of the Arecibo telescope's dome and one of its antennas.

EXPLORING ASTEROIDS An asteroid's crashing into Earth may seem like the subject of a science fiction movie. Yet asteroids pose a real danger to humans. Some asteroids could cause widespread destruction if they struck our planet.

Astronomers are tracking these asteroids to determine how close they will pass to Earth in the future.

Asteroids are too faint to be viewed clearly with optical telescopes on Earth. However, radio telescopes can provide detailed images of asteroids. Inside the dome of the Arecibo telescope is the world's most powerful radar transmitter. The transmitter can bounce a beam of radio waves off the telescope's dish to reach an asteroid millions of miles away. The telescope picks up returning signals, which are converted into images.

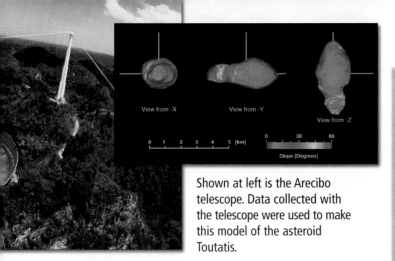

Shown at left is the Arecibo telescope. Data collected with the telescope were used to make this model of the asteroid Toutatis.

learn about the characteristics of asteroids. The Arecibo telescope in Puerto Rico is an important tool for studying asteroids. The largest radio dish in the world, it allows scientists to determine the motions and shapes of asteroids. Computer models and tests with real materials provide additional information about the mass, materials, and structure of each asteroid.

If scientists ever find an asteroid headed toward Earth, these studies may help us change the asteroid's course safely. Remember the comet that struck Jupiter in many pieces? If an asteroid broke apart before reaching Earth, pieces hitting different locations could cause even more dam-age than a single impact. Before using a bomb or laser to change the course of an asteroid, govern-ments must make sure that the asteroid will not break apart. Fortunately, scientists would have decades to study a dangerous asteroid and figure out what action to take.

UNANSWERED Questions

Scientists are learning about the risk of an aster-oid's colliding with Earth. The more we learn about collisions in space, the more questions we have.

- What methods can be used to change the course of an asteroid that threatens Earth?

- How can we make sure that an asteroid will not break apart because of our efforts to change its course?

- How many smaller but still dangerous objects may be headed toward Earth?

UNIT PROJECTS

As you study this unit, work alone or with a group on one of these projects.

Observe the Sky

Choose a space object or part of the distant sky to observe over a month. Keep an observation journal of what you see and think.

- Pay special attention to any changes relative to other objects in the sky.

- Look up information or construct tools to help you observe.

- Copy your best drawings for a display board. Explain your observations.

Multimedia Presentation

The Arecibo telescope is not used only for studying asteroids. Prepare a multimedia presentation on other research that is being carried out with the giant radio telescope.

- Find information about the research from Internet sites and other sources.

- Prepare both audio and visual compo-nents for your presentation.

Map a Space Object

Use a large potato to represent a newly explored space object. Draw lines of latitude and longitude. Then identify features, and make a flat map.

- Use roller-ball pens to mark poles, an equator, and lines of longitude and lati-tude. Try not to pierce the potato's skin.

- Do the potato's eyes seem like craters or volcanoes? Decide how to name the different types of features.

- Make a flat map of the space object.

CAREER CENTER
CLASSZONE.COM

Learn about careers in astronomy.

CHAPTER 1

Exploring Space

the **BIG** idea

People develop and use technology to explore and study space.

Key Concepts

SECTION
1.1 **Some space objects are visible to the human eye.**
Learn about views of space from Earth and about the arrangement of the universe.

SECTION
1.2 **Telescopes allow us to study space from Earth.**
Learn how astronomers gather information about space from different kinds of radiation.

SECTION
1.3 **Spacecraft help us explore beyond Earth.**
Learn how astronauts and instruments provide information about space.

SECTION
1.4 **Space exploration benefits society.**
Learn about the benefits of space exploration.

Internet Preview

CLASSZONE.COM

Chapter 1 online resources: Content Review, Simulation, Visualization, two Resource Centers, Math Tutorial, Test Practice

What challenges must be overcome in space exploration?

EXPLORE (the **BIG** idea)

Why Does the Sun Appear to Move Around Earth?

Stand in front of a floor lamp, and turn around slowly. Notice how the lamp moves within your field of vision.

Observe and Think Why did the lamp seem to move?

What Colors Are in Sunlight?

In bright sunlight, hold a clear plastic pen over a box. Move the pen until a rainbow pattern appears.

Observe and Think What colors did you see? What might have caused them to appear?

Internet Activity: Universe

Go to **ClassZone.com** to simulate moving through different levels of scale in the universe.

Observe and Think How much of the universe could you see without a telescope?

NSTA scilinks.org SCI*LINKS*

Space Probes **Code: MDL057**

Getting Ready to Learn

◀ CONCEPT REVIEW

- There are more stars in the sky than anyone can easily count.
- Telescopes magnify the appearance of distant objects in the sky.
- Once an invention exists, people are likely to think up new ways of using it.

◀ VOCABULARY REVIEW

See Glossary for definitions.

data

energy

gravity

technology

 CONTENT REVIEW
CLASSZONE.COM
Review concepts and vocabulary.

▶ TAKING NOTES

MAIN IDEA WEB

Write each new blue heading, or main idea, in the center box. In the boxes around it, take notes about important terms and details that relate to the main idea.

VOCABULARY STRATEGY

Think about a vocabulary term as a **magnet word** diagram. Write the other terms or ideas related to that term around it.

See the Note-Taking Handbook on pages R45–R51.

SCIENCE NOTEBOOK

The constellations change position in the night sky as Earth rotates.

Polaris is located straight over the North Pole.

The sky seems to turn as Earth rotates.

Polaris can help you figure out direction and location.

ORBIT

path around another object

influence of gravity

Moon orbits Earth

planets orbit Sun

space telescopes

satellites

KEY CONCEPT

Some space objects are visible to the human eye.

◀ BEFORE, you learned

- Earth is one of nine planets that orbit the Sun
- The Moon orbits Earth
- Earth turns on its axis every 24 hours

▶ NOW, you will learn

- How the universe is arranged
- How stars form patterns in the sky
- How the motions of bodies in space appear from Earth

VOCABULARY

orbit p. 10
solar system p. 10
galaxy p. 10
universe p. 10
constellation p. 12

EXPLORE Distance

How far is the Moon from Earth?

PROCEDURE

(1) Tie one end of the string around the middle of the tennis ball. The tennis ball will represent Earth.

(2) Wrap the string 9.5 times around the tennis ball, and make a mark on the string at that point. Wrap the aluminum foil into a ball around the mark. The foil ball will represent the Moon.

(3) Stretch out the string to put the model Moon and Earth at the right distance compared to their sizes.

MATERIALS

- tennis ball
- aluminum foil (5 cm strip)
- string (250 cm)
- felt marker

WHAT DO YOU THINK?

- How does the scale model compare with your previous idea of the distance between Earth and the Moon?
- How many Earths do you estimate would fit between Earth and the Moon?

We see patterns in the universe.

MAIN IDEA WEB
Record details about patterns in space.

For most of history, people had very limited knowledge of space. They saw planets and stars as points of light in the night sky. However, they did not know how far those bodies were from Earth or from each other. Early observers made guesses about planets and stars on the basis of their appearance and the ways they seemed to move in the sky. Different peoples around the world connected the patterns they saw in the sky with stories about imaginary beings.

We still have much to learn about the universe. Within the last few hundred years, however, new tools and scientific theories have greatly increased our knowledge. In this chapter you will learn about the arrangement of planets and stars. You will also learn about the ways in which astronomers explore and study space.

Arrangement of the Universe

If you look up at the sky on a clear night, you will see only a tiny fraction of the planets and stars that exist. The number of objects in the universe and the distances between them are greater than most people can imagine. Yet these objects are not spread around randomly. Gravity causes objects in space to be grouped together in different ways.

The images on page 11 show some basic structures in the universe. Like a camera lens zooming out, the images provide views of space at different levels of size.

READING TIP

The word *orbit* can be a noun or a verb.

1 Earth Our planet's diameter is about 13,000 kilometers (8000 mi). This is almost four times the diameter of the Moon, which orbits Earth. An **orbit** is the path of an object in space as it moves around another object because of gravity.

2 Solar System Earth and eight other major planets orbit the Sun. The Sun, the planets, and various smaller bodies make up the **solar system.** The Sun is about 100 times greater in diameter than Earth. You could fit more than 4000 bodies the size of the Sun between the Sun and the solar system's outermost planet at its average distance from the Sun. The Sun is one of countless stars in space. Astronomers have detected planets orbiting some of these other stars.

3 The Milky Way Our solar system and the stars you can see with your bare eyes are part of a galaxy called the Milky Way. A **galaxy** is a group of millions or billions of stars held together by their own gravity. If the solar system were the size of a penny, the Milky Way would stretch from Chicago to Dallas. Most stars in the Milky Way are so far away that our galaxy appears to us as a hazy band of light.

4 The Universe The **universe** is everything—space and all the matter and energy in it. The Milky Way is just one of many billions of galaxies in the universe. These galaxies extend in all directions.

Astronomers study space at each of these different levels. Some focus on planets in the solar system. Other astronomers study distant galaxies. To learn how the universe formed, astronomers even study the smallest particles that make up all matter.

CHECK YOUR READING What is the relationship between the solar system and the Milky Way?

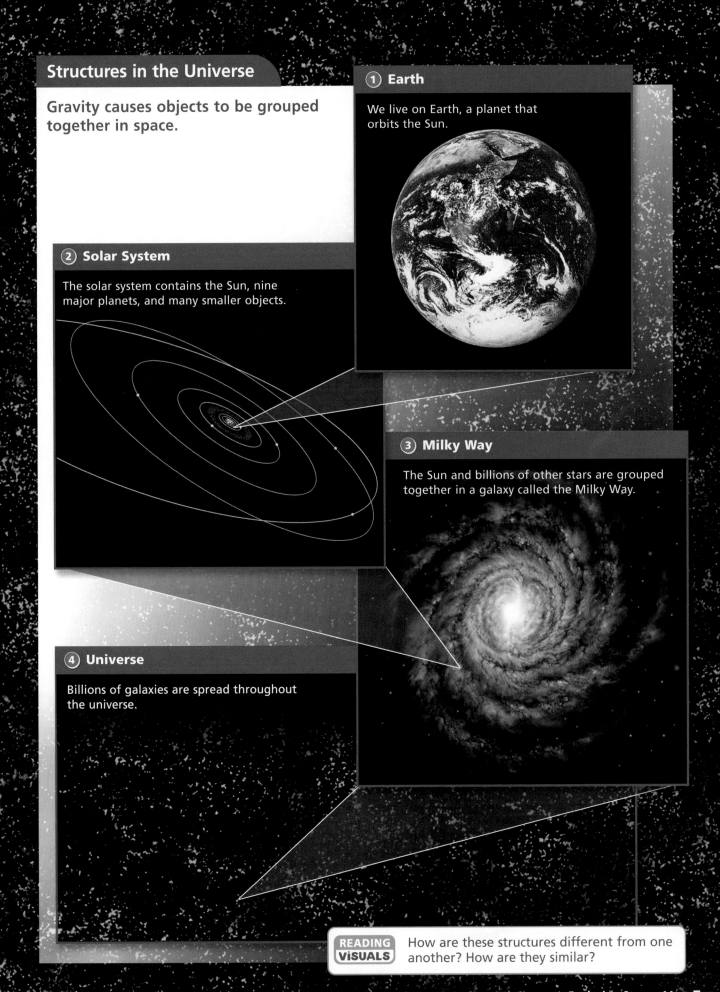

Structures in the Universe

Gravity causes objects to be grouped together in space.

① **Earth**

We live on Earth, a planet that orbits the Sun.

② **Solar System**

The solar system contains the Sun, nine major planets, and many smaller objects.

③ **Milky Way**

The Sun and billions of other stars are grouped together in a galaxy called the Milky Way.

④ **Universe**

Billions of galaxies are spread throughout the universe.

READING VISUALS How are these structures different from one another? How are they similar?

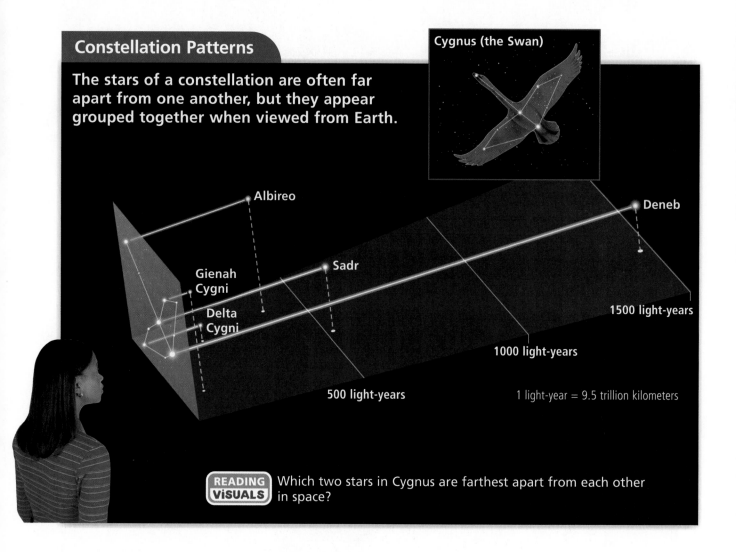

Constellation Patterns

The stars of a constellation are often far apart from one another, but they appear grouped together when viewed from Earth.

Cygnus (the Swan)

Albireo

Gienah Cygni

Sadr

Delta Cygni

Deneb

1500 light-years

1000 light-years

500 light-years

1 light-year = 9.5 trillion kilometers

READING VISUALS Which two stars in Cygnus are farthest apart from each other in space?

Constellations

If you want to find a particular place in the United States, it helps to know the name of the state it is in. Astronomers use a similar system to describe the locations of objects in the sky. They have divided the sky into 88 areas named for the constellations.

A **constellation** is a group of stars that form a pattern in the sky. In the constellation Cygnus, for example, a group of bright stars form the shape of a flying swan. Any other objects in that area of the sky, such as galaxies, are said to be located in Cygnus, even if they are not parts of the swan pattern. The ancient Greeks named many of the constellations for animals and imaginary beings.

Unlike the planets in the solar system, the stars in a constellation are usually not really close to each other. They seem to be grouped together when viewed from Earth. But as the illustration above shows, you would not see the same pattern in the stars if you viewed them from another angle.

CHECK YOUR READING What relationship exists among the stars in a constellation?

VISUALIZATION
CLASSZONE.COM

View images of the night sky taken throughout the year.

The sky seems to turn as Earth rotates.

You cannot see all of the constellations at once, because Earth blocks half of space from your view. However, you can see a parade of constellations each night as Earth rotates. As some constellations slowly come into view over the eastern horizon, others pass high in the sky above you, and still others set at the western horizon. Throughout the ages, many peoples have observed these changes and used them to help in navigation and measuring time.

If you extended the North Pole into space, it would point almost exactly to a star called Polaris, or the North Star. If you were standing at the North Pole, Polaris would be directly over your head. As Earth rotates through the night, the stars close to Polaris seem to move in circles around it. Although not the brightest star in the sky, Polaris is fairly bright and easy to find. You can use Polaris to figure out direction and location.

The stars in this image were photographed over several hours to show how they move across the night sky.

 CHECK YOUR READING What causes constellations to change positions during the night?

INVESTIGATE Constellation Positions

How does time of day affect the positions of constellations?

PROCEDURE

1. Cut out both diagrams on the Constellation Wheel Sheet and assemble them as shown.

2. Rotate the wheel so that the current month is aligned with 9 P.M. Observe the positions of the constellations.

3. Align the current month with other times to determine how the positions of the constellations change during the night.

WHAT DO YOU THINK?

- How do the positions of the constellations change during the night?

- In which direction does the northern sky seem to turn?

CHALLENGE Earth's rotation makes the sky seem to turn. What does the model tell you about the direction of Earth's rotation?

SKILL FOCUS
Analyzing

MATERIALS
- Constellation Wheel Sheet
- scissors
- brass fastener

TIME
20 minutes

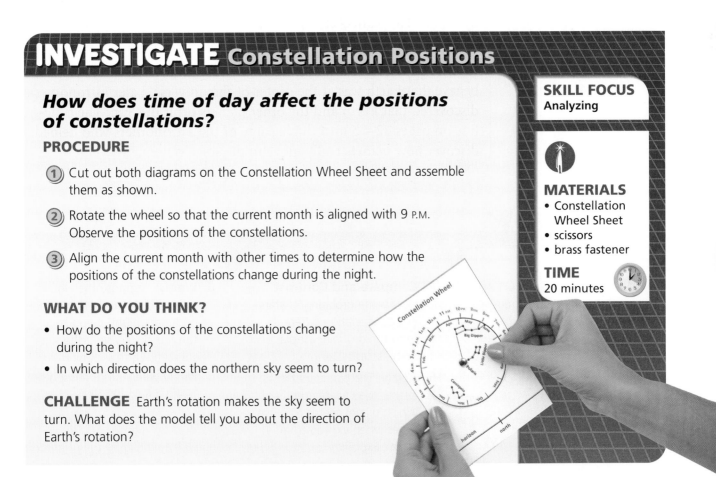

The movements of planets and other nearby objects are visible from Earth.

A jet plane travels at a greater speed and altitude than a bird. Yet if a bird and a plane flew overhead at the same time, you might think that the bird was faster. You would have this impression because the farther away a moving object is from you, the less it seems to move.

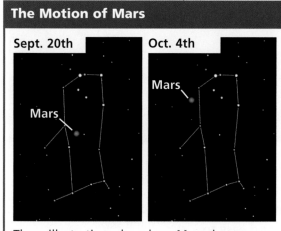

The Motion of Mars

Sept. 20th

Mars

Oct. 4th

Mars

These illustrations show how Mars changes positions in the constellation Gemini over a period of two weeks.

Stars are always moving, but they are so far away that you cannot see their movements. Observers have seen the same constellation patterns for thousands of years. Only over a much longer period does the motion of stars gradually change constellation patterns.

By contrast, the Moon moves across the star background a distance equal to its width every hour as it orbits Earth. The Moon is our closest neighbor. The planets are farther away, but you can see their gradual movements among the constellations over a period of weeks or months.

Planet comes from a Greek word that means "wanderer." Ancient Greek astronomers used this term because they noticed that planets move among the constellations. It is easiest to see the movements of Venus and Mars, the two planets closest to Earth. They change their positions in the sky from night to night.

The apparent movement of the sky led early astronomers to believe that Earth was at the center of the universe. Later astronomers discovered that Earth and the other planets orbit the Sun. The time-line on pages 72–75 introduces some of the astronomers who helped discover how planets really move in the solar system.

1.1 Review

KEY CONCEPTS

1. What are the basic structures in which objects are grouped together in space?
2. What is a constellation?
3. How does Earth's rotation affect our view of stars?

CRITICAL THINKING

4. **Compare and Contrast** How is the grouping of stars in a constellation different from the grouping of planets in the solar system?

5. **Apply** The planet Jupiter is farther than Mars from Earth. Which planet seems to move faster when viewed from Earth? Explain.

○ CHALLENGE

6. **Predict** Suppose that you are standing at the North Pole on a dark night. If you keep turning clockwise at the same speed as Earth's rotation, how would your movement affect your view of the stars?

KEY CONCEPT

Telescopes allow us to study space from Earth.

◀ **BEFORE, you learned**

- Objects in the universe are grouped together in different ways
- The motions of planets and other nearby objects are visible from Earth

▶ **NOW, you will learn**

- About light and other forms of radiation
- How astronomers gather information about space

VOCABULARY

electromagnetic radiation p. 15

spectrum p. 16

wavelength p. 16

telescope p. 17

EXPLORE Distortion of Light

How can light become distorted?

PROCEDURE

① Place a white sheet of paper behind a glass filled with plain water. Shine a flashlight through the glass, and observe the spot of light on the paper.

② Pour a spoonful of salt into the water. Stir the water, and observe the spot of light.

WHAT DO YOU THINK?

- How did the spot of light change after you mixed the salt into the water?
- How could Earth's atmosphere cause similar changes in light from space?

MATERIALS

- flashlight
- glass filled with water
- sheet of white paper
- spoon
- salt

Light and other forms of radiation carry information about space.

VOCABULARY
Add a magnet word diagram for *electromagnetic radiation* to your notebook.

When you look at an object, your eyes are gathering light from that object. Visible light is a form of **electromagnetic radiation** (ih-LEHK-troh-mag-NEHT-ihk), which is energy that travels across distances as certain types of waves. There are other forms of electromagnetic radiation that you cannot see directly, such as radio waves and x-rays. Scientists have developed instruments to detect these other forms.

Electromagnetic radiation travels in all directions throughout space. Almost everything we know about the universe has come from our study of radiation. Astronomers can often learn about the size, distance, and movement of an object by studying its radiation. Radiation can also reveal what an object is made of and how it has changed.

The Electromagnetic Spectrum

The different forms of electromagnetic radiation vary in their wavelengths.

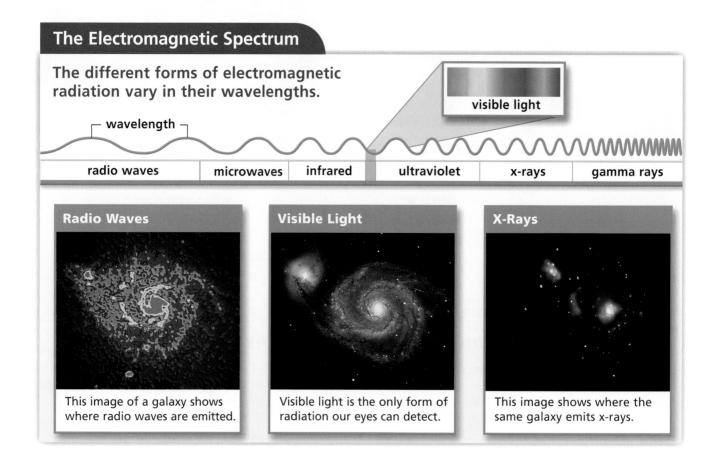

visible light

wavelength

| radio waves | microwaves | infrared | ultraviolet | x-rays | gamma rays |

Radio Waves

This image of a galaxy shows where radio waves are emitted.

Visible Light

Visible light is the only form of radiation our eyes can detect.

X-Rays

This image shows where the same galaxy emits x-rays.

READING TIP

A prism is a transparent object that is used to separate the wavelengths of light.

If you shine a flashlight through a prism, the beam of white light will separate into a range of colors called a **spectrum** (SPEHK-truhm). The colors that make up visible light are red, orange, yellow, green, blue, indigo, and violet. These are the colors in a rainbow, which appears when light spreads out as it passes through raindrops.

In a spectrum, the colors of visible light appear in the order of their wavelengths. **Wavelength** is the distance between one wave peak and the next wave peak. Red light has the longest wavelength. Violet light has the shortest.

As you can see in the illustration above, visible light is just a tiny part of a larger spectrum called the electromagnetic spectrum. The electromagnetic spectrum includes all the forms of electromagnetic radiation. Notice that the wavelength of infrared radiation is longer than the wavelength of visible light but not as long as the wavelength of microwaves or radio waves. The wavelength of ultraviolet radiation is shorter than the wavelength of visible light but not as short as the wavelength of x-rays or gamma rays.

CHECK YOUR READING How is visible light different from other forms of electromagnetic radiation?

Astronomers use telescopes to collect information about space.

A **telescope** is a device that gathers electromagnetic radiation. If you have ever looked through a telescope, it was probably one that gathers visible light. Such telescopes provide images that are much clearer than what is seen with the naked eye. Images from other types of telescopes show radiation that your eyes cannot detect. Each form of radiation provides different information about objects in space.

Astronomers usually record images from telescopes electronically, which allows them to use computers to analyze images. Different colors or shades in an image reveal patterns of radiation. For example, in the right-hand image on page 16, the colors yellow and red indicate where the galaxy is emitting large amounts of x-rays.

Most types of telescopes gather radiation with a glass lens or a reflecting surface, such as a mirror. Larger lenses and reflecting surfaces produce brighter and more detailed images. You can magnify an image from a telescope to any size. However, enlarging an image will not bring out any more details of an object. If the image is fuzzy at a small size, it will remain fuzzy no matter how much it is enlarged.

Visible-Light, Infrared, and Ultraviolet Telescopes

There are two types of visible-light telescopes: reflecting telescopes and refracting telescopes. Reflecting telescopes can also be built to gather infrared or ultraviolet radiation.

- **Reflecting Telescope** This type of telescope has a curved mirror that gathers light. The image comes into focus in front of the mirror. Many reflecting telescopes have a second mirror that reflects the image to recording equipment or to a lens called an eyepiece.

- **Refracting Telescope** This type of telescope has an objective lens, or curved piece of glass, at one end of a long tube. The lens gathers light and focuses it to form an image near the other end of the tube. An eyepiece magnifies this image.

Reflecting Telescope
- eyepiece
- main mirror
- secondary mirror

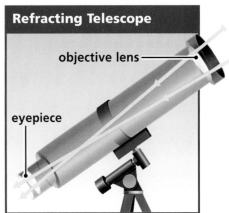

Refracting Telescope
- objective lens
- eyepiece

Most powerful visible-light telescopes are built on mountaintops in rural areas. Rural areas offer a much better view of the night sky than cities do, because the many electric lights in cities make dim space objects hard to see. By locating telescopes on mountaintops, astronomers reduce problems caused by Earth's atmosphere. The atmosphere interferes with light coming in from space. In fact, movements of the air are what make stars appear to twinkle. At high altitudes there is less air above the ground to interfere with light.

Radio Telescope

Radio Telescopes

Radio telescopes show where radio waves are being emitted by objects in space. A radio telescope has a curved metal surface, called a dish, that gathers radio waves and focuses them onto an antenna. The dish works in the same way as the main mirror of a reflecting telescope. Some radio telescopes have dishes made of metal mesh rather than solid metal.

Because radio waves are so long, a single radio telescope must be very large to produce useful images. To improve the quality of images, astronomers often aim a group of radio telescopes at the same object. Signals from the telescopes are combined and then converted into an image. Groups of radio telescopes, like the Very Large Array in New Mexico, can show more detail than even the largest single dish.

Signals from these radio telescopes in New Mexico can be combined to produce clearer images.

Unlike visible-light telescopes, radio telescopes are not affected by clouds or bad weather. They even work well in daylight. In addition, radio telescopes can be located at low altitudes because most radio waves pass freely through Earth's atmosphere.

○ **CHECK YOUR READING** What is the function of the dish in a radio telescope?

RESOURCE CENTER
CLASSZONE.COM
Find out more about telescopes.

Telescopes in Space

Many exciting images have come from the Hubble Space Telescope and other telescopes in space. The Hubble telescope is a reflecting telescope. It was placed in orbit around Earth in 1990. Astronomers operate it from the ground, although astronauts have visited it to make repairs and improvements. The telescope sends images and measurements back to Earth electronically.

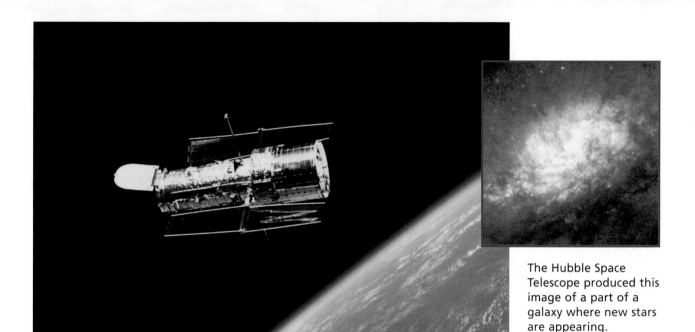

The Hubble Space Telescope produced this image of a part of a galaxy where new stars are appearing.

Because the Hubble telescope is located in space, Earth's atmosphere does not interfere with light from objects the telescope is aimed at. This lack of interference allows it to obtain clearer images than ground-based telescopes with much larger mirrors. In addition to collecting visible light, the Hubble telescope produces images of ultraviolet and infrared radiation.

The Hubble Space Telescope is part of a group of telescopes that orbit Earth. The telescopes allow astronomers to gain information from the full range of electromagnetic radiation. The Compton Gamma-Ray Observatory was sent into orbit in 1991. The Chandra X-Ray Observatory was launched eight years later. These telescopes were placed in space because Earth's atmosphere blocks most x-rays and gamma rays.

 CHECK YOUR READING Why does the Hubble telescope produce clearer images than a telescope of the same size on Earth?

1.2 Review

KEY CONCEPTS

1. How are visible light, radio waves, and other forms of electromagnetic radiation different from each other?

2. What function do mirrors serve in reflecting telescopes?

3. Why are some telescopes placed on mountains or in orbit around Earth?

CRITICAL THINKING

4. **Compare and Contrast** What are the similarities and differences between refracting telescopes and reflecting telescopes?

5. **Analyze** Why would it be difficult to build radio telescopes if they did not work well at low altitudes?

CHALLENGE

6. **Analyze** Why might astronomers use different types of telescopes to obtain images of the same object in space?

CHAPTER INVESTIGATION

Observing Spectra

OVERVIEW AND PURPOSE Visible light is made up of different colors that can be separated into a rainbow band called a spectrum. Astronomers gain information about the characteristics of stars by spreading their light into spectra (*spectra* is the plural form of *spectrum*). A spectroscope is a device that produces spectra. In most spectroscopes, diffraction gratings are used to separate light into different colors. The colors with the longest wavelengths appear farthest from the slit in a spectroscope. The colors with the shortest wavelengths appear closest to the slit. In this investigation you will

- build a spectroscope and observe the spectra of three different light sources
- identify ways in which the spectra of light sources differ

MATERIALS
- shoebox with lid
- ruler
- scissors
- diffraction grating
- tape
- index card
- pencils or markers in a variety of colors
- incandescent light
- fluorescent light
for Challenge:
- cellophane in several colors

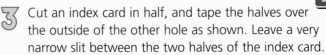

▶ Procedure

1. Cut a hole measuring 3 cm by 1.5 cm in each end of a shoebox. Make sure that the holes line up.

2. On the inside of the box, tape a piece of diffraction grating over one of the holes. Handle the diffraction grating by its edges so that you do not get finger-prints on it.

step 1

3. Cut an index card in half, and tape the halves over the outside of the other hole as shown. Leave a very narrow slit between the two halves of the index card.

4 Put the lid on the shoebox. Then turn off the overhead lights in the classroom.

5 Look through the hole covered with the diffraction grating, aiming the spectroscope's slit at the sky through a window. **Caution:** *Never look directly at the Sun.* Observe the spectrum you see to the left of the slit.

step 5

6 Repeat step 5 while aiming the spectroscope at an incandescent light and then at a fluorescent light.

▶ Observe and Analyze
Write It Up

1. **RECORD OBSERVATIONS** For each light source, draw in your data table the spectrum you see to the left of the slit. Describe the colors and patterns in the spectrum, and label the light source.

2. **IDENTIFY LIMITS** What problems, if any, did you experience in observing the spectra? Why was it important to turn off overhead lights for this activity?

▶ Conclude
Write It Up

1. **COMPARE AND CONTRAST** How did the spectra differ from one another? Did you notice any stripes of color that were brighter or narrower than other colors in the same spectrum? Did you notice any lines or spaces separating colors?

2. **ANALYZE** The shorter the wavelength of a color, the closer it appears to the slit in a spectroscope. On the basis of your observations, which color has the shortest wavelength? Which color has the longest wavelength?

3. **INFER** How might the spectra look different if the slit at the end of the spectroscope were curved instead of a straight line?

▶ INVESTIGATE Further

CHALLENGE Cover the slit on your spectroscope with a piece of colored cellophane. Aiming the spectroscope at a fluorescent light or another light source, observe and draw the resulting spectrum. Then repeat with cellophane of other colors. List the colors that each piece of cellophane transmitted. Did these results surprise you? If so, why?

Observing Spectra

Observe and Analyze

Table 1. Spectra of Different Light Sources

Light Source	Drawing	Description

Conclude

Spacecraft help us explore beyond Earth.

◀ **BEFORE, you learned**

- The motions of planets and other nearby objects are visible from Earth
- Light and other forms of radiation carry information about the universe

▶ **NOW, you will learn**

- How astronauts explore space near Earth
- How different types of spacecraft are used in exploration

VOCABULARY

satellite p. 23
space station p. 24
lander p. 28
probe p. 29

EXPLORE Viewing Space Objects

How do objects appear at different distances?

PROCEDURE

1. Crumple the paper into a ball and place it on your desk.

2. Sketch the ball at the same time as another student sketches it. One of you should sketch it from a distance of 1 m. The other should sketch it from 5 m away.

WHAT DO YOU THINK?

- How do the details in the two drawings compare?
- What details might be easier to see on a planet if you were orbiting the planet?

MATERIALS

- paper
- pencils

Astronauts explore space near Earth.

RESOURCE CENTER
CLASSZONE.COM

Learn more about space exploration.

Space travel requires very careful planning. Astronauts take everything necessary for survival with them, including air, water, and food. Spacecraft need powerful rockets and huge fuel tanks to lift all their weight upward against Earth's gravity. The equipment must be well designed and maintained, since any breakdown can be deadly.

Once in space, astronauts must get used to a special environment. People and objects in an orbiting spacecraft seem to float freely unless they are fastened down. This weightless condition occurs because they are falling in space at the same rate as the spacecraft. In addition, to leave their airtight cabin, astronauts must wear special protective suits. Despite these conditions, astronauts have managed to perform experiments and make important observations about space near Earth.

Moon Missions

For about a decade, much of space exploration was focused on a race to the Moon. This race was driven by rivalry between the United States and the Soviet Union, which included Russia. In 1957 the Soviet Union launched the first artificial satellite to orbit Earth. A **satellite** is an object that orbits a more massive object. The Soviet Union also sent the first human into space in 1961. Although the United States lagged behind in these early efforts, it succeeded in sending the first humans to the Moon.

Preparation Many steps had to be taken before astronauts from the United States could visit the Moon. The National Aeronautics and Space Administration (NASA) sent spacecraft without crews to the Moon to find out whether it was possible to land on its surface. NASA also sent astronauts into space to practice important procedures.

Landings The NASA program to reach the Moon was called Apollo. During early Apollo missions, astronauts tested spacecraft and flew them into orbit around the Moon. On July 20, 1969, crew members from *Apollo 11* became the first humans to walk on the Moon's surface. NASA achieved five more Moon landings between 1969 and 1972. During this period, the Soviet Union sent spacecraft without crews to get samples of the Moon's surface.

Scientific Results The Apollo program helped scientists learn about the Moon's surface and interior. Much of the information came from 380 kilograms (weighing 840 lb) of rock and soil that astronauts brought back to Earth. These samples are still being studied.

Powerful booster rockets were used to launch the Apollo spacecraft. Beginning with *Apollo 15*, astronauts rode in lunar roving vehicles to explore greater areas of the Moon's surface.

Orbiting Earth

A **space station** is a satellite in which people can live and work for long periods. The United States and the Soviet Union launched the first space stations in the early 1970s. After the breakup of the Soviet Union in 1991, the Russian space agency and NASA began to act as partners rather than rivals. Russian and U. S. astronauts carried out joint missions aboard *Mir* (meer), the Russian space station.

The *Mir* missions helped prepare for the International Space Station (ISS). The United States, Russia, and 15 other nations are working together to build the ISS. When completed, it will cover an area about as large as two football fields. The ISS is too large to launch into space in one piece. Instead, sections of the space station are being launched separately and assembled in orbit over a period of years.

Construction of the ISS began in 1998. The first three-member crew arrived at the station in 2000. In addition to constructing the station, crew members make observations of Earth and perform experiments. Some experiments are much more effective when they are performed in space, where gravity affects them differently. For example, scientists can grow cell tissue more easily in space than they can on Earth. Research on cell tissue grown in space may increase our understanding of cancer and other diseases.

International Space Station

Each section of the space station has a specific function.

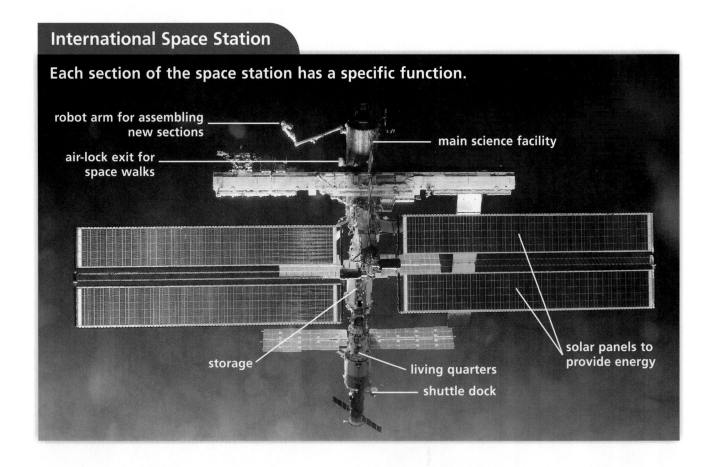

robot arm for assembling new sections

air-lock exit for space walks

main science facility

storage

living quarters

shuttle dock

solar panels to provide energy

Research and technological advances from the space station may lay the groundwork for new space exploration. ISS crew members study how living in space affects the human body over long periods. This research may provide useful information for future efforts to send astronauts to other planets.

Most crews have flown to the ISS aboard space shuttles. Unlike earlier spacecraft, a space shuttle can be used again and again. At the end of a mission, it reenters Earth's atmosphere and glides down to a runway. The large cargo bay of a space shuttle can carry satellites, equipment, and laboratories.

NASA has launched space shuttles more than 100 times since 1981. Space shuttles are much more sophisticated than the Apollo spacecraft that carried astronauts to the Moon. However, space travel remains a dangerous activity.

Two booster rockets and an external fuel tank are needed to lift a space shuttle into orbit.

CHECK YOUR READING Why might some researchers choose to perform experiments aboard a space station rather than on Earth?

INVESTIGATE Launch Planning

How does Earth's rotation affect launches of spacecraft?

PROCEDURE

1. Tightly wad 14 sheets of paper into balls, and place the balls in a small bucket.

2. Stand 1.5 m away from a large bucket placed on a desk. Try tossing 7 balls into the bucket.

3. While turning slowly, try tossing the remaining 7 balls into the bucket.

WHAT DO YOU THINK?

- How much more difficult was it to toss the paper balls into the bucket while you were turning than when you were standing still?

- Why does Earth's rotation make launching rockets into space more complicated?

CHALLENGE How would you design an experiment to show the variables involved in a launch from Earth toward another rotating body in space, such as the Moon?

MATERIALS
- paper
- small bucket
- large bucket

TIME
10 minutes

Spacecraft carry instruments to other worlds.

Currently, we cannot send humans to other planets. One obstacle is that such a trip would take years. A spacecraft would need to carry enough air, water, and other supplies needed for survival on the long journey. Another obstacle is the harsh conditions on other planets, such as extreme heat and cold. Some planets do not even have surfaces to land on.

Because of these obstacles, most research in space is accomplished through the use of spacecraft without crews aboard. These missions pose no risk to human life and are less expensive than missions involving astronauts. The spacecraft carry instruments that test the compositions and characteristics of planets. Data and images are sent back to Earth as radio signals. Onboard computers and radio signals from Earth guide the spacecraft.

Spacecraft have visited all the major planets in our solar system except Pluto. NASA has also sent spacecraft to other bodies in space, such as comets and moons. Scientists and engineers have designed different types of spacecraft to carry out these missions.

CHECK YOUR READING What questions do you still have about space exploration?

Flybys

The first stage in space exploration is to send out a spacecraft that passes one or more planets or other bodies in space without orbiting them. Such missions are called flybys. After a flyby spacecraft leaves Earth's orbit, controllers on Earth can use the spacecraft's small rockets to adjust its direction. Flyby missions may last for decades. However, because a spacecraft flies by planets quickly, it can collect data and images from a particular planet only for a brief period.

As a flyby spacecraft passes a planet, the planet's gravity can be used to change the spacecraft's speed or direction. During the flyby of the planet, the spacecraft can gain enough energy to propel it to another planet more quickly. This method allowed *Voyager 2* to fly past Saturn, Uranus, and Neptune, even though the spacecraft left Earth with only enough energy to reach Jupiter.

Many complex mathematical calculations are needed for a flyby mission to be successful. Experts must take into account Earth's rotation and the positions of the planets that the spacecraft will pass. The period of time when a spacecraft can be launched is called a launch window.

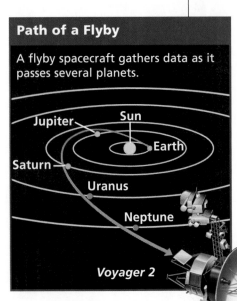

Path of a Flyby

A flyby spacecraft gathers data as it passes several planets.

Jupiter — Sun
Saturn
Earth
Uranus
Neptune
Voyager 2

Orbiters

The second stage in space exploration is to study a planet over a long period of time. Spacecraft designed to accomplish this task are called orbiters. As an orbiter approaches its target planet, rocket engines are fired to slow the spacecraft down. The spacecraft then goes into orbit around the planet.

In an orbiter mission, a spacecraft orbits a planet for several months to several years. Since an orbiter remains near a planet for a much longer period of time than a flyby spacecraft, it can view most or all of the planet's surface. An orbiter can also keep track of changes that occur over time, such as changes in weather and volcanic activity.

Orbiters allow astronomers to create detailed maps of planets. Most orbiters have cameras to photograph planet surfaces. Orbiters may also carry other instruments, such as a device for determining the altitudes of surface features or one for measuring temperatures in different regions.

Some orbiters are designed to explore moons or other bodies in space instead of planets. It is also possible to send a spacecraft to orbit a planet and later move it into orbit around one of the planet's moons.

▽ REMINDER

Remember that objects orbit, or move around, other objects in space because of the influence of gravity.

△ **CHECK YOUR READING** What is the main difference between a flyby spacecraft and an orbiter?

How an Orbiter Provides Data

Data from an orbiter are sent to Earth in the form of radio waves.

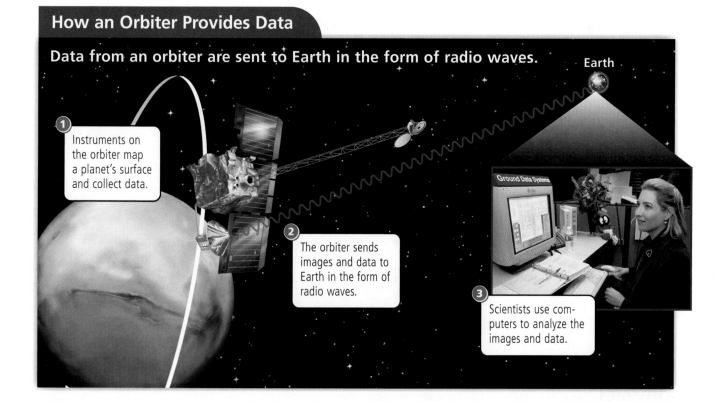

Earth

1. Instruments on the orbiter map a planet's surface and collect data.

2. The orbiter sends images and data to Earth in the form of radio waves.

Ground Data Systems

3. Scientists use computers to analyze the images and data.

Landers and Probes

The third stage in space exploration is to land instruments on a planet or to send instruments through its atmosphere. Such a mission can tell us more about the features and properties of a planet. It can also provide clues to what the planet was like in the past.

A **lander** is a craft designed to land on a planet's surface. After a lander touches down, controllers on Earth can send it commands to collect data. Landers have been placed successfully on the Moon, Venus, and Mars. Some have operated for months or years at a time.

The images taken by a lander are more detailed than those taken by an orbiter. In addition to providing close-up views of a planet's surface, a lander can measure properties of the planet's atmosphere and surface. A lander may have a mechanical arm for gathering soil and rock samples. It may also contain a small vehicle called a rover, which can explore beyond the landing site.

1 The spacecraft slows down as it moves through the atmosphere.

Landing Sequence

Parachutes and air bags can be used to slow a lander as it descends to a planet's surface.

2 A parachute opens, and the lander is lowered from the spacecraft. Air bags are inflated shortly before landing.

3 The lander bounces on the surface and rolls to a stop.

4 The air bags are deflated and pulled back.

5 A rover from the lander begins to move across the surface.

One of the most successful space missions was that of *Mars Pathfinder,* which landed on Mars in 1997. *Mars Pathfinder* and its rover sent back thousands of photographs. These images provided evidence that water once flowed over the surface of Mars. Unfortunately, another lander, sent two years later, failed to work after it reached Mars.

Some spacecraft are designed to work only for a short time before they are destroyed by conditions on a planet. The term **probe** is often used to describe a spacecraft that drops into a planet's atmosphere. As the probe travels through the atmosphere, its instruments identify gases and measure properties such as pressure and temperature. Probes are especially important for exploring the deep atmospheres of giant planets, such as Jupiter.

 CHECK YOUR READING What is the difference between a probe and a lander?

Combining Missions

A lander or a probe can work in combination with an orbiter. For example, in 1995 the orbiter *Galileo* released a probe into Jupiter's atmosphere as it began orbiting the planet. The probe sent data back to the orbiter for nearly an hour before it was destroyed. The orbiter passed the data on to Earth. *Galileo* continued to orbit Jupiter for eight years.

Future space missions may involve even more complex combinations of spacecraft. Planners hope to send groups of landers to collect soil and rock samples from the surface of Mars. A rocket will carry these samples to an orbiter. The orbiter will then bring the samples to Earth for study.

1.3 Review

KEY CONCEPTS

1. Why are space stations important for scientific research?
2. How is information sent between Earth and a spacecraft?
3. What are the three main stages in exploring a planet?

CRITICAL THINKING

4. **Analyze** Why is most space exploration accomplished with spacecraft that do not have astronauts on board?
5. **Infer** Why is it important to map a planet's surface before planning a lander mission?

CHALLENGE

6. **Predict** Early space exploration was influenced by political events, such as the rivalry between the United States and the Soviet Union. What circumstances on Earth might interfere with future space missions?

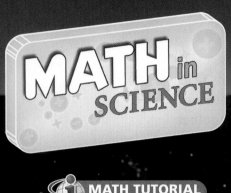

MATH in **SCIENCE**

MATH TUTORIAL
CLASSZONE.COM
Click on Math Tutorial
for more help with
powers and exponents.

SKILL: USING EXPONENTS

Distances in Space

Astronomers often deal with very large numbers. For example, the planet Venus is about 100 million kilometers from the Sun. Written out, 100 million is 100,000,000. To use fewer zeros and to make the number easier to write and read, you could write 100 million as 10^8, which is the same value in exponent form.

Example

PROBLEM Write 1000 km, using an exponent.

To find the exponent of a number, you can write the number as a product. For example,

1000 km = 10 $\times$ 10 $\times$ 10 km

This product has 3 factors of 10. When whole numbers other than zero are multiplied together, each number is a factor of the product. To write a product that has a repeated factor, you can use an exponent. The exponent is the number of times the factor is repeated. With factors of 10, you can also determine the exponent by counting the zeros in the given number.

There are 3   **The factor 10 is**
zeros in 1000.   **repeated 3 times.**

1000   =   **10 $\times$ 10 $\times$ 10**

ANSWER The exponent form of 1000 km is 10^3 km.

Write each distance, using an exponent.

1. 10,000 km

2. 1,000,000 km

3. 100,000,000,000 km

4. 10,000,000,000,000 km

5. 100,000,000,000,000,000 km

6. 10 km

CHALLENGE The galaxy shown on this page is about 10^{18} kilometers across. Write the value of 10^{18} without using an exponent.

Galaxy M83, which is roughly the same size as the Milky Way, has a diameter of about 10^{18} kilometers.

Space exploration benefits society.

◀ **BEFORE, you learned**

- Light and other radiation carry information about space
- Astronauts explore space near Earth

▶ **NOW, you will learn**

- How space exploration has helped us to learn more about Earth
- How space technology is used on Earth

VOCABULARY

impact crater p. 32

THINK ABOUT

How does Earth look from space?

This photograph of Earth over the Moon was taken by the crew of *Apollo 8*. The Apollo missions provided the first images of our planet as a whole. What do you think we can learn about Earth from photographs taken from space?

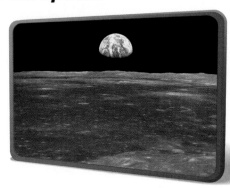

Space exploration has given us new viewpoints.

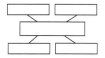

MAIN IDEA WEB
Record in your notes important information that space exploration has provided about Earth.

Space exploration enriches us in many ways. Throughout history, the study of stars and planets has inspired new ideas. As we meet the challenges of space exploration, we gain valuable technology. Space exploration is also an exciting adventure.

Space science has advanced knowledge in other scientific fields, such as physics. For example, observations of the Moon and other bodies in space helped scientists understand how gravity works. Scientists figured out that the same force that causes an object to fall to the ground causes the Moon to orbit Earth.

Finally, the study of other worlds can teach us about our own. Earth has changed considerably since its formation. By comparing Earth with different worlds, scientists can learn more about the history of Earth's surface features and atmosphere.

 CHECK YOUR READING Identify some benefits of space exploration.

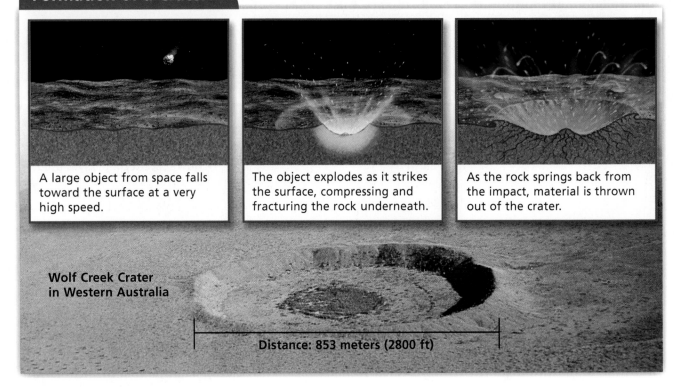

Formation of a Crater

A large object from space falls toward the surface at a very high speed.

The object explodes as it strikes the surface, compressing and fracturing the rock underneath.

As the rock springs back from the impact, material is thrown out of the crater.

Wolf Creek Crater in Western Australia

Distance: 853 meters (2800 ft)

Surface Features

Exploration of other worlds has helped us learn about the impacts of space objects. When an object strikes the surface of a larger object in space, it explodes and leaves behind a round pit called an **impact crater.** The illustration above shows how an impact crater forms.

Earth has little evidence of impacts because its surface is constantly being worn down by wind and water and altered by forces beneath the surface. However, impact craters remain on the Moon, Mercury, and many other bodies that have no wind or liquid water.

Atmosphere

We are also learning about Earth's atmosphere from space exploration. Earth's temperature allows liquid water to remain on the surface. Mars and Venus, the planets closest to Earth, have no liquid water on their surfaces. By comparing Earth with those planets, we can see how liquid water has affected the development of Earth's atmosphere.

Another area of study involves the energy Earth receives from the Sun. Many scientists think that small changes visible on the Sun's surface can affect weather on Earth. These changes may have caused periods of cooling in Earth's atmosphere.

 CHECK YOUR READING What have scientists learned about Earth's past from studying bodies in space?

INVESTIGATE Weathering

How does weather affect evidence of impacts on Earth?

PROCEDURE

1. Fill a shoebox lid halfway with sand, and smooth the surface with a ruler.

2. Create three craters by dropping a golf ball into the sand from a height of 70 cm. Remove the ball carefully. Leave the lid inside the classroom.

3. Repeat steps 1 and 2 outdoors, leaving the lid in an area where it will be exposed to the weather.

4. Check both lids after 24 hours. Observe changes in each one.

WHAT DO YOU THINK?

- How did the craters in the sand that you left outdoors differ in appearance from the craters in the sand that remained inside?

- What aspect of weather caused any differences you observed?

CHALLENGE What natural processes besides weather can affect evidence of impacts from space objects on Earth?

Space technology has practical uses.

Space exploration has done more than increase our knowledge. It has also provided us with technology that makes life on Earth easier. Each day you probably benefit from some material or product that was developed for the space program.

Satellite Views of Earth

One of the most important benefits of space exploration has been the development of satellite technology. Satellites collect data from every region of our planet. The data are sent to receivers on Earth and converted into images. Scientists have learned from the space program how to enhance such images to gain more information.

Weather satellites show conditions throughout Earth's atmosphere. Images and data from weather satellites have greatly improved weather forecasting. Scientists can now provide warnings of dangerous storms long before they strike populated areas.

Other satellites collect images of Earth's surface to show how it is being changed by natural events and human activity. Satellite data are also used for wildlife preservation, conservation of natural resources, and mapping.

Technology Spinoffs

Have you ever come up with a new way to use something that was designed for a different purpose? NASA often creates advanced technology to meet the special demands of space travel. Many spinoffs of technology from the space program can be found in homes, offices, schools, and hospitals.

NASA designers helped develop a system that allows this boy to communicate by using eye movements.

Everything on a spacecraft must be as small and lightweight as possible because the heavier a spacecraft is, the more difficult it is to launch. Design techniques developed to meet this need have improved devices used on Earth, such as tools for diagnosing diseases and devices that help people overcome disabilities.

Materials and parts on a spacecraft have to endure harsh conditions, such as extreme heat and cold. Many new homes and buildings contain fire-resistant materials developed for the space program. Firefighters wear protective suits made from fabric originally used in space suits. NASA has also helped design devices that allow firefighters to avoid injury from inhaling smoke.

Humans need a safe environment in spacecraft and space stations. NASA has developed systems for purifying air, water, and food. These systems now help protect people on Earth as well as in space.

1.4 Review

KEY CONCEPTS

1. How has space exploration helped us learn about impacts of space objects on Earth?

2. How do satellites provide images of Earth's surface and atmosphere?

3. Give two examples of technology we use on Earth that is a result of space exploration.

CRITICAL THINKING

4. **Infer** Hurricanes form in the middle of the ocean. Why would satellites be useful in tracking hurricanes?

5. **Apply** What space-technology spinoffs might be used in a school?

⬤ CHALLENGE

6. **Predict** It takes over a year for a spacecraft to reach Mars and return to Earth. If astronauts ever travel to Mars, they will need a spacecraft that can recycle air and water. How might such technology be adapted for use on Earth?

How Earth's Gravity Affects Plants

One of the most important issues in biology is understanding how plants grow. By applying the results of research on this issue, American farmers now grow twice as much food as they did 50 years ago.

One aspect of plant growth is the direction in which plants grow. After a plant sprouts from a seed, some of its cells form a shoot that grows upward. Other cells grow downward, becoming roots. How does this happen? Biologists think that plants usually respond to signals from the Sun and from the force of gravity.

Gravity and Plant Growth

To test the importance of sunlight, biologists can grow plants in the dark on Earth. Testing the impact of gravity, though, is more difficult. In 1997, a space shuttle carried moss plants into space. The plants grew for two weeks in microgravity, an environment in which objects are almost weightless. When the shuttle returned the plants to Earth, biologists studied how they had grown.

Prediction

Biologists had predicted that the moss would grow randomly. They expected that without signals from sunlight or the force of gravity, the moss would grow in no particular pattern.

Results

The biologists were surprised by what they saw. The moss had not grown randomly. Instead, the plants had spread out in a clear pattern. Each plant had formed a clockwise spiral.

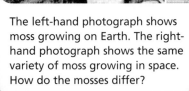

The left-hand photograph shows moss growing on Earth. The right-hand photograph shows the same variety of moss growing in space. How do the mosses differ?

Significance

The moss experiment may be important for future space exploration. Can plants provide the food and oxygen that astronauts will need on long voyages to other planets? Experiments with moss are among the first steps in finding out.

EXPLORE

1. **PROVIDE EXAMPLES** Make a list of other spiral formations that occur in nature. Discuss why spirals may be common.
2. **CHALLENGE** Use library or Internet resources to learn about other experiments that test the effects of microgravity on plants and seeds.

Chapter Review

CONTENT REVIEW
CLASSZONE.COM

◄ KEY CONCEPTS SUMMARY

1.1 Some space objects are visible to the human eye.

- Gravity causes objects in space to be grouped together in different ways.
- Stars form patterns in the sky.
- The sky seems to turn as Earth rotates.

VOCABULARY
orbit p. 10
solar system p. 10
galaxy p. 10
universe p. 10
constellation p. 12

1.2 Telescopes allow us to study space from Earth.

Each form of electromagnetic radiation provides different information about objects in space. Astronomers use different types of telescopes to gather visible light and other forms of radiation.

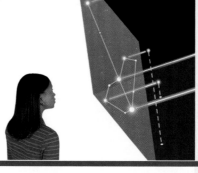

VOCABULARY
electromagnetic radiation p. 15
spectrum p. 16
wavelength p. 16
telescope p. 17

1.3 Spacecraft help us explore beyond Earth.

Astronauts can explore space near Earth. Spacecraft without crews carry instruments to other worlds. A flyby mission usually provides data from several bodies in space. Orbiters, landers, and probes gather data from one planet or body.

VOCABULARY
satellite p. 23
space station p. 24
lander p. 28
probe p. 29

1.4 Space exploration benefits society.

Space exploration has taught us about Earth's development. It has also provided technology that has important uses on Earth.

VOCABULARY
impact crater p. 32

Reviewing Vocabulary

Write a definition of each word. Use the meaning of the underlined word part to help you.

Word	Root Meaning	Definition
EXAMPLE satellite	person of lesser rank	an object that orbits a more massive object
1. orbit	circle	
2. solar system	Sun	
3. universe	one	
4. constellation	star	
5. electro-magnetic radiation	to emit rays	
6. spectrum	to look at	
7. probe	test	
8. impact crater	bowl	

Reviewing Key Concepts

Multiple Choice *Choose the letter of the best answer.*

9. Stars in a galaxy are held together by
  a. light   **c.** gravity
  b. radiation   **d.** satellites

10. Astronomers use constellations to
  a. locate objects in the sky
  b. calculate the distances of objects
  c. calculate the masses of objects
  d. classify spectra

11. Stars rise and set in the night sky because
  a. Earth orbits the Sun
  b. Earth rotates
  c. the North Pole points toward Polaris
  d. the stars are moving in space

12. In the electromagnetic spectrum, different forms of radiation are arranged according to their
  a. colors   **c.** wavelengths
  b. distances   **d.** sizes

13. Astronomers often locate telescopes on mountains to
  a. lessen the interference of Earth's atmosphere
  b. save money on land
  c. keep their discoveries secret
  d. get closer to space objects

14. A reflecting telescope gathers light with a
  a. lens   **c.** refractor
  b. eyepiece   **d.** mirror

15. What was the goal of the Apollo program?
  a. to view Earth from space
  b. to explore the Sun
  c. to explore the Moon
  d. to explore other planets

16. Which type of mission produces detailed maps of a planet?
  a. flyby   **c.** lander
  b. orbiter   **d.** probe

17. What causes an impact crater to form on a planet's surface?
  a. Gravity pulls soil and rock downward.
  b. Wind and water wear away the surface.
  c. Forces beneath the surface push upward.
  d. An object from space strikes the surface.

Short Answer *Write a short answer to each question.*

18. Why is it easier to see the motions of planets than to see the motions of stars?

19. How do astronomers obtain most of their information about space?

20. How does the size of a telescope's main lens or mirror affect its performance?

21. Why have lightweight materials been developed for space travel?

Copy the Venn diagram below, and use it to help you answer the next two questions.

Reflecting Telescope   Radio Dish

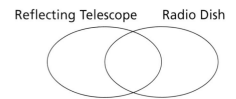

22. COMPARE AND CONTRAST Fill in the Venn diagram to show similarities and differences between a reflecting telescope and a radio dish.

23. APPLY Suppose that you live in an area that has frequent storms. Which would be more suitable for your location, a reflecting telescope or a radio dish? Explain.

24. COMPARE AND CONTRAST What are the similarities and differences between visible light and radio waves?

25. HYPOTHESIZE Many of the constellations named by ancient peoples are now hard to see from populated areas. Why might it have been easier to see them hundreds or thousands of years ago?

26. ANALYZE What may be the advantages of electronically recording an image from a telescope instead of looking at the object directly through the telescope's eyepiece?

27. SYNTHESIZE Suppose it became possible to send astronauts to explore a nearby planet. What concerns would need to be taken into account before deciding whether to send a spacecraft with astronauts or a spacecraft with no crew aboard?

28. COMPARE AND CONTRAST Compare and contrast the development of the International Space Station with the Apollo missions to the Moon.

29. ANALYZE If you were designing a medical device to be implanted in a patient's body, why might you seek help from designers of space technology?

30. EVALUATE Do you think that the United States should continue to maintain its own space program, or should it combine its space program with the programs of other nations? Explain.

31. SEQUENCE Astronomers have learned that some stars other than the Sun have planets orbiting them. Imagine that you are planning a program to explore one of these planet systems. Copy the chart below. Use the chart to identify stages in the exploration of the system and to describe what would occur during each stage.

Stage of Exploration	Description

the BIG idea

32. PROVIDE EXAMPLES Look again at the photograph on pages 6–7. Now that you have finished the chapter, how would you change your response to the question on the photograph?

33. EVALUATE In the United States billions of dollars are spent each year on space exploration. Do you think that this expense is justified? Why or why not?

UNIT PROJECTS

If you are doing a unit project, make a folder for your project. Include in your folder a list of the resources you will need, the date on which the project is due, and a schedule to track your progress. Begin gathering data.

Analyzing a Star Map

Use the star map to answer the next five questions.

1. Constellations are represented on the map as dots that are
   a. surrounded by planets
   b. grouped in a spiral pattern
   c. connected by lines
   d. scattered in a random pattern

2. How would a map showing the same portion of the sky two hours later compare with the map above?
   a. Almost all the space objects would have changed position noticeably.
   b. No space objects would have changed position.
   c. Only the moon would have changed position.
   d. Only the planets would have changed position.

3. Why would the map for two hours later be different from this map?
   a. The Moon is rotating on its axis.
   b. Earth is rotating on its axis.
   c. The solar system is part of the Milky Way.
   d. The planets move in relation to the stars.

4. A map showing the same portion of the sky exactly one year later would look very similar to this map. What would probably be different?
   a. the shapes of the constellations
   b. the names of the constellations
   c. the positions of the Moon and the planets
   d. the radiation of the stars

5. Which statement best describes the location of the stars shown on the map?
   a. They are outside the solar system but within the Milky Way galaxy.
   b. They are within the solar system.
   c. They are outside the Milky Way galaxy but within the universe.
   d. They are outside the universe.

Extended Response

Answer the two questions below in detail. Include some of the terms shown in the word box. In your answer, underline each term you use.

electromagnetic radiation	solar system
Milky Way	radio waves
universe	visible light

6. What is the relationship between Earth, our solar system, the Milky Way, and the universe?

7. What do visible-light telescopes and radio telescopes have in common? How are they different?

CHAPTER 2

Earth, Moon, and Sun

the **BIG** idea

Earth and the Moon move in predictable ways as they orbit the Sun.

Key Concepts

SECTION

2.1 Earth rotates on a tilted axis and orbits the Sun.
Learn what causes day and night and why there are seasons.

SECTION

2.2 The Moon is Earth's natural satellite.
Learn about the structure and motion of Earth's Moon.

SECTION

2.3 Positions of the Sun and Moon affect Earth.
Learn about phases of the Moon, eclipses, and tides.

What would you see if you looked at the Moon with a telescope?

Internet Preview

CLASSZONE.COM

Chapter 2 online resources: Content Review, two Visualizations, two Resource Centers, Math Tutorial, Test Practice

EXPLORE the BIG idea

How Do Shadows Move?

Place a small sticky note on a window that sunlight shines through. At several different times of day, sketch the location of the note's shadow in the room.

Observe and Think
Does the shadow move in a clockwise or counterclockwise direction? Does the shadow's distance from the window change?

What Makes the Moon Bright?

On a day when you see the Moon in the sky, compare it with a round object. Hold the object in line with the Moon. Make sure that your hand does not block the sunlight. Notice the part of the object that is bright.

Observe and Think
How does the sunlight on the object compare with the light on the Moon?

Internet Activity: Seasons

Go to **ClassZone.com** to explore seasons. Find out how sunlight affects the temperature in different places at different times of year.

Observe and Think
Does the picture show Earth in June or in December?

NSTA scilinks.org **SCiLINKS**
The Moon Code: MDL058

Getting Ready to Learn

◀ CONCEPT REVIEW

- The sky seems to turn as Earth rotates.
- The motions of nearby space objects are visible from Earth.
- Light and other radiation carry information about space.

◀ VOCABULARY REVIEW

orbit p. 10

electromagnetic radiation p. 15

satellite p. 23

See Glossary for definitions.

force, gravity, mass

CONTENT REVIEW
C L A S S Z O N E . C O M
Review concepts and vocabulary.

▶ TAKING NOTES

COMBINATION NOTES

To take notes about a new concept, first make an informal outline of the information. Then make a sketch of the concept and label it so you can study it later.

VOCABULARY STRATEGY

Write each new vocabulary term in the center of a **frame game** diagram. Decide what information to frame the term with. Use examples, descriptions, pictures, or sentences in which the term is used in context. You can change the frame to fit each term.

See the Note-Taking Handbook on pages R45–R51.

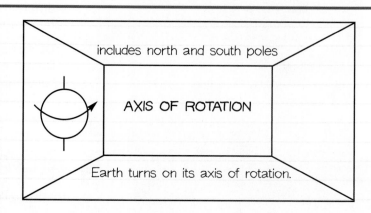

SCIENCE NOTEBOOK

NOTES

Earth turns.
- It turns on an imaginary axis.
  - Poles are ends of axis.
  - Equator is halfway.
- Rotation takes 24 hours.
- Sun shines on one side only.
  - Light side is daytime.
  - Dark side is night.

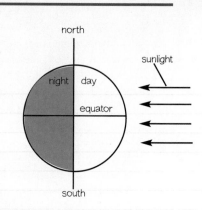

north / sunlight / night / day / equator / south

includes north and south poles

AXIS OF ROTATION

Earth turns on its axis of rotation.

Earth rotates on a tilted axis and orbits the Sun.

 BEFORE, you learned

- Stars seem to rise, cross the sky, and set because Earth turns
- The Sun is very large and far from Earth
- Earth orbits the Sun

 NOW, you will learn

- Why Earth has day and night
- How the changing angles of sunlight produce seasons

VOCABULARY

axis of rotation p. 44
revolution p. 45
season p. 46
equinox p. 46
solstice p. 46

EXPLORE Time Zones

What time is it in Iceland right now?

PROCEDURE

MATERIAL
time zone map

(1) Find your location and Iceland on the map. Identify the time zone of each.

(2) Count the number of hours between your location and Iceland. Add or subtract that number of hours from the time on your clock.

WHAT DO YOU THINK?

- By how much is Iceland's time earlier or later than yours?
- Why are clocks set to different times?

Earth's rotation causes day and night.

When astronauts explored the Moon, they felt the Moon's gravity pulling them down. Their usual "down"—Earth—was up in the Moon's sky.

As you read this book, it is easy to tell which way is down. But is down in the same direction for a person on the other side of Earth? If you both pointed down, you would be pointing toward each other. Earth's gravity pulls objects toward the center of Earth. No matter where you stand on Earth, the direction of down will be toward Earth's center. There is no bottom or top. Up is out toward space, and down is toward the center of the planet.

As Earth turns, so do you. You keep the same position with respect to what is below your feet, but the view above your head changes.

 In what direction does gravity pull objects near Earth?

The directions north, south, east, and west are based on the way the planet rotates, or turns. Earth rotates around an imaginary line running through its center called an **axis of rotation.** The ends of the axis are the north and south poles. Any location on the surface moves from west to east as Earth turns. If you extend your right thumb and pretend its tip is the North Pole, then your fingers curve the way Earth rotates.

At any one time, about half of Earth is in sunlight and half is dark. However, Earth turns on its axis in 24 hours, so locations move through the light and darkness in that time. When a location is in sunlight, it is daytime there. When a location is in the middle of the sunlit side, it is noon. When a location is in darkness, it is night there, and when the location is in the middle of the unlit side, it is midnight.

The globe and the flat map show the progress of daylight across Earth in two ways. This location is experiencing sunrise.

noon

night moves westward

midnight

CHECK YOUR READING If it is noon at one location, what time is it at a location directly on the other side of Earth?

INVESTIGATE Rotation

What causes day and night?

In this model the lamp represents the Sun, and your head represents Earth. The North Pole is at the top of your head. You will need to imagine locations on your head as if your head were a globe.

PROCEDURE

1. Face the lamp and hold your hands to your face as shown in the photograph. Your hands mark the horizon. For a person located at your nose, the Sun would be high in the sky. It would be noon.

2. Face away from the lamp. Determine what time it would be at your nose.

3. Turn to your left until you see the lamp along your left hand.

4. Continue turning to the left, through noon, until you just stop seeing the lamp.

WHAT DO YOU THINK?

• What times was it at your nose in steps 2, 3, and 4?

• When you face the lamp, what time is it at your right ear?

CHALLENGE How can a cloud be bright even when it is dark on the ground?

SKILL FOCUS
Making models

MATERIALS
lamp

TIME
15 minutes

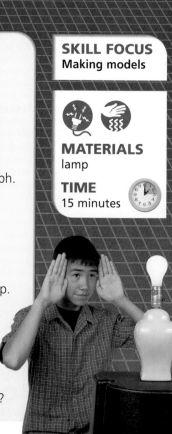

Earth's tilted axis and orbit cause seasons.

Just as gravity causes objects near Earth to be pulled toward Earth's center, it also causes Earth and other objects near the Sun to be pulled toward the Sun's center. Fortunately, Earth does not move straight into the Sun. Earth moves sideways, at nearly a right angle to the Sun's direction. Without the Sun's gravitational pull, Earth would keep moving in a straight line out into deep space. However, the Sun's pull changes Earth's path from a straight line to a round orbit about 300 million kilometers (200,000,000 mi) across.

Just as a day is the time it takes Earth to rotate once on its axis, a year is the time it takes Earth to orbit the Sun once. In astronomy, a **revolution** is the motion of one object around another. The word *revolution* can also mean the time it takes an object to go around once.

Earth's rotation and orbit do not quite line up. If they did, Earth's equator would be in the same plane as Earth's orbit, like a tiny hoop and a huge hoop lying on the same tabletop. Instead, Earth rotates at about a 23° angle, or tilt, from this lined-up position.

READING **TiP**

Use the second vowel in each word to help you remember that an object r<u>o</u>tates on its own <u>a</u>xis, but rev<u>o</u>lves around another <u>o</u>bject.

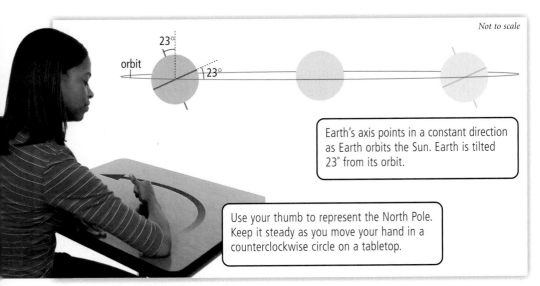

Not to scale

Earth's axis points in a constant direction as Earth orbits the Sun. Earth is tilted 23° from its orbit.

Use your thumb to represent the North Pole. Keep it steady as you move your hand in a counterclockwise circle on a tabletop.

As Earth moves, its axis always points in the same direction in space. You could model Earth's orbit by moving your right fist in a circle on a desktop. You would need to point your thumb toward your left shoulder and keep it pointing that way while moving your hand around the desktop.

Earth's orbit is not quite a perfect circle. In January, Earth is about 5 million kilometers closer to the Sun than it is in July. You may be surprised to learn that this distance makes only a tiny difference in temperatures on Earth. However, the combination of Earth's motion around the Sun with the tilt of Earth's axis does cause important changes of temperature. Turn the page to find out how.

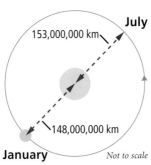

July

153,000,000 km

148,000,000 km

January *Not to scale*

Earth's orbit is almost a circle. Earth's distance from the Sun varies by only about 5,000,000 km—about 3%—during a year.

VOCABULARY
Remember to put each
new term into a frame
game diagram.

Seasonal Patterns

Most locations on Earth experience **seasons,** patterns of temperature changes and other weather trends over the course of a year. Near the equator, the temperatures are almost the same year-round. Near the poles, there are very large changes in temperatures from winter to summer. The temperature changes occur because the amount of sunlight at each location changes during the year. The changes in the amount of sunlight are due to the tilt of Earth's axis.

Look at the diagram on page 47 to see how the constant direction of Earth's tilted axis affects the pattern of sunlight on Earth at different times of the year. As Earth travels around the Sun, the area of sunlight in each hemisphere changes. At an **equinox** (EE-kwuh-NAHKS), sunlight shines equally on the northern and southern hemispheres. Half of each hemisphere is lit, and half is in darkness. As Earth moves along its orbit, the light shifts more into one hemisphere than the other. At a **solstice** (SAHL-stihs), the area of sunlight is at a maximum in one hemisphere and a minimum in the other hemisphere. Equinoxes and solstices happen on or around the 21st days of certain months of the year.

1 September Equinox When Earth is in this position, sunlight shines equally on the two hemispheres. You can see in the diagram that the North Pole is at the border between light and dark. The September equinox marks the beginning of autumn in the Northern Hemisphere and of spring in the Southern Hemisphere.

2 December Solstice Three months later, Earth has traveled a quarter of the way around the Sun, but its axis still points in the same direction into space. The North Pole seems to lean away from the direction of the Sun. The solstice occurs when the pole leans as far away from the Sun as it will during the year. You can see that the North Pole is in complete darkness. At the same time, the opposite is true in the Southern Hemisphere. The South Pole seems to lean toward the Sun and is in sunlight. It is the Southern Hemisphere's summer solstice and the Northern Hemisphere's winter solstice.

3 March Equinox After another quarter of its orbit, Earth reaches another equinox. Half of each hemisphere is lit, and the sunlight is centered on the equator. You can see that the poles are again at the border between day and night.

4 June Solstice This position is opposite the December solstice. Earth's axis still points in the same direction, but now the North Pole seems to lean toward the Sun and is in sunlight. The June solstice marks the beginning of summer in the Northern Hemisphere. In contrast, it is the winter solstice in the Southern Hemisphere.

READING TiP

The positions and lighting can be hard to imagine, so you might use a model as well as the diagram on the next page to help you understand.

CHECK YOUR READING In what month does winter begin in the Southern Hemisphere?

Earth's orbit and steady, tilted axis produce seasons.

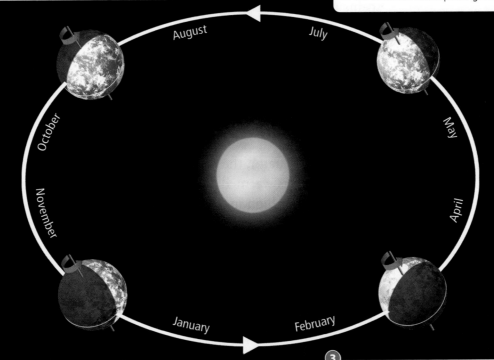

① **September Equinox** Half of the sunlight is in each hemisphere. The strongest sunlight is on the equator.

④ **June Solstice** More than half of the Northern Hemisphere is in sunlight. The strongest sunlight is north of the equator, so the Northern Hemisphere grows warmer.

August July October November May April

Not to scale

January February

② **December Solstice** Less than half of the Northern Hemisphere is in sunlight. The strongest sunlight is south of the equator, so the Southern Hemisphere grows warmer.

③ **March Equinox** Half of the sunlight is in each hemisphere. The strongest sunlight is on the equator.

View from the Sun

If you could stand on the Sun and look at Earth, you would see different parts of Earth at different times of year.

fall — spring —

winter — summer —

spring — fall —

summer — winter —

① September Equinox   **②** December Solstice   **③** March Equinox   **④** June Solstice

The equinoxes and solstices mark the beginnings of seasons in the two hemispheres. Warmer seasons occur when more of a hemisphere is in sunlight.

READING VISUALS Look at the poles to help you see how each hemisphere is lit. When is the South Pole completely in sunlight?

Angles of Sunlight

RESOURCE CENTER
CLASSZONE.COM

Learn more about
seasons.

You have seen that seasons change as sunlight shifts between hemispheres during the year. On the ground, you notice the effects of seasons because the angle of sunlight and the length of daylight change over the year. The effects are greatest at locations far from the equator. You may have noticed that sunshine seems barely warm just before sunset, when the Sun is low in the sky. At noon the sunshine seems much hotter. The angle of light affects the temperature.

When the Sun is high in the sky, sunlight strikes the ground at close to a right angle. The energy of sunlight is concentrated. Shadows are short. You may get a sunburn quickly when the Sun is at a high angle. When the Sun is low in the sky, sunlight strikes the ground at a slant. The light is spread over a greater area, so it is less concentrated and produces long shadows. Slanted light warms the ground less.

Near the equator, the noonday Sun is almost overhead every day, so the ground is warmed strongly year-round. In the middle latitudes, the noon Sun is high in the sky only during part of the year. In winter the noon Sun is low and warms the ground less strongly.

CHECK YOUR READING How are temperatures throughout the year affected by the angles of sunlight?

Sun Height and Shadows

Winter Solstice, 12 P.M.

Winter shadows are long because sunlight is spread out. The Sun appears low in the sky even at noon.

location on Earth

Spring Equinox, 12 P.M.

Spring and fall shadows are of medium length, and the noon Sun appears higher in the sky.

Summer Solstice, 12 P.M.

Summer shadows are short because the light is concentrated in a small area. The noon Sun appears high in the sky.

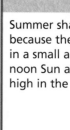

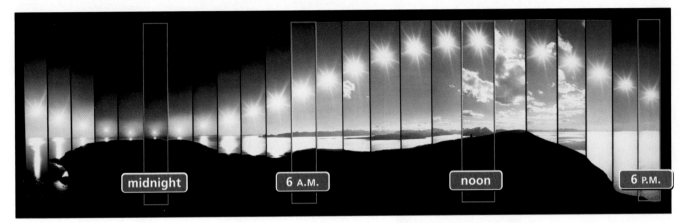

midnight | 6 A.M. | noon | 6 P.M.

Near the pole in the summer, the Sun stays above the horizon, so there is no night. This series of photographs was taken over the course of a day.

Lengths of Days

Seasonal temperatures depend on the amount of daylight, too. In Chicago, for example, the summer Sun heats the ground for about 15 hours a day, but in winter there may be only 9 hours of sunlight each day. The farther you get from the equator, the more extreme the changes in day length become. As you near one of the poles, summer daylight may last for 20 hours or more.

Very close to the poles, the Sun does not set at all for six months at a time. It can be seen shining near the horizon at midnight. Tourists often travel far north just to experience the midnight Sun. At locations near a pole, the Sun sets on an equinox and then does not rise again for six months. Astronomers go to the South Pole in March to take advantage of the long winter night, which allows them to study objects in the sky without the interruption of daylight.

Very near the equator, the periods of daylight and darkness are almost equal year-round—each about 12 hours long. Visitors who are used to hot weather during long summer days might be surprised when a hot, sunny day ends suddenly at 6 P.M. At locations away from the equator, daylight lasts 12 hours only around the time of an equinox.

READING TiP

Equinox means "equal night"—daylight and night-time are equal in length.

2.1 Review

KEY CONCEPTS

1. What causes day and night?
2. What happens to Earth's axis of rotation as Earth orbits the Sun?
3. How do the areas of sunlight in the two hemispheres change over the year?

CRITICAL THINKING

4. **Apply** If you wanted to enjoy longer periods of daylight in the summertime, would you head closer to the equator or farther from it? Why?

5. **Compare and Contrast** How do the average temperatures and the seasonal changes at the equator differ from those at the poles?

CHALLENGE

6. **Infer** If Earth's axis were tilted so much that the North Pole sometimes pointed straight at the Sun, how would the hours of daylight be affected at your location?

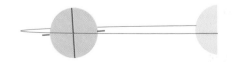

CHAPTER INVESTIGATION

Modeling Seasons

OVERVIEW AND PURPOSE Why is the weather in North America so much colder in January than in July? You might be surprised to learn that it has nothing to do with Earth's distance from the Sun. In fact, Earth is closest to the Sun in January. In this lab, you will model the cause of seasons as you
- orient a light source at different angles to a surface
- determine how the angles of sunlight at a location change as Earth orbits the Sun

▶ Problem

How does the angle of light affect the amount of solar energy a location receives at different times of year?

▶ Hypothesize

After performing step 3, write a hypothesis to explain how the angles of sunlight affect the amounts of solar energy your location receives at different times of year. Your hypothesis should take the form of an "If . . . , then . . . , because . . ." statement.

▶ Procedure

MATERIALS
- graph paper
- flashlight
- meter stick
- protractor
- globe
- stack of books
- sticky note

PART A

1. Mark an *X* near the center of the graph paper. Shine the flashlight onto the paper from about 30 cm straight above the X—at an angle of 90° to the surface. Observe the size of the spot of light.

2. Shine the flashlight onto the X at different angles. Keep the flashlight at the same distance. Write down what happens to the size of the spot of light as you change angles.

3. Repeat step 2, but observe just one square near the X. Write down what happens to the brightness of the light as you change the angle. The brightness shows how much energy the area receives from the flashlight.

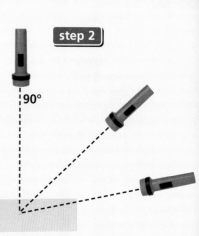

step 2

90°

4. Think about the temperatures at different times of year at your location, then write your hypothesis.

PART B

5 Set up the globe, books, and flashlight as shown in the photograph. Point the globe's North Pole to the right. This position represents solstice A.

solstice A

6 Find your location on the globe. Place a folded sticky note onto the globe at your location as shown in the photograph. Rotate the globe on its axis until the note faces toward the flashlight.

7 The flashlight beam represents noonday sunlight at your location. Use the protractor to estimate the angle of the light on the surface.

light
steps 6–7

8 Move the globe to the left side of the table and the flashlight and books to the right side of the table. Point the North Pole to the right. This position represents solstice B.

9 Repeat step 7 for solstice B.

solstice B

▶ Observe and Analyze
Write It Up

1. **RECORD** Draw the setup of your materials in each part of the investigation. Organize your notes.

2. **ANALYZE** Describe how the angle of the flashlight in step 2 affected the area of the spot of light. Which angle concentrated the light into the smallest area?

3. **EVALUATE** At which angle did a square of the graph paper receive the most energy?

4. **COMPARE** Compare the angles of light in steps 7 and 9. In which position was the angle of light closer to 90°?

▶ Conclude
Write It Up

1. **EVALUATE** How did the angle of sunlight at your location differ at the two times of year? At which position is sunlight more concentrated at your location?

2. **APPLY** The amount of solar energy at a location affects temperature. Which solstice—A or B—represents the summer solstice at your location?

3. **INTERPRET** Do your results support your hypothesis? Explain why or why not.

▶ INVESTIGATE Further

CHALLENGE What happens in the other hemisphere at the two times of year? Use the model to find out.

Modeling Seasons

Problem How does the angle of light affect the amount of solar energy a location receives at different times of year?

Hypothesize

Observe and Analyze

Table 1. Solstices A and B

	Solstice A	Solstice B
Drawing		
Angle of light (°)		
Observations		

Conclude

2.2 The Moon is Earth's natural satellite.

◀ **BEFORE, you learned**

- Earth turns as it orbits the Sun
- The day side of Earth is the part in sunlight
- The Moon is the closest body to Earth

▶ **NOW, you will learn**

- How the Moon moves
- What the Moon's dark-colored and light-colored features are
- About the inside structure of the Moon

VOCABULARY

mare p. 53

EXPLORE The Moon's Motion

How much does the Moon turn?

PROCEDURE

1. Draw a circle to represent the Moon's orbit with Earth at the center. The compass represents the Moon.

2. Move the compass around the circle. Keep the side of the compass marked *E* always facing Earth.

3. Observe the positions of the *E* and the compass needle at several positions on the circle.

WHAT DO YOU THINK?
What does the model tell you about the Moon's motion?

MATERIALS
- paper
- magnetic compass

The Moon rotates as it orbits Earth.

When you look at the disk of the Moon, you may notice darker and lighter areas. Perhaps you have imagined them as features of a face or some other pattern. People around the world have told stories about the animals, people, and objects they have imagined while looking at the light and dark areas of the Moon. As you will read in this chapter, these areas tell a story to scientists as well.

The pull of gravity keeps the Moon, Earth's natural satellite, in orbit around Earth. Even though the Moon is Earth's closest neighbor in space, it is far away compared to the sizes of Earth and the Moon.

The Moon's diameter is about 1/4 Earth's diameter, and the Moon is about 30 Earth diameters away.

Earth ————————————————————————•

Moon

The distance between Earth and the Moon is roughly 380,000 kilometers (240,000 mi)—about a hundred times the distance between New York and Los Angeles. If a jet airliner could travel in space, it would take about 20 days to cover a distance that huge. Astronauts, whose spaceships traveled much faster than jets, needed about 3 days to reach the Moon.

You always see the same pattern of dark-colored and light-colored features on the Moon. Only this one side of the Moon can be seen from Earth. The reason is that the Moon, like many other moons in the solar system, always keeps one side turned toward its planet. This means that the Moon turns once on its own axis each time it orbits Earth.

 CHECK YOUR READING Why do you see only one side of the Moon?

The Moon's craters show its history.

The half of the Moon's surface that constantly faces Earth is called the near side. The half that faces away from Earth is called the far side. Much of the Moon's surface is light-colored. Within the light-colored areas are many small, round features. There are also dark-colored features, some of which cover large areas. Much of the near side of the Moon is covered with these dark-colored features. In contrast, the far side is mostly light-colored with just a few of the darker features.

Just as on Earth, features on the Moon are given names to make it easier to discuss them. The names of the larger surface features on the Moon are in the Latin language, because centuries ago scientists from many different countries used Latin to communicate with one another. Early astronomers thought that the dark areas might be bodies of water, so they used the Latin word for "sea." Today, a dark area on the Moon is still called a lunar **mare** (MAH-ray). The plural form is *maria* (MAH-ree-uh).

The maria are not bodies of water, however. All of the features that can be seen on the Moon are different types of solid or broken rock. The Moon has no air, no oceans, no clouds, and no life.

Moon

The side of the Moon that constantly faces Earth has large, dark areas called maria.

Mass 1% of Earth's mass
Diameter 27% of Earth's diameter
**Average distance
    from Earth** 380,000 km
Orbits in 27.3 Earth days
Rotates in 27.3 Earth days

READING TiP

Lunar means "having to do with the Moon." The word comes from *luna,* the Latin word for the Moon.

Craters and Maria

The light-colored areas of the Moon are higher—at greater altitudes—than the maria, so they are called the lunar highlands. The ground of the lunar highlands is rocky, and some places are covered with a powder made of finely broken rock.

The highlands have many round features, called impact craters, that formed when small objects from space hit the Moon's surface. Long ago, such collisions happened more often than they do today. Many impact craters marked the surfaces of the Moon, Earth, and other bodies in space. On Earth, however, most craters have been worn away by water and wind. On the dry, airless Moon, impact craters from a long time ago are still visible.

Long ago, some of the largest craters filled with molten rock, or lava, that came from beneath the Moon's surface. The lava filled the lowest areas and then cooled, forming the large, flat plains called maria. Smaller impacts have continued to occur, so the dark plains of the maria do contain some craters. Most of the large maria are on the near side of the Moon. However, the widest and deepest basin on the Moon is on the far side, near the Moon's south pole.

 CHECK YOUR READING How did the maria form? List the steps.

Lunar Map

Light-colored highlands and dark maria form a familiar pattern on the near side of the Moon and a very different pattern on the far side.

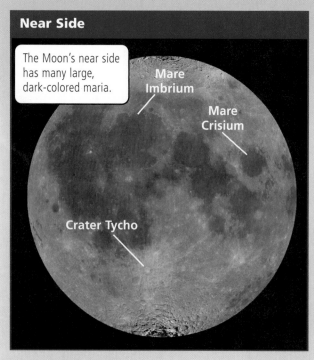

Near Side

The Moon's near side has many large, dark-colored maria.

Mare Imbrium

Mare Crisium

Crater Tycho

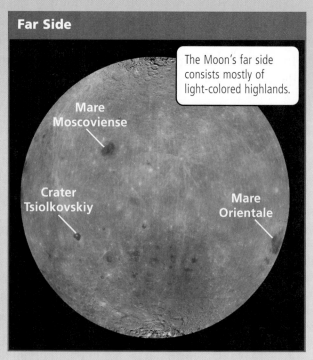

Far Side

The Moon's far side consists mostly of light-colored highlands.

Mare Moscoviense

Crater Tsiolkovskiy

Mare Orientale

INVESTIGATE Moon Features

How did the Moon's features form?

In this model, you will use a paper towel to represent the Moon's surface and gelatin to represent molten rock from inside the Moon.

PROCEDURE

1. Pour about 1 cm of partly cooled liquid gelatin into the cup.

2. Hold the paper towel by bringing its corners together. Push the towel into the cup until the center of the towel touches the bottom of the cup. Open the towel slightly.

3. Place the cup in the bowl of ice, and allow the gelatin time to solidify.

WHAT DO YOU THINK?

- What part of the towel did the gelatin affect?

- When you look down into the cup, what can the smooth areas tell you about heights?

CHALLENGE Early astronomers thought there might be oceans on the Moon. How does your model lava resemble an ocean?

Moon Rocks

Moon rocks have different ages. Some of the surface rock of the Moon is about 4.5 billion years old—as old as the Moon itself. This very old rock is found in the lunar highlands. The rock in the maria is younger because it formed from lava that solidified later, 3.8–3.1 billion years ago. These two main types of rock and their broken pieces cover most of the Moon's surface. Astronauts explored the Moon and brought back samples of as many different types of material as they could.

Impacts from space objects leave craters, and they also break the surface material into smaller pieces. This breaking of material is called weathering, even though it is not caused by wind and water. Weathered material on the Moon forms a type of dry, lifeless soil. The lunar soil is more than 15 meters (50 ft) deep in some places. Impacts can also toss lunar soil into different places, compact it into new rocks, or melt it and turn it into a glassy type of rock.

The dark-colored rock that formed from lava is called basalt (buh-SAWLT). Lunar basalt is similar to the rock deep beneath Earth's oceans. The basalt of the lunar maria covers large areas but is often only a few hundred meters in depth. However, the basalt can be several kilometers deep at the center of a mare, a depth similar to that of Earth's oceans.

Almost 400 kg (weighing more than 800 lb) of Moon rocks and soil were collected and brought back to Earth by astronauts.

highland rock

basalt

The Moon has layers.

Scientists on Earth have analyzed the lunar rocks and soil to determine their ages and materials. These results told scientists a story about how the Moon changed over time. During an early stage of the Moon's history, impacts happened often and left craters of many different sizes. That stage ended about 3.8 billion years ago, and impacts have happened much less often since then. The highland rocks and soil come from the original surface and impacts. Shortly after the impacts slowed, lava flooded the low-lying areas and formed the maria. Then the flooding stopped. During the last 3 billion years, the Moon has gained new impact craters from time to time but has remained mostly unchanged.

COMBINATION NOTES
Remember to take notes and make diagrams when you read about new ideas and terms.

Structure

Scientists have used information from lunar rocks and other measurements to figure out what is inside the Moon. Beneath its thin coating of crushed rock, the Moon has three layers—a crust, a mantle, and a core. As on Earth, the crust is the outermost layer. It averages about 70 kilometers (about 40 mi) thick and contains the least dense type of rock.

The Moon's interior resembles Earth's interior in several ways.

crust
mantle
core

Beneath the crust is a thick mantle that makes up most of the Moon's volume. The mantle is made of dense types of rock that include the elements iron and magnesium. The basalt on the lunar surface contains these same elements, so scientists infer that the material of the basalt came from the mantle.

In the middle of the Moon is a small core, approximately 700 kilometers (400 mi) across. Although dense, it makes up only a tiny fraction of the Moon's mass. Scientists have less information about the core than the mantle because material from the core did not reach the Moon's surface. The core seems to consist of iron and other metals.

CHECK YOUR READING What are your own questions about the Moon?

Formation

Scientists develop models to help them understand their observations, such as the observed similarities and differences between Earth and the Moon. The two objects have similar structures and are made of similar materials. However, the materials are in different proportions. The Moon has more materials like Earth's crust and mantle and less material like Earth's core.

Scientists have used these facts to develop models of how the Moon formed. A widely accepted model of the Moon's origin involves a giant collision. In this model, an early version of Earth was hit by a

Formation of the Moon

Collision

An early version of Earth is struck by a slightly smaller space body.

Re-Forming

The many pieces pull each other into orbits. Most of the material forms a new version of Earth.

Earth and Moon

The Moon forms from material that orbits the new version of Earth.

smaller space body. Much of the material from both bodies, especially the cores, combined to form a new version of Earth. The energy of the collision also threw material out, away from Earth. Bits of material from the crusts and mantles of both bodies went into orbit around the new Earth. Much of this orbiting material clumped together and became the Moon. Computer simulations of these events show that the Moon may have formed quickly—perhaps within just one year.

Evidence from fossils and rocks on Earth show that, whether the Moon formed from a giant collision or in some other way, it was once much closer to Earth than it is today. The Moon has been moving slowly away from Earth. It now moves 3.8 centimeters (1.5 in.) farther from Earth each year. However, this change is so slow that you will not notice any difference in your lifetime.

2.2 Review

KEY CONCEPTS

1. How many times does the Moon rotate on its axis during one trip around Earth?

2. What are the dark spots and the light areas on the Moon called?

3. Describe the Moon's layers.

CRITICAL THINKING

4. **Compare and Contrast** How are the Moon's dark-colored areas different from its light-colored areas?

5. **Draw Conclusions** How have the Moon rocks that astronauts brought back to Earth helped scientists understand the history of the Moon?

○ CHALLENGE

6. **Analyze** Scientists use indirect methods to learn about the cores of Earth and the Moon. Imagine you have several Styrofoam balls, some with steel balls hidden inside. Without breaking a ball open, how might you tell whether it contains a steel ball?

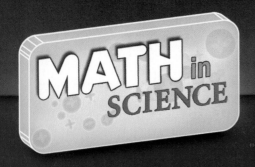

MATH TUTORIAL
CLASSZONE.COM
Click on Math Tutorial for
more help with line graphs.

Graphing Sunlight

The location of the Moon and the Sun in the sky depend on your location on Earth and when you look. In summer, the noon Sun is at a greater angle above the horizon—closer to 90°—than it is in winter. In summer, the Sun rises earlier and sets later than in winter. Longer days and steeper angles of sunlight combine to make summer days much warmer than winter days. Plot the data for Washington, D.C. (latitude 39° N) to see the changing patterns of sunlight.

Washington, D.C.

Month	Sunlight Each Day (h)	Angle of Sun at Noon (°)
Jan.	9.9	31.4
Feb.	11.0	40.8
Mar.	12.2	51.6
Apr.	13.5	63.2
May	14.5	71.4
June	14.9	74.6
July	14.5	71.4
Aug.	13.5	63.0
Sept.	12.2	51.6
Oct.	11.0	40.2
Nov.	9.9	31.1
Dec.	9.5	27.7

This is a series of images of the Sun photographed at exactly the same time of day every few days over most of a year. The bottom of the photograph is from just one of the days and includes a stone circle calendar.

Example

You can make a double line graph to see patterns in the data. Use a colored pencil to label the second y-axis.

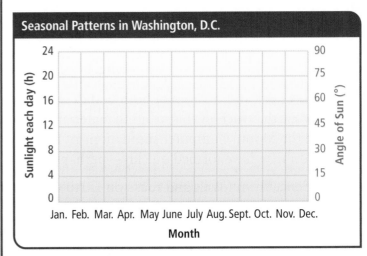

(1) Copy all three graph axes onto graph paper.

(2) Use the y-axis on the left to plot the data for the hours of daylight. Draw line segments to connect the points.

(3) Use the y-axis on the right and a colored pencil to plot the data for the angle of the Sun. Draw line segments to connect the points.

Answer the following questions.

1. During which time period do days get shorter?

2. About how many degrees higher in the sky is the noon Sun in June than in December? About how many more hours of sunlight are there each day in June than in December?

3. Does the angle of the Sun change more quickly between June and July or between September and October? How can you tell?

CHALLENGE Copy the axes again, then graph the data your teacher gives you for a location near the North Pole. Use your graphs to compare daylight patterns at the two latitudes.

2.3 Positions of the Sun and Moon affect Earth.

BEFORE, you learned

- The Moon orbits Earth
- Sunlight shines on Earth and the Moon

NOW, you will learn

- Why the Moon has phases
- What causes eclipses
- Why Earth's oceans have tides

VOCABULARY

eclipse p. 63
umbra p. 63
penumbra p. 63

THINK ABOUT

Have you seen the Moon in daylight?

Many people think that the Moon is visible only at night. This idea is not surprising, because the Moon is the brightest object in the sky at night. In the daytime the Moon is only as bright as a tiny, thin cloud. It is easy to miss, even in a cloudless blue sky. You can see the Moon sometimes in the day-time, sometimes at night, often at both times, and sometimes not at all. Why does the Moon sometimes disappear from view?

Phases are different views of the Moon's sunlit half.

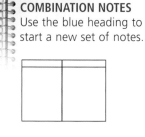

COMBINATION NOTES
Use the blue heading to start a new set of notes.

What you see as moonlight is really light from the Sun reflected by the Moon's surface. At any time, sunlight shines on half of the Moon's surface. Areas where sunlight does not reach look dark, just as the night side of Earth looks dark from space. As the Moon turns on its axis, areas on the surface move into and out of sunlight.

When you look at the Moon, you see a bright shape that is the lit part of the near side of the Moon. The unlit part is hard to see. Lunar phases are the patterns of lit and unlit portions of the Moon that you see from Earth. It takes about a month for the Moon to orbit Earth and go through all the phases.

 CHECK YOUR READING Why do you sometimes see only part of the near side of the Moon?

The Moon's position in its monthly orbit determines how it appears from Earth. The diagram on page 61 shows how the positions of the Moon, the Sun, and Earth affect the shapes you see in the sky.

Waxing Moon

First Week The cycle begins with a new moon. From Earth, the Moon and the Sun are in the same direction. If you face a new moon, you face the Sun. Your face and the far side of the Moon are in sunlight. The near side of the Moon is unlit, so you do not see it. During a new moon, there appears to be no Moon.

As the Moon moves along its orbit, sunlight begins falling on the near side. You see a thin crescent shape. During the first week, the Moon keeps moving farther around, so more of the near side becomes lit. You see thicker crescents as the Moon waxes, or grows.

Second Week When half of the near side of the Moon is in sunlight, the Moon has completed one-quarter of its cycle. The phase is called the first quarter, even though you might describe the shape as a half-moon. You can see in the diagram that the Moon is 90 degrees—at a right angle—from the Sun. If you face the first-quarter moon when it is high in the sky, sunlight will shine on the right side of your head and the right side of the Moon.

You see more of the Moon as it moves along its orbit during the second week. The phase is called gibbous (GIHB-uhs) when the near side is more than half lit but not fully lit. The Moon is still waxing, so the phases during the second week are called waxing gibbous moons.

 CHECK YOUR READING Why does the Moon sometimes seem to have a crescent shape?

Waning Moon

Third Week Halfway through its cycle, the whole near side of the Moon is in sunlight—a full moon. You might think of it as the second quarter. Viewed from Earth, the Moon and the Sun are in opposite directions. If you face a full moon at sunset, sunlight from behind you lights the back of your head and the near side of the Moon.

As the Moon continues around during the third week, less and less of the near side is in sunlight. The Moon seems to shrink, or wane, so these phases are called waning gibbous moons.

Fourth Week When the near side is again only half in sunlight, the Moon is three-quarters of the way through its cycle. The phase is called the third quarter. The Moon is again 90 degrees from the Sun. If you face the third-quarter moon when it is high in the sky, sunlight will shine on the left side of your head and the left side of the Moon.

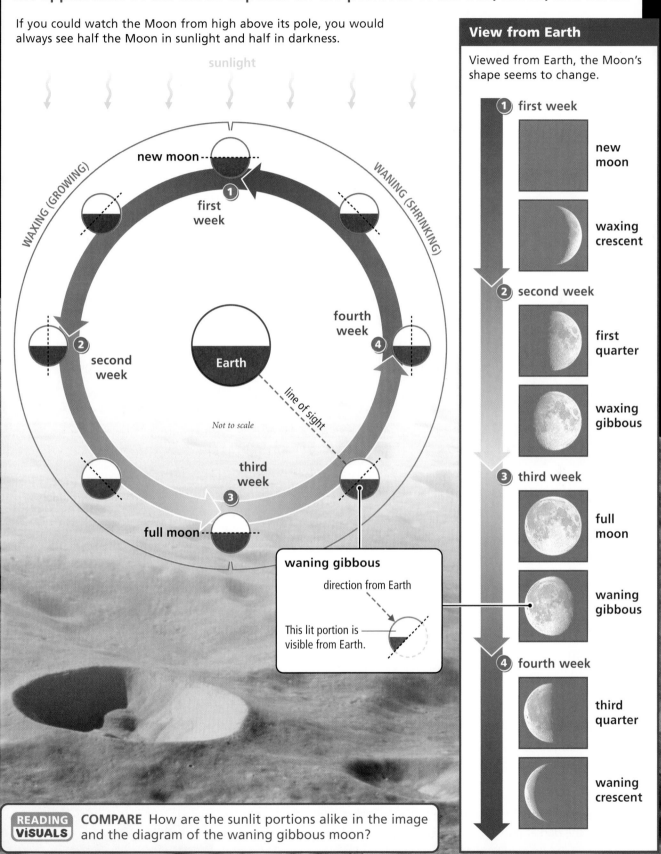

Lunar Phases

The appearance of the Moon depends on the positions of the Sun, Moon, and Earth.

If you could watch the Moon from high above its pole, you would always see half the Moon in sunlight and half in darkness.

sunlight

WAXING (GROWING)

WANING (SHRINKING)

new moon

1

first week

2

second week

Earth

Not to scale

line of sight

fourth week

4

third week

3

full moon

waning gibbous

direction from Earth

This lit portion is visible from Earth.

View from Earth

Viewed from Earth, the Moon's shape seems to change.

1 first week

new moon

waxing crescent

2 second week

first quarter

waxing gibbous

3 third week

full moon

waning gibbous

4 fourth week

third quarter

waning crescent

READING ViSUALS **COMPARE** How are the sunlit portions alike in the image and the diagram of the waning gibbous moon?

As the Moon continues to move around Earth during the fourth week, less and less of the near side is in sunlight. The waning crescent moon grows thinner and thinner. At the end of the fourth week, the near side is again unlit, and the new moon begins a new cycle.

Crescent and Gibbous Moons

Think through the waxing lunar phases again. The Moon waxes from new to crescent to gibbous during the first half of its cycle. Then it wanes from full to gibbous to crescent during the second half of its cycle.

The amount of the Moon that you see from Earth depends on the angle between the Moon and the Sun. When this angle is small, you see only a small amount of the Moon. Crescent moons occur when the Moon appears close to the Sun in the sky. As a result, they are visible most often in the daytime or around the time of sunrise or sunset. When the angle between the Sun and the Moon is large, you see a large amount of the Moon. Gibbous and full moons appear far from the Sun in the sky. You may see them in the daytime, but you are more likely to notice them at night.

 CHECK YOUR READING What shape does the Moon appear to be when it is at a small angle to the Sun?

INVESTIGATE Phases of the Moon

Why does the Moon seem to change shape?

PROCEDURE

1. Place the ball on the stick, which will act as a handle. The ball will represent the Moon, and your head will represent Earth.

2. Hold the ball toward the light, then move it to your left until you see a bright edge. Draw what you see.

3. Move the ball farther around until half of what you see is lit. Draw it.

4. Keep moving the ball around to your left until the side you see is fully lit, then half lit, then lit only a little bit. Each time, face the ball and draw it.

WHAT DO YOU THINK?

- In step 2, which side of the ball was lit? Explain why.
- How are your drawings like the photographs of the Moon's phases? Label each drawing with the name of the corresponding lunar phase.

CHALLENGE When the Moon is a crescent, sometimes you can dimly see the rest of the Moon if you look closely. Where might the light that makes the darker part of the Moon visible come from?

SKILL FOCUS
Making models

MATERIALS
- foam ball
- stick
- lamp

TIME
20 minutes

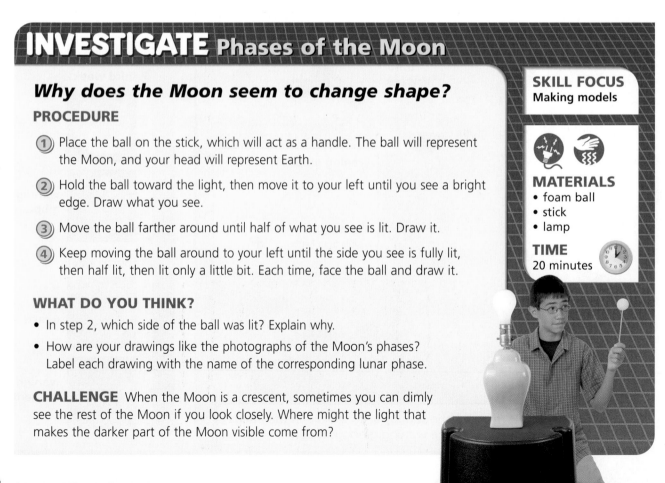

Shadows in space cause eclipses.

Sunlight streams past Earth and the Moon, lighting one side of each body. Beyond each body is a long, thin cone of darkness where no sunlight reaches—a shadow in space. The two bodies are far apart, so they usually miss each other's shadow as the Moon orbits Earth. However, if the Moon, the Sun, and Earth line up exactly, a shadow crosses Earth or the Moon. An **eclipse** occurs when a shadow makes the Sun or the Moon seem to grow dark. In a lunar eclipse, the Moon darkens. In a solar eclipse, the Sun seems to darken.

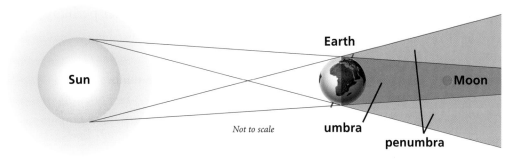

Sun

Earth

Moon

Not to scale   umbra

penumbra

Lunar Eclipses

The Moon becomes dark during a lunar eclipse because it passes through Earth's shadow. There are two parts of Earth's shadow, as you can see in the diagram above. The **umbra** is the darkest part. Around it is a spreading cone of lighter shadow called the **penumbra.**

Just before a lunar eclipse, sunlight streaming past Earth produces a full moon. Then the Moon moves into Earth's penumbra and becomes slightly less bright. As the Moon moves into the umbra, Earth's dark shadow seems to creep across and cover the Moon. The entire Moon can be in darkness because the Moon is small enough to fit entirely within Earth's umbra. After an hour or more, the Moon moves slowly back into the sunlight that is streaming past Earth.

A total lunar eclipse occurs when the Moon passes completely into Earth's umbra. If the Moon misses part or all of the umbra, part of the Moon stays light and the eclipse is called a partial lunar eclipse.

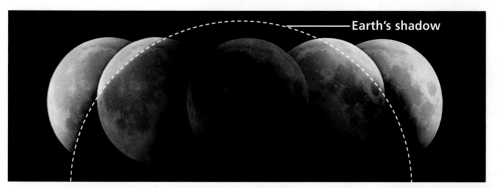

Earth's shadow

The Moon starts getting dark on one side as it passes into Earth's umbra. Even when the Moon is completely within Earth's umbra, some red sunlight, bent by Earth's atmosphere, may still reach the Moon.

Solar Eclipses

In a solar eclipse, the Sun seems to darken because the Moon's shadow falls onto part of Earth. Imagine that you are in the path of a solar eclipse. At first, you see a normal day. You cannot see the dark Moon moving toward the Sun. Then part of the Sun seems to disappear as the Moon moves in front of it. You are in the Moon's penumbra. After several hours of growing darkness, the Moon covers the Sun's disk completely. The sky becomes as dark as night, and you may see constellations. In place of the Sun is a black disk—the new moon— surrounded by a pale glow. You are in the Moon's umbra, the darkest part of the shadow, experiencing a total solar eclipse. After perhaps a minute, the Sun's bright surface starts to appear again.

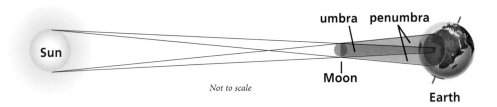

Sun

umbra   penumbra

Moon

Earth

Not to scale

A solar eclipse occurs when the Moon passes directly between Earth and the Sun. As you can see in the diagram above, the side of the Moon that faces Earth is unlit, so solar eclipses occur only during new moons.

If you could watch a solar eclipse from space, it might seem more like a lunar eclipse. You would see the Moon's penumbra, with the dark umbra in the center, move across Earth's daylight side. However, the Moon is smaller than Earth, so it casts a smaller shadow. As you can see in the diagram above, the Moon's umbra covers only a fraction of Earth's surface at a time.

June 21, 2001, Eclipse

total eclipse

In this time-lapse photograph, the Sun's disk appears darker as the Moon passes in front. When the Moon is exactly in front of the Sun, the sky grows as dark as night.

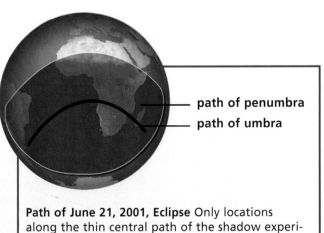

path of penumbra

path of umbra

Path of June 21, 2001, Eclipse Only locations along the thin central path of the shadow experience a total eclipse. Other locations experience a partial eclipse.

Only locations in the path of the Moon's shadow experience a solar eclipse. Some people travel thousands of miles to be in the thin path of the Moon's umbra so that they can experience a total solar eclipse. Locations near the path of the umbra get an eclipse that is less than total. If only the penumbra moves over your location, you experience a partial solar eclipse. The Moon covers just part of the Sun.

Bright light from the Sun's disk can damage your eyes if you look directly at it. The Sun is unsafe to look at even when the Moon covers most of the Sun's disk. If you have the chance to experience a solar eclipse, use a safe method to view the Sun.

CHECK YOUR READING Where is the Moon during a solar eclipse? Find a way to remember the difference between the two types of eclipses.

COMBINATION NOTES
Remember to make notes about new ideas.

The Moon's gravity causes tides on Earth.

If you have spent time near an ocean, you may have experienced the usual pattern of tides. At first, you might see dry sand that slopes down to the ocean. Then, waves creep higher and higher onto the sand. The average water level rises slowly for about 6 hours. The highest level is called high tide. Then the water level slowly drops for about 6 hours. The lowest level is called low tide. Then the water level rises and falls again. The entire pattern—two high tides and two low tides—takes a little more than 24 hours.

CHECK YOUR READING How many high tides do you expect per day?

In areas with tides, the water generally reaches its lowest level twice a day and its highest level twice a day.

Tides occur because the Moon's gravity changes the shape of Earth's oceans. The Moon pulls on different parts of Earth with different amounts of force. It pulls hardest on the side of Earth nearest it, a little less hard on the center of Earth, and even less hard on the farthest side of Earth. If Earth were flexible, it would be pulled into a football shape. Earth's crust is hard enough to resist being pulled into a different shape, but Earth's oceans do change shape.

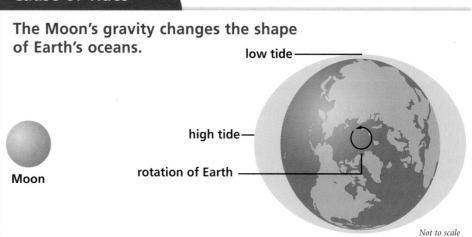

Cause of Tides

The Moon's gravity changes the shape of Earth's oceans.

low tide

high tide

rotation of Earth

Moon

Not to scale

RESOURCE CENTER
CLASSZONE.COM
Learn more about tides.

The diagram above shows what would happen if Earth were covered with a thick layer of water. The Moon's pull produces a bulge of thicker ocean water on the side of Earth nearest the Moon. Another bulge of water is produced on the side of Earth farthest from the Moon because the Moon pulls the center of Earth away from that side. The layer of water is thinnest in the middle, between the bulges.

A location moves past different thicknesses of water as Earth turns on its axis. As a result, the water level there rises and falls. The thickest water produces the highest level, which is high tide. A quarter of a rotation—6 hours—later, the location has moved to the thinnest layer of water, or low tide. Another high tide and low tide complete the cycle. Because the Moon is orbiting while Earth is turning, the cycle takes a little longer than the 24 hours in a day.

 CHECK YOUR READING Why does a cycle of tides take about 24 hours?

2.3 Review

KEY CONCEPTS

1. When the Moon is full, where is it in its orbit around Earth?

2. Where is the Moon in its orbit at the time of a solar eclipse?

3. If it is high tide where you are, is the tide high or low on the side of Earth directly opposite you?

CRITICAL THINKING

4. **Apply** If you were on the Moon's near side during a new moon, how much of the side of Earth facing you would be sunlit?

5. **Predict** If Earth did not turn, how would the pattern of tides be affected?

● CHALLENGE

6. **Predict** Would we see lunar phases if the Moon did not rotate while it orbits Earth?

Astronomy in Archaeology

In order to understand how people lived and thought long ago, archaeologists study the buildings and other physical remains of ancient cultures. Archaeologists often think about what needs people had in order to figure out how they used the things they built. For example, people needed to know the time of year in order to decide when to plant crops, move to a different location for winter, or plan certain ceremonies.

Archaeologists can use their knowledge about objects in the sky to hypothesize about the purpose of an ancient structure. They can also use knowledge and models from astronomy to test their hypotheses. For example, archaeologists found some structures at Chimney Rock that were built at times of special events in the sky.

Antikythera Computer

A device with gears and dials was found in an ancient Greek shipwreck. While examining the device, a scientist noticed terms, patterns, and numbers from astronomy. These observations led him to form a hypothesis that ancient Greeks used the instrument to calculate the positions of the Sun, Moon, and other bodies in space. Gamma-ray images of the instrument's interior later supported this hypothesis.

Chimney Rock

Chimney Rock, in Colorado, is topped by two natural pillars of rock. The Moon appears to rise between the pillars under special circumstances that happen about every 18 years. Near the pillars are ruins of buildings of the Anasazi people. In order to construct the buildings and live here, the builders had to haul materials and water much farther than was usual. Some archaeologists hypothesize that the Anasazi built here in order to watch or celebrate special events in the sky.

Stonehenge

Stonehenge is an arrangement of stones in Britain. The first stones were placed there around 3100 B.C. The way that the Sun and Moon line up with the stones has led some archaeologists to think that they were designed to help people predict solstices and eclipses. Solstices tell people the time of year, so Stonehenge has sometimes been called a calendar.

path of rising Sun on solstice

Stonehenge as seen from above

EXPLORE

1. **COMPARE** How is each archaeological example related to astronomy?

2. **CHALLENGE** Make a list of five print or television advertisements that feature the Sun or other objects in the sky. Bring in copies of the advertisements if you can. Why might the advertisers have chosen these objects?

Ruins of buildings were found on a high, narrow ridge at Chimney Rock.

the **BIG** idea

Earth and the Moon move in predictable ways as they orbit the Sun.

CONTENT REVIEW
CLASSZONE.COM

◀ KEY CONCEPTS SUMMARY

2.1 **Earth rotates on a tilted axis and orbits the Sun.**

Earth's rotation in sunlight causes day and night.

The changing angles of sunlight on Earth cause seasons.

VOCABULARY
axis of rotation p. 44
revolution p. 45
season p. 46
equinox p. 46
solstice p. 46

2.2 **The Moon is Earth's natural satellite.**

Dark-colored maria formed from lava-filled craters.

Light-colored highlands are old and cratered.

The Moon's near side always faces Earth.

crust ——
mantle ——
core ——

VOCABULARY
mare p. 53

2.3 **Positions of the Sun and Moon affect Earth.**

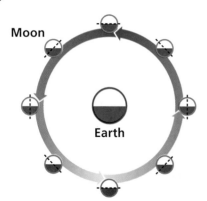

Moon

Earth

Lunar phases are different views of the Moon's sunlit half.

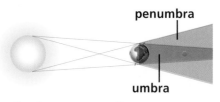

penumbra

umbra

Shadows cause eclipses.

The Moon's gravity causes tides as Earth turns.

VOCABULARY
eclipse p. 63
umbra p. 63
penumbra p. 63

Reviewing Vocabulary

Use words and diagrams to show the relationship between the terms in each the following pairs. Underline the two terms in each answer.

1. revolution, rotation

2. revolution, season

3. solstice, equinox

4. mare, impact crater

5. eclipse, umbra

6. umbra, penumbra

Reviewing Key Concepts

Multiple Choice *Choose the letter of the best answer.*

7. How long does it take Earth to turn once on its axis of rotation?
   a. an hour
   b. a day
   c. a month
   d. a year

8. How long does it take Earth to orbit the Sun?
   a. an hour
   b. a day
   c. a month
   d. a year

9. About how long does it take the Moon to revolve once around Earth?
   a. an hour
   b. a day
   c. a month
   d. a year

10. Why is it hotter in summer than in winter?
    a. Earth gets closer to and farther from the Sun.
    b. Sunlight strikes the ground at higher angles.
    c. Earth turns faster in some seasons.
    d. Earth revolves around the Sun more times in some seasons.

11. The dark maria on the Moon formed from
    a. dried-up seas
    b. finely-broken rock
    c. large shadows
    d. lava-filled craters

12. The lunar highlands have more impact craters than the maria, so scientists know that the highlands
    a. are older than the maria
    b. are younger than the maria
    c. are flatter than the maria
    d. are darker than the maria

13. Why is just one side of the Moon visible from Earth?
    a. The Moon does not rotate on its axis as it orbits Earth.
    b. The Moon rotates once in the same amount of time that it orbits.
    c. Half of the Moon is always unlit by the Sun.
    d. Half of the Moon does not reflect light.

14. Why does the Moon seem to change shape from week to week?
    a. Clouds block part of the Moon.
    b. The Moon moves through Earth's shadow.
    c. The Moon is lit in different ways.
    d. Different amounts of the dark-colored side of the Moon face Earth.

15. Which words describe the different shapes that the Moon appears to be?
    a. waning and waxing
    b. waning and crescent
    c. waxing and gibbous
    d. crescent and gibbous

16. During a total eclipse of the Moon, the Moon is
    a. in Earth's umbra
    b. in Earth's penumbra
    c. between Earth and the Sun
    d. casting a shadow on Earth

Short Answer *Write a short answer to each question.*

17. What motion produces two high tides in a day? Explain your answer.

18. How are the structure of the Moon and the structure of Earth similar?

Use the lunar map below to answer the next four questions.

Near Side   **Far Side**

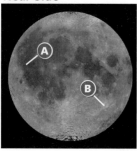

19. **APPLY** Which points are at higher elevations? Explain how you know.

20. **COMPARE** During a first-quarter moon, will point A, point B, both, or neither be in sunlight? **Hint:** Use the diagram on page 61.

21. **INFER** During a total lunar eclipse, which points will be in darkness?

22. **INFER** During a total solar eclipse, the Moon is new. Which points will be in darkness?

23. **CONNECT** Use your knowledge of the motions of Earth and the Moon to determine how long it takes the Moon to travel once around the Sun.

24. **ANALYZE** Which two parts of the Moon have important chemical elements in common? Choose from the following: core, mantle, crust, maria, highlands.

25. **APPLY** If it is noon for you, what time is it for someone directly on the opposite side of Earth?

26. **CLASSIFY** On what part or parts of Earth are winter and summer temperatures the most different from each other?

27. **APPLY** If it is the winter solstice in New York, what solstice or equinox is it in Sydney, Australia, in the Southern Hemisphere?

28. **PREDICT** If Earth stayed exactly the same distance from the Sun throughout the year, would the seasons be different? Explain what you think would happen.

29. **PREDICT** If Earth's axis were not tilted with respect to the orbit, would the seasons be different? Explain what you think would happen.

30. **PROVIDE EXAMPLES** How do the positions of the Sun and the Moon affect what people do? Give three examples of the ways that people's jobs or other activities are affected by the positions of the Sun, the Moon, or both.

31. **PREDICT** Which shape of the Moon are you most likely to see during the daytime? **Hint:** Compare the directions of the Sun and Moon from Earth in the diagram on page 61.

32. **CLASSIFY** What types of information have scientists used to make inferences about the Moon's history?

South Pole

33. **ANALYZE** The photograph above shows the side of Earth in sunlight at a particular time. The location of the South Pole is indicated. Was the photograph taken in March, in June, in September, or in December?

the BIG idea

34. **APPLY** Look again at the photograph on pages 40–41. Now that you have finished the chapter, how would you change your response to the question on the photograph?

35. **SYNTHESIZE** If you were an astronaut in the middle of the near side of the Moon during a full moon, how would the ground around you look? How would Earth, high in your sky, look? Describe what is in sunlight and what is in darkness.

UNIT PROJECTS

If you need to do an experiment for your unit project, gather the materials. Be sure to allow enough time to observe results before the project is due.

Analyzing a Diagram

The sketches show the phases of the Moon one week apart. The diagram shows the Moon's orbit around Earth. Use the diagram and the sketches to answer the questions below.

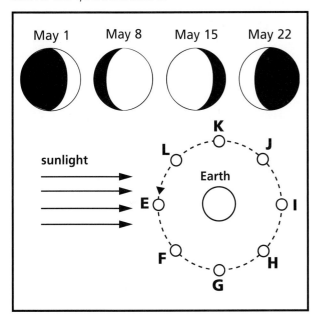

1. At which letter on the diagram might a full moon occur?

  a. E   **c.** I

  b. G   **d.** J

2. Which letter on the diagram shows the position of the Moon on May 8?

  a. E   **c.** G

  b. F   **d.** H

3. Approximately when was the Moon full?

  a. May 4   **c.** May 18

  b. May 11   **d.** May 29

4. At which letter on the diagram might a solar eclipse occur?

  a. E   **c.** I

  b. H   **d.** L

5. How much of the sunlit part of the Moon was visible from Earth on May 8?

  a. None of the sunlit part was visible.

  b. About one-quarter of the sunlit part was visible.

  c. About three-quarters of the sunlit part was visible.

  d. All of the sunlit part was visible.

6. Which of these sketches show Earth's shadow on the Moon?

  a. those for May 1 and May 22

  b. those for May 8 and May 15

  c. all 4 of them

  d. none of them

7. Which factor is most directly responsible for determining how often a full moon appears?

  a. the size of the Moon

  b. the size of Earth

  c. how quickly the Moon orbits Earth

  d. how quickly the Moon turns on its axis

Extended Response

Answer the two questions below in detail. A diagram may help you to answer.

8. The Moon was once much closer to Earth. What effect do you think that this distance had on eclipses?

9. What do you think would happen to tides on Earth if Earth stopped rotating? Why?

TIMELINES in Science

THE STORY OF ASTRONOMY

Around the year A.D. 140, an astronomer named Ptolemy wrote down his ideas about the motion of bodies in space. Ptolemy shared the view of many Greek astronomers that the Sun, the Moon, and the planets orbit Earth in perfect circles. The Greeks had observed that planets sometimes seem to reverse direction in their motion across the sky. Ptolemy explained that the backward movements are smaller orbits within the larger orbits. For 1400 years, Europeans accepted this Earth-centered model. In the mid-1500s, however, astronomers began to challenge and then reject Ptolemy's ideas.

The timeline shows a few events in the history of astronomy. Scientists have developed special tools and procedures to study objects in the sky. The boxes below the timeline show how technology has led to new knowledge about space and how that knowledge has been applied.

1543
Sun Takes Center Stage
Nicolaus Copernicus, a Polish astronomer, proposes that the planets orbit the Sun rather than Earth. His Sun-centered model shocks many because it conflicts with the traditional belief that Earth is the center of the universe.

EVENTS

| 1500 | 1520 | 1540 | 1560 |

APPLICATIONS AND TECHNOLOGY

APPLICATION

Navigating by Sunlight and Starlight
For thousands of years, sailors studied the sky to find their way at sea. Because the Sun and stars move in predictable ways, sailors used them to navigate across water. During the 1400s, sailors began to use a device called a mariner's astrolabe to observe the positions of the Sun and stars. Later devices allowed sailors to make more accurate measurements.

This mariner's astrolabe was made in the 1600s.

1609
Scientist Pinpoints Planet Paths

German astronomer Johannes Kepler concludes that the orbits of planets are not circles but ellipses, or flattened circles. Kepler, formerly the assistant of Tycho Brahe, reached his conclusion by studying Brahe's careful observations of the motions of planets.

1863
Stars and Earth Share Elements

English astronomer William Huggins announces that stars are made of hydrogen and other elements found on Earth. Astronomers had traditionally believed that stars were made of a unique substance. Huggins identified the elements in stars by studying their spectra.

1687
Laws of Gravity Revealed

English scientist Isaac Newton explains that gravity causes planets to orbit the Sun. His three laws of motion explain how objects interact on Earth as well as in space.

| 1600 | 1620 | 1640 | 1660 | 1680 | | 1860 |

TECHNOLOGY
Viewing Space

The telescope was probably invented in the early 1600s, when an eyeglass maker attached lenses to both ends of a tube. Soon afterward, Italian scientist Galileo Galilei copied the invention and used it to look at objects in space. Galileo's telescope allowed him to study features never seen before, such as mountains on the Moon. Most astronomers now use telescopes that gather visible light with mirrors rather than lenses. There are also special telescopes that gather other forms of electromagnetic radiation.

1912
Cycles of Stars Are Key to Distances
Certain types of stars, called Cepheid variables, get brighter and then dimmer in a regular cycle. Astronomer Henrietta Leavitt finds that brighter stars have longer cycles. This discovery will allow the distances to these stars to be calculated.

1929
Big Is Getting Bigger
Edwin Hubble has already used Cepheid variables to show that some objects in the sky are actually distant galaxies. Now he finds that galaxies are generally moving apart, at rates that increase with distance. Many astronomers conclude that the universe is expanding.

1916
Time, Space, and Mass Are Connected
The general theory of relativity expands Newton's theory of gravitation. Albert Einstein shows that mass affects time and space. According to this theory, gravity will affect the light we receive from objects in space.

1880	1900	1920	1940	1960

TECHNOLOGY
Colliding Particles Give Details About the Start of the Universe
Scientists think that all matter and energy was in an extremely hot, dense state and then exploded rapidly in an event called the big bang. Some scientists are attempting to re-create some of the conditions that existed during the first billionth of a second after the big bang. They use devices called particle accelerators to make tiny particles move almost at the speed of light. When the particles crash into each other, they produce different types of particles and radiation. Scientists use what they learn from the particles and the radiation to develop models of conditions at the beginning of the universe.

1998

Fast Is Getting Faster

Two groups of astronomers studying exploding stars called supernovae come to the same remarkable conclusion. Not only is the universe expanding, but the rate of expansion is increasing. In the diagram below, the rate of expansion is shown by the distances between rings and between galaxies.

The expanding universe

Present

Expansion slows down   Expansion speeds up

Big Bang

Farthest supernova

~15 billion years

RESOURCE CENTER
CLASSZONE.COM
Learn more about current advances in astronomy.

1980   2000

TECHNOLOGY

Measuring the Big Bang

In 1965 two researchers noticed radio waves that came from all directions instead of from just one direction, like a signal from a space object. They inferred that the radiation was left over from the big bang. In 1989 and again in 2001, NASA launched spacecraft to study the radiation. Data gathered using these telescopes in space are still being used to test different models of the big bang, including the arrangement of matter in the universe. In this map of the sky, red and yellow show the areas that were hottest after the big bang.

INTO THE FUTURE

Throughout history, people have learned about the universe from visible light and other radiation. New and better measurements have been made as technologies improved. Better and more complex models are filling in details that cannot be measured directly. In the future, improvements will continue. Computers, telescopes in space, and other instruments will allow astronomers to collect better data and make better models.

Some matter in the universe does not give off or reflect any detectable radiation. This is called dark matter. Astronomers infer its existence from its effects on matter that is detected. In the future, astronomers hope to determine what dark matter is, exactly where it is, and how it moves in the universe. In a similar way, astronomers will learn more about why the universe is expanding faster with time and what energy is involved in this acceleration.

ACTIVITIES

Reliving History

Some early astronomers observed the Moon in order to develop and test their ideas about space. For two weeks or more, make frequent observations of the Moon and keep your notes, sketches, and thoughts in a notebook. You might look for the Moon at a certain time each day or night or perhaps record the direction in which the Moon sets. A newspaper may list the times of moonrise and moonset for your location.

Compare your observations and thoughts with those of other students. You might also find out what people in other cultures thought of the patterns of change they saw in the Moon.

Writing About Science

Choose one of these famous astronomers and research his or her story. Write a biographical profile or an imaginary interview with that person.

Our Solar System

the **BIG** idea

Planets and other objects form a system around our Sun.

Key Concepts

SECTION

Planets orbit the Sun at different distances. Learn about the sizes and the distances of objects in the solar system and about its formation.

SECTION

The inner solar system has rocky planets. Learn about the processes that shape Earth and other planets.

SECTION

The outer solar system has four giant planets. Learn about the largest planets.

SECTION

Small objects are made of ice and rock. Learn about moons, asteroids, and comets.

Internet Preview

CLASSZONE.COM

Chapter 3 online resources: Content Review, Visualization, two Resource Centers, Math Tutorial, Test Practice

This image shows Jupiter with one of its large moons. How big are these objects compared with Earth?

EXPLORE (the BIG idea)

How Big Is Jupiter?

Measure 1.4 mL of water (about 22 drops) into an empty 2 L bottle to represent Earth. Use a full 2 L bottle to represent Jupiter. Lift each one.

Observe and Think How big is Jupiter compared with Earth? Using this scale, you would need more than nine hundred 2 L bottles to represent the Sun. How big is the Sun compared with Jupiter?

How Round Is an Orbit?

Tie a loop 10 cm long in a piece of string. Place two thumbtacks 2 cm apart in the center of a piece of paper. Loop the string around the thumbtacks and use a pencil to draw an oval the shape of Pluto's orbit. Remove one thumbtack. The remaining thumbtack represents the Sun.

Observe and Think How would you describe the shape of this orbit? How different is it from a circle?

Internet Activity: Spacing

Go to **ClassZone.com** to take a virtual spaceflight through the solar system. Examine distances between planets as your virtual spaceship travels at a constant speed.

Observe and Think What do you notice about the relative distances of the planets?

NSTA
scilinks.org

SC*i*LINKS

The Solar System **Code: MDL059**

Getting Ready to Learn

◀ CONCEPT REVIEW

- The planets we see are much closer than the stars in constellations.
- The Sun, the planets, and smaller bodies make up the solar system.
- Scientists observe different types of electromagnetic radiation from space objects.

◀ VOCABULARY REVIEW

orbit p. 10

solar system p. 10

satellite p. 23

impact crater p. 32

axis of rotation p. 44

 CONTENT REVIEW
CLASSZONE.COM
Review concepts and vocabulary.

▶ TAKING NOTES

MAIN IDEA AND DETAILS

Make a two-column chart. Write **main ideas,** such as those in the blue headings, in the column on the left. Write **details** about each of those main ideas in the column on the right.

VOCABULARY STRATEGY

Draw a **word triangle** diagram for each new vocabulary term. In the bottom row write and define the term. In the middle row, use the term correctly in a sentence. At the top, draw a small picture to help you remember the term.

See the Note-Taking Handbook on pages R45–R51.

SCIENCE NOTEBOOK

MAIN IDEAS	DETAIL NOTES
1. Planets have different sizes and distances.	1. Objects in the solar system • Sun • planets • moons • comets and asteroids
2.	2.

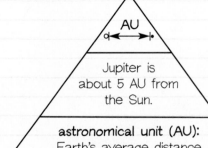

AU

Jupiter is about 5 AU from the Sun.

astronomical unit (AU): Earth's average distance from the Sun

Planets orbit the Sun at different distances.

◀ **BEFORE, you learned**

- Earth orbits the Sun
- The Moon is Earth's natural satellite
- The Moon's features tell us about its history

▶ **NOW, you will learn**

- What types of objects are in the solar system
- About sizes and distances in the solar system
- How the solar system formed

VOCABULARY

astronomical unit (AU) p. 81

ellipse p. 81

EXPLORE Planet Formation

How do planets form?

PROCEDURE

1 Fill the bowl about halfway with water.

2 Stir the water quickly, using a circular motion, and then remove the spoon.

3 Sprinkle wax pieces onto the swirling water.

WHAT DO YOU THINK?

- In what direction did the wax move?
- What else happened to the wax?

MATERIALS

- bowl
- water
- spoon
- wax pieces

Planets have different sizes and distances.

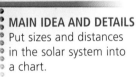

MAIN IDEA AND DETAILS
Put sizes and distances in the solar system into a chart.

You may have seen some planets in the sky without realizing it. They are so far from Earth that they appear as tiny dots of light in the darkened sky. If you have seen something that looks like a very bright star in the western sky in the early evening, you have probably seen the planet Venus. Even if you live in a city, you may have seen Mars, Jupiter, or Saturn but thought that you were seeing a star. Mercury is much more difficult to see. You need a telescope to see three of the planets in our solar system—Uranus, Neptune, and Pluto.

Like the Moon, planets can be seen because they reflect sunlight. Planets do not give off visible light of their own. Sunlight is also reflected by moons and other objects in space, called comets and asteroids. However, these objects are usually too far away and not bright enough to see without a telescope.

 CHECK YOUR READING Why do planets look bright?

Objects in the Solar System

The sizes of objects in the solar system range from very small to very large.

asteroids

Sun
On this scale, the Sun is about a meter across.

Mars

Saturn

Saturn's moons

Earth

Venus

Mercury

Jupiter's moons

Neptune

Neptune's moons

Jupiter

Uranus

Uranus's moons

comets

0   20,000   40,000 kilometers

Pluto

Objects smaller than about 100 kilometers are represented as dots.

Distances of Planets

Sun Venus Mars   Jupiter   Saturn   Uranus

Mercury Earth   asteroids

0   2   4 AU

Objects in the solar system have very different sizes. An asteroid may be as small as a mountain, perhaps 1/1000 Earth's diameter. In contrast, the largest planets are about 10 Earth diameters across. The Sun's diameter is about 100 times Earth's. If the planets were the sizes shown on page 80, the Sun would be about a meter across.

Distances

The distances between most objects in space are huge in comparison with the objects' diameters. If Earth and the Sun were the sizes shown on page 80, they would be more than 100 meters from each other.

VOCABULARY
Draw word triangles in your notebook for new terms.

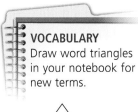

Astronomers understand huge distances by comparing them with something more familiar. One **astronomical unit,** or AU, is Earth's average distance from the Sun. An AU is about 150 million kilometers (93 million mi). Mercury is less than 0.5 AU from the Sun, Jupiter is about 5 AU from the Sun, and Pluto gets nearly 50 AU from the Sun at times. You can use the diagram at the bottom of pages 80–81 to compare these distances. However, the planets are not arranged in a straight line—they move around the Sun.

You can see that the planets are spaced unevenly. The first four planets are relatively close together and close to the Sun. They define a region called the inner solar system. Farther from the Sun is the outer solar system, where the planets are much more spread out.

CHECK YOUR READING What are the two regions of the solar system?

Orbits

More than 99 percent of all the mass in the solar system is in the Sun. The gravitational pull of this huge mass causes planets and most other objects in the solar system to move around, or orbit, the Sun.

The shape of each orbit is an **ellipse**—a flattened circle or oval. A circle is a special type of ellipse, just as a square is a special type of rectangle. Most of the planets' orbits are very nearly circles. Only one planet—Pluto—has an orbit that looks a little flattened instead of round.

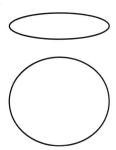

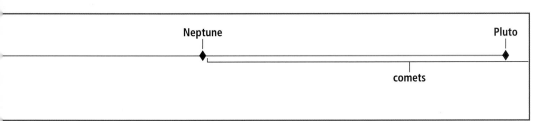

Neptune

Pluto

comets

INVESTIGATE Distances

How far apart are the planets?

PROCEDURE

(1) Mark one sheet from the end of the roll of paper as the location of the Sun. Mark an *X* and write the word *Sun* with dots rather than lines.

(2) Use the Distance Table data sheet to mark the distances for the rest of the solar system. Count sheets and estimate tenths of a sheet as necessary. Re-roll or fold the paper neatly.

(3) Go to a space where you can unroll the paper. Compare the distances of planets as you walk along the paper and back again.

WHAT DO YOU THINK?

- How does the distance between Earth and Mars compare with the distance between Saturn and Uranus?

- How would you use the spacing to sort the planets into groups?

CHALLENGE If it took two years for the *Voyager 2* spacecraft to travel from Earth to Jupiter, about how long do you think it took for *Voyager 2* to travel from Jupiter to Neptune?

SKILL FOCUS
Using models

MATERIALS
- roll of toilet paper
- felt-tipped pen
- Distance Table

TIME
30 minutes

The solar system formed from a swirling cloud of gas and dust.

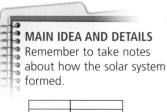

MAIN IDEA AND DETAILS
Remember to take notes about how the solar system formed.

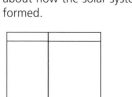

The planets orbit the Sun in similar ways. Their paths are almost in a flat plane, like the rings of a target. They all orbit the Sun in the same direction—counterclockwise as seen from above Earth's North Pole. Most of the planets rotate on their axes in this direction, too. Many other objects in the solar system also orbit and rotate in this same direction. These similar motions have given scientists clues about how the solar system formed.

According to the best scientific model, the solar system formed out of a huge cloud of different gases and specks of dust. The cloud flattened into a disk of whirling material. Most of the mass fell to the center and became a star—the Sun. At the same time, tiny bits of dust and frozen gases in the disk stuck together into clumps. The clumps stuck together and became larger. Large clumps became planets. They moved in the same direction that the flat disk was turning.

Not all the clumps grew big enough to be called planets. However, many of these objects still orbit the Sun the same way that planets orbit. Some of the objects close to the Sun are like rocks or mountains in space and are called asteroids. Other objects, farther from the Sun, are more like enormous snowballs or icebergs. They are called comets.

Formation of the Solar System

The Sun and other objects formed out of material in a flat disk.

① Nebula

Part of a huge cloud of material, called a nebula, collapsed into a flattened disk.

② Disk

The Sun formed at the center of the disk. Other objects formed from the whirling material of the disk.

③ Solar System

Much of the material was cleared away. The Sun, planets, and other objects remained.

Some objects orbit planets instead of orbiting the Sun directly, so they are considered moons. You will read more about asteroids, comets, and moons in Section 3.4.

You can tell a little bit about the size of an object in space from its shape. Lumpy objects are usually much smaller than round objects. As a space object starts to form, the clumps come together from many directions and produce an uneven shape. The gravity of each part affects every other part. The pieces pull each other closer together. When an object has enough mass, this pulling becomes strong enough to make the object round. Any parts that would stick far out are pulled in toward the center until the object becomes a sphere.

 CHECK YOUR READING Why do planets and large moons have a spherical shape?

 **Review**

KEY CONCEPTS

1. What are the types of space objects in the solar system?

2. Why is the unit of measurement used for the distances of planets from the Sun different from the unit used for their sizes?

3. How did planets and other objects in the solar system form out of material in a disk?

CRITICAL THINKING

4. **Analyze** Why do the planets all orbit in one direction?

5. **Infer** Which of the two moons below has more mass? Explain why you think so.

⬤ CHALLENGE

6. **Apply** Could you model all the sizes of objects in the solar system by using sports balls? Explain why or why not.

MATH TUTORIAL
CLASSZONE.COM

Click on Math Tutorial
for more help with the
percent equation.

This picture of Buzz Aldrin on
the Moon was taken by Neil
Armstrong, who can be seen
reflected in Aldrin's helmet.

SKILL: USING PERCENTAGES

How Much Would You Weigh on Other Worlds?

When astronauts walked on the Moon, they felt much lighter than they felt when they were on Earth. Neil Armstrong's total mass—about 160 kilograms with space suit and backpack—did not change. However, the Moon did not pull as hard on him as Earth did, so he weighed less on the Moon. At the surface, the Moon's gravitational pull is only 17% of Earth's gravitational pull. You can use percentages to calculate Neil Armstrong's weight on the Moon.

Example

On Earth, with his heavy space suit and backpack, Neil Armstrong weighed about 1600 newtons (360 lb). To calculate his weight on the Moon, find 17% of 1600 newtons.

"Of" means "multiply."	17% of 1600 N = 17% × 1600 N
Change the percent to a decimal fraction.	= 0.17 × 1600 N
Simplify.	= 272 N

ANSWER With his suit and backpack, Neil Armstrong weighed about 270 newtons on the Moon.

Use the percentages in the table to answer the following questions.

1. A backpack weighs 60 newtons (13 lb) on Earth. **(a)** How much would it weigh on Jupiter? **(b)** How much would it weigh on Jupiter's moon Io?

2. **(a)** How much would a student weighing 500 newtons (110 lb) on Earth weigh on Saturn? **(b)** on Venus?

3. On which planet or moon would you be lightest?

CHALLENGE A pencil weighs 0.3 newtons (1 oz) on Earth. How much would it weigh on the Moon? If an astronaut let go of the pencil on the Moon, would the pencil fall? Explain.

Percent of Weight on Earth	
Planet or Moon	**%**
Mercury	38
Venus	91
Earth	100
Moon (Earth)	17
Mars	38
Jupiter	236
Io (Jupiter)	18
Europa (Jupiter)	13
Ganymede (Jupiter)	15
Callisto (Jupiter)	13
Saturn	92
Titan (Saturn)	14
Uranus	89
Neptune	112
Triton (Neptune)	8.0
Pluto	6.7
Charon (Pluto)	2.8

3.2

The inner solar system has rocky planets.

BEFORE, you learned

- Planets are closer together in the inner solar system than in the outer solar system
- Planets formed along with the Sun
- Gravity made planets round

NOW, you will learn

- How four processes change the surfaces of solid planets
- How atmospheres form and then affect planets
- What the planets closest to the Sun are like

VOCABULARY

terrestrial planet p. 85
tectonics p. 86
volcanism p. 86

EXPLORE Surfaces

How does a planet's mantle affect its surface?

PROCEDURE

1. Dampen a paper towel and place it on top of two blocks to model a crust and a mantle.

2. Move one block. Try different amounts of motion and different directions.

WHAT DO YOU THINK?

- What happened to the paper towel?
- What landforms like this have you seen?

MATERIALS

- 2 blocks
- paper towel
- newspaper

The terrestrial planets have rocky crusts.

Scientists study Earth to learn about other planets. They also study other planets to learn more about Earth. The **terrestrial planets** are Mercury, Venus, Earth, and Mars—the four planets closest to the Sun. They all have rocky crusts and dense mantles and cores. Their insides, surfaces, and atmospheres formed in similar ways and follow similar patterns. One planet—Earth—can be used as a model to understand the others. In fact, the term *terrestrial* comes from *terra*, the Latin word for Earth.

Earth

Most of Earth's rocky surface is hidden by water. More details about Earth and other planets are listed in the Appendix at the back of this book.

Mass 6×10^{24} kg
Diameter 12,800 km
Average distance from Sun 1 AU

Orbits in 365 days
Rotates in 24 hours

Processes and Surface Features

All terrestrial planets have layers. Each planet gained energy from the collisions that formed it. This energy heated and melted the planet's materials. The heaviest materials were metals, which sank to the center and formed a core. Lighter rock formed a mantle around the core. The lightest rock rose to the surface and cooled into a crust.

Four types of processes then shaped each planet's rocky crust. The processes acted to different extents on each planet, depending on how much the crust and inside of the planet cooled.

READING TiP

Compare what you read about each type of feature with the pictures and diagrams on page 87.

① **Tectonics** Earth's crust is split into large pieces called tectonic plates. These plates are moved by Earth's hot mantle. Mountains, valleys, and other features form as the plates move together, apart, or along each other. The crusts of other terrestrial planets are not split into plates but can be twisted, wrinkled up, or stretched out by the mantle. **Tectonics** is the processes of change in a crust due to the motion of hot material underneath. As a planet cools, the crust gets stiffer and the mantle may stop moving, so this process stops.

② **Volcanism** A second process, called **volcanism,** occurs when molten rock moves from a planet's hot interior onto its surface. The molten rock is called lava when it reaches the surface through an opening called a volcano. On Earth, lava often builds up into mountains. Volcanoes are found on Earth, Venus, and Mars. Lava can also flow onto large areas and cool into flat plains like the lunar maria. When the inside of a planet cools enough, no more molten rock reaches the surface.

③ **Weathering and Erosion** You have read about weathering on Earth and the Moon. Weather or small impacts break down rocks. The broken material is moved by a group of processes called erosion. The material may form dunes, new layers of rock, or other features. On Earth, water is important for weathering and erosion. However, similar things happen even without water. Wind can carry sand grains that batter at rocks and form new features. Even on a planet without air, rock breaks down from being heated in the daylight and cooled at night. The material is pulled downhill by gravity.

RESOURCE CENTER
CLASSZONE.COM

Find out more about impact craters on Earth and other space objects.

④ **Impact Cratering** A small object sometimes hits a planet's surface so fast that it causes an explosion. The resulting impact crater is often ten times larger than the object that produced it. On Earth, most craters have been erased by other processes. Impact craters are easier to find on other planets. If a planet or part of a planet is completely covered with impact craters, then the other processes have not changed the surface much in billions of years.

CHECK YOUR READING What processes affect the surfaces of terrestrial planets?

The processes that shape features on a planet's surface can be divided into four types. The features can tell you different things about the planet.

① Tectonics

A hot mantle can move and distort the crust above it. This system of mountains and valleys on **Earth** formed as the crust was stretched.

② Volcanism

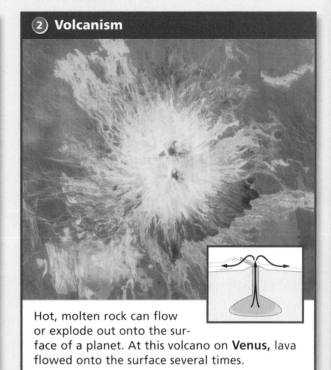

Hot, molten rock can flow or explode out onto the surface of a planet. At this volcano on **Venus,** lava flowed onto the surface several times.

③ Weathering and Erosion

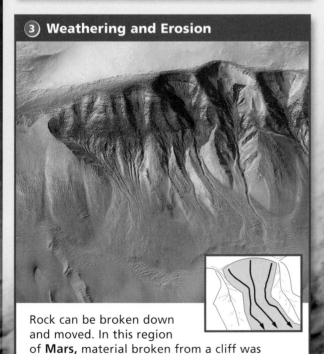

Rock can be broken down and moved. In this region of **Mars,** material broken from a cliff was moved by erosion into new slopes and dunes.

④ Impact Cratering

A small space object can hit a planet's surface and leave a crater. Because the other processes on **Mercury** are weak, newer craters can be seen on a background of older, more eroded craters.

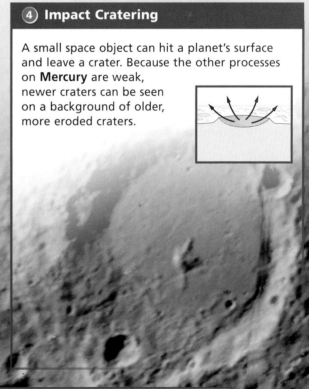

READING ViSUALS Which two processes happen because of hot material beneath the surface?

How do the layers inside of planets form?

In this model, the materials you use represent different rocks and metals that make up the solid planets.

PROCEDURE

1. Put pieces of gelatin into the container until it is about one-quarter full.

2. Mix in a spoonful each of sand and wax. Use the spoon to break the gelatin into small pieces as you mix. Remove the spoon.

3. Place the container in a bowl of hot tap water (about 70°C) and observe what happens as the gelatin melts.

WHAT DO YOU THINK?

- What happened to each of the materials when the gelatin melted?
- How do the results resemble the core, mantle, and crust of Earth and other planets?

CHALLENGE How might you improve this model?

SKILL FOCUS
Using models

MATERIALS
- container
- spoon
- firm gelatin
- sand
- wax pieces
- bowl of hot tap water

TIME
40 minutes

Atmospheres

Atmospheres on terrestrial planets mainly formed from gases that poured out of volcanoes. If a planet's gravity is strong enough, it pulls the gases in and keeps them near the surface. If a planet's gravity is too weak, the gases expand into outer space and are lost.

Venus, Earth, and Mars each had gravity strong enough to hold heavy gases such as carbon dioxide. However, the lightest gases—hydrogen and helium—escaped into outer space. The atmospheres of Venus and Mars are mostly carbon dioxide.

An atmosphere can move energy from warmer places to cooler places. This movement of heat energy makes temperatures more uniform between a planet's day side and its night side and between its equator and its poles. An atmosphere can also make a planet's whole surface warmer by slowing the loss of energy from the surface.

After Earth formed, its atmosphere of carbon dioxide kept the surface warm enough for water to be liquid. Oceans covered most of Earth's surface. The oceans changed the gases of the atmosphere, and living organisms caused even more changes. Earth's atmosphere is now mostly nitrogen with some oxygen.

 CHECK YOUR READING Why is the solid Earth surrounded by gases?

Craters cover the surface of Mercury.

Mercury, like the Moon, has smooth plains and many craters. The processes at work on Earth also affected Mercury.

Tectonics Long, high cliffs stretch across Mercury's surface. Scientists think that Mercury's huge core of iron shrank when it cooled long ago. The crust wrinkled up, forming cliffs, as the planet got a little smaller.

Volcanism Parts of the surface were covered with lava long ago. Large, smooth plains formed. The plains are similar to lunar maria.

Weathering and Erosion Small impacts and temperature changes have broken rock. Gravity has moved broken material downhill.

Impact Cratering Round features cover much of the surface. These craters show that the other processes have not changed Mercury's surface very much for a long time.

Mercury has the longest cycle of day and night of the terrestrial planets—three months of daylight and three months of darkness. There is no atmosphere to move energy from the hot areas to the cold areas. In the long daytime, it can get hotter than 420°C (about 800°F)—hot enough to melt lead. During the long, cold night, the temperature can drop lower than −170°C (about −280°F).

CHECK YOUR READING How is Mercury similar to the Moon?

—no data

Mercury

This map of Mercury was made from many images taken by one spacecraft. The blank patches show areas that were not mapped by the spacecraft.

Mass 6% of Earth's mass

Diameter 38% of Earth's diameter

Average distance from Sun 0.39 AU

Orbits in 88 Earth days

Rotates in 59 Earth days

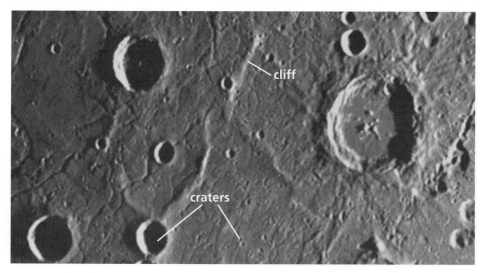

Craters of all sizes cover Mercury's surface, but there are also flat lava plains and cliffs from long ago.

cliff

craters

Volcanoes shape the surface of Venus.

The planet Venus is only a little smaller than Earth and orbits a little closer to the Sun. As a result, Venus is sometimes called Earth's sister planet. However, Venus is different from Earth in important ways.

Venus takes about eight months to turn just once on its axis. Unlike most other planets, Venus rotates and orbits in opposite directions. The rotation and orbit together produce very long days and nights—two months of daylight followed by two months of darkness.

The atmosphere of Venus is very dense. Air pressure on Venus is 90 times that on Earth. Venus's atmosphere is mostly carbon dioxide. This gas slows the loss of energy and makes the surface very hot. The ground temperature on Venus is about 470°C (about 870°F). The atmosphere of Venus moves energy around so well that the long nights are as hot as the days and the poles are as hot as the equator. In addition, there are droplets of sulfuric acid, a corrosive chemical, in the atmosphere. These droplets form thick white clouds that completely cover the planet and hide the surface.

Like Mercury, Venus is affected by the same four types of processes that change Earth's surface. Scientists think that tectonics and volcanism may still be changing Venus's surface today.

Tectonics Patterns of cracks and cliffs have formed as movements of the hot mantle have stretched, wrinkled, and twisted the surface.

Volcanism Most of the surface of Venus has been covered with lava in the last billion years or so. Volcanoes and flat lava plains are found all over the surface.

Thick clouds make it impossible to see Venus's surface in visible light. This inset shows a map of Venus that scientists made using radio waves.

Venus

Venus is nearly the size of Earth but has a thicker atmosphere and is much hotter than Earth. The surface is rocky, as you can see in the image below.

Mass 82% of Earth's mass
Diameter 95% of Earth's diameter
Average distance from Sun 0.72 AU

Orbits in 225 Earth days
Rotates in 243 Earth days

weathered and eroded rock

spacecraft

Weathering and Erosion Venus is too hot to have liquid water, and the winds do not seem to move much material. Erosion may be slower on Venus than on Earth.

Impact Cratering Round craters mark the surface here and there. Older craters have been erased by the other processes. Also, Venus's thick atmosphere protects the surface from small impacts.

 Why is Venus not covered with craters?

Erosion changes the appearance of Mars.

Mars is relatively small, with a diameter about half that of Earth. The orange color of some of the surface comes from molecules of iron and oxygen—rust. Mars has two tiny moons. They were probably once asteroids that were pulled into orbit around Mars.

Surface of Mars

The same processes that affect the other terrestrial planets affect Mars.

Tectonics Valleys and raised areas formed on Mars as the mantle moved. One huge system of valleys, called Valles Marineris, is long enough to stretch across the United States.

Volcanism Most of the northern hemisphere has smooth plains of cooled lava. Several volcanoes are higher than any mountain on Earth. The lava must have built up in the same spot for a long time, so scientists have inferred that the crust of Mars has cooled more than Earth's crust. On Earth, the tectonic plates move, so chains of smaller volcanoes form instead of single larger volcanoes.

Weathering and Erosion Fast winds carry sand that breaks down rocks. Wind and gravity move the broken material, forming new features such as sand dunes. There are also landforms that look like the results of gigantic flash floods that happened long ago.

Impact Cratering Round craters cover much of the southern hemisphere of Mars. Many craters are very old and eroded. A few impact craters on the volcanoes make scientists think that the volcanoes have not released lava for a long time.

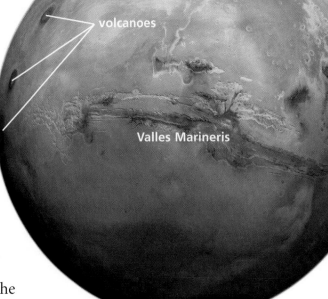

Mars

The atmosphere of Mars is thin but causes weathering and erosion.

Mass 11% of Earth's mass
Diameter 53% of Earth's diameter
Average distance from Sun 1.5 AU
Orbits in 1.9 Earth years
Rotates in 25 hours

volcanoes

Valles Marineris

red dust carried by wind

distant hills

weathered and eroded rock

The sky of Mars is made red by dust that the wind picks up and carries to new places.

Gases and Water on Mars

The atmosphere of Mars is mostly carbon dioxide. The air pressure is only about 1 percent of the air pressure on Earth. The gas is not dense enough to keep the surface warm or to move much energy from cold areas to warmer areas. Therefore, temperatures may reach almost 20°C (about 60°F) in the daytime and −90°C (−130°F) at night. The large differences in temperature produce fast winds. The winds cause gigantic dust storms that sometimes cover most of the planet.

Like Earth, Mars has polar caps that grow in winter and shrink in summer. However, the changing polar caps of Mars are made mostly of frozen carbon dioxide—dry ice. The carbon dioxide of the atmosphere can also form clouds, fog, and frost on the ground.

There is no liquid water on the surface of Mars today. Any water would quickly evaporate or freeze. However, there were floods in the past, and there is still frozen water in the ground and in one polar cap. Water is important for life and will also be needed to make rocket fuel if humans are ever to make trips to Mars and back.

 CHECK YOUR READING In what ways is Mars different from Earth?

3.2 Review

KEY CONCEPTS

1. What are the four types of processes that shape planets' surfaces? For each, give one example of a feature that the process can produce.

2. How can an atmosphere affect the temperature of a planet's surface?

3. Which terrestrial planet has the oldest, least-changing surface?

CRITICAL THINKING

4. **Compare and Contrast** Make a chart with columns for the four types of processes and for an atmosphere. Fill out a row for each planet.

5. **Apply** If a planet had a surface with craters but no other features, what could you say about the inside of the planet?

◯ CHALLENGE

6. **Infer** Describe how a hot mantle can affect a planet's atmosphere. **Hint**: Which of the four processes is involved?

What Shapes the Surface of Mars?

Many features on Mars, when seen close up, look a lot like features found on Earth. Astronomers use their knowledge of the four types of processes that affect the terrestrial planets to hypothesize about the features on Mars. Using what you know about the processes, make your own hypotheses to explain the features in the image to the left.

▶ Results of Research

- Small objects hit the surface, producing craters.
- Volcanoes erupt, creating mountains and flows of lava.
- The mantle moves the crust, producing mountains and valleys.
- Wind, water, and gravity move material on the surface, eroding some places and building up others.

▶ Observations

- Dark, raised triangles point roughly east.
- Patterns of light stripes run mostly north-south between the dark hills.
- The features are inside a huge impact crater.

dark hills

light stripes

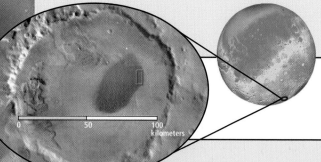

The large image shows details of the area in the red rectangle.

0   50   100 kilometers

The black oval on the globe shows the location of the crater.

0   0.5   1.0 kilometers

▶ Form a Hypothesis

On Your Own Consider one or more processes that might produce the hills and stripes seen in the image at left.

As a Group With a small group discuss possible hypotheses to explain the formation of these features. See if the group can agree on which one is most reasonable.

CHALLENGE Create a model that you can use to test your hypothesis. What will you use to represent the surface of Mars and the forces acting on it?

The outer solar system has four giant planets.

◀ **BEFORE, you learned**

- Planets formed along with the Sun
- Vast distances separate planets
- The gravity of a terrestrial planet may be strong enough to hold the heavier gases

▶ **NOW, you will learn**

- About the four giant planets in the solar system
- What the atmospheres of giant planets are like
- About the rings of giant planets

VOCABULARY

gas giant p. 94
ring p. 97

THINK ABOUT

What is Jupiter like inside?

Most of Jupiter's huge mass is hidden below layers of clouds. Scientists learn about Jupiter by studying its gravity, its magnetic field, its motions, and its radiation. Scientists also use data from other space bodies to make models, from which they make predictions. Then they observe Jupiter to test their predictions. What might it be like under Jupiter's clouds?

VOCABULARY
Remember to draw a word triangle when you read a new term.

The gas giants have very deep atmospheres.

You have already read about the four rocky planets in the inner solar system, close to the Sun. Beyond Mars stretches the outer solar system, where the four largest planets slowly orbit the Sun. The **gas giants**—Jupiter, Saturn, Uranus (YUR-uh-nuhs), and Neptune—are made mainly of hydrogen, helium, and other gases.

When you think of gases, you probably think of Earth's air, which is not very dense. However, the giant planets are so large and have such large amounts of these gases that they have a lot of mass. The huge gravitational force from such a large mass is enough to pull the gas particles close together and make the atmosphere very dense. Inside the giant planets, the gases become more dense than water. The outermost parts are less dense and more like Earth's atmosphere.

CHECK YOUR READING Why are the gas giants dense inside?

The atmosphere of a giant planet is very deep. Imagine traveling into one. At first, the atmosphere is thin and very cold. There may be a haze of gases. A little lower is a layer of clouds that reflect sunlight, just like clouds on Earth. There are strong winds and other weather patterns. Lower down, it is warmer and there are layers of clouds of different materials. As you go farther, the atmosphere gradually becomes dense enough to call a liquid. It also gets thousands of degrees hotter as you get closer to the center of the planet. The materials around you become more and more dense until they are solid. Scientists think that each of the four gas giants has a solid core, larger than Earth, deep in its center.

Interior of a Giant Planet

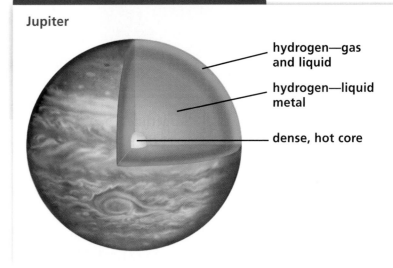

Jupiter

hydrogen—gas and liquid

hydrogen—liquid metal

dense, hot core

Jupiter is a world of storms and clouds.

Jupiter is the largest planet in the solar system. It is more than 10 times larger than Earth in diameter and more than 1200 times larger in volume. A jet plane that could circle Earth in about 2 days would take 23 days to circle Jupiter. If you could weigh the planets on a cosmic scale, all the other planets put together would weigh less than half as much as Jupiter.

Jupiter is more than five times farther from the Sun than Earth is. It moves more slowly through space than Earth and has a greater distance to travel in each orbit. Jupiter takes 12 Earth years to go once around the Sun.

Even though it is big, Jupiter takes less than 10 hours to turn once on its axis. This fast rotation produces fast winds and stormy weather. Like Earth, Jupiter has bands of winds that blow eastward and westward, but Jupiter has many more bands than Earth does.

Jupiter

Jupiter's colorful stripes are produced by clouds at different levels in Jupiter's deep atmosphere.

Mass 318 Earth masses
Diameter 11 Earth diameters
Average distance from Sun 5.2 AU
Orbits in 12 Earth years
Rotates in 9.9 hours

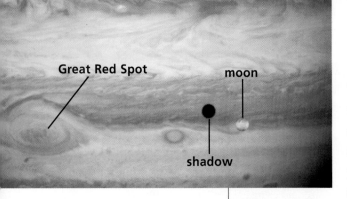

Great Red Spot

moon

shadow

This image shows one of Jupiter's moons casting a shadow on Jupiter. If you were in that shadow, you would experience a solar eclipse.

Stripes of cold clouds form along the bands. The clouds look white because they are made of crystals that reflect sunlight. The crystals in these high white clouds are frozen ammonia rather than frozen water, as on Earth. Between Jupiter's white bands of clouds, you can see down to the next layer. The lower clouds are brown or red and made of different chemicals. Sometimes there are clear patches in the brown clouds, where the next layer of bluish clouds shows through.

CHECK YOUR READING What are Jupiter's white stripes?

Storms can form between bands of winds that blow in opposite directions. Because Jupiter has no land to slow the storms, they can last for a long time. The largest of these storms is the Great Red Spot, which is twice as wide as Earth and at least 100 years old. Its clouds rise even higher than the white ammonia-ice clouds. Scientists are trying to find out which chemicals produce the spot's reddish color.

Saturn has large rings.

REMINDER

Density is the amount of mass in a given volume. An object of low density can still have a great total mass if it has a large volume.

The sixth planet from the Sun is Saturn. Saturn is only a little smaller than Jupiter, but its mass is less than one-third that of Jupiter. Because there is less mass, the gravitational pull is weaker, so the gas particles can spread out more. As a result, Saturn has a much lower density than Jupiter. The storms and stripes of clouds form deeper in Saturn's atmosphere than in Jupiter's, so the details are harder to see.

Saturn

Saturn has an average density less than that of liquid water on Earth. The diameter of Saturn's ring system is almost as great as the distance from Earth to the Moon.

Mass 95 Earth masses

Diameter 9 Earth diameters

Average distance from Sun 9.5 AU

Orbits in 29 Earth years

Rotates in 11 hours

Saturn was the first planet known to have rings. A planetary **ring** is a wide, flat zone of small particles that orbit a planet. All four gas giants have rings around their equators. Saturn's rings are made of chunks of water ice the size of a building or smaller. Larger chunks, considered to be tiny moons, orbit within the rings. Saturn's main rings are very bright. The outermost ring is three times as wide as the planet, but it is usually too faint to see. Saturn's rings have bright and dark stripes that change over time.

You can use Saturn's rings to see the planet's seasons. Like Earth's axis of rotation, Saturn's axis is tilted. The angle is 27 degrees. When the image on this page was taken, sunlight shone more on the northern hemisphere, so the north side of the rings was bright. The shadow of the rings fell on the southern hemisphere. Winter started in Saturn's northern hemisphere in May 2003 and will last more than seven Earth years. Saturn is almost ten times farther from the Sun than Earth is, so Saturn takes almost 30 Earth years to go around the Sun once.

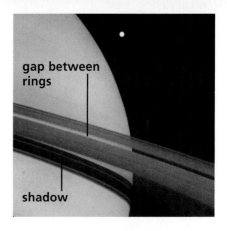

gap between rings

shadow

Sunlight shines from the upper right of this image. The rings cast shadows on Saturn's clouds.

INVESTIGATE Giant Planets

Why do Saturn's rings seem to change size?

PROCEDURE

1. Poke the stick through the plate and cut off the plate's rim. Shape the clay onto both sides of the plate to make a model of a planet with rings.

2. Model Saturn's orbit for your partner. Stand between your partner and the classroom clock. Point one end of the stick at the clock. Hold the model at the same height as your partner's eyes. Have your partner watch the model with just one eye open.

3. Move one step counterclockwise around your partner and point the stick at the clock again. Make sure the model is as high as your partner's eyes. Your partner may need to turn to see the model.

4. Continue taking steps around your partner and pointing the stick at the clock until you have moved the model all the way around your partner.

5. Switch roles with your partner and repeat steps 2, 3, and 4.

WHAT DO YOU THINK?

- How did your view of the rings change as the model planet changed position?

- How many times per orbit do the rings seem to vanish?

CHALLENGE How do Saturn's axis and orbit compare with those of Earth?

SKILL FOCUS
Observing

MATERIALS
- ice-cream stick
- disposable plate
- scissors
- clay

TIME
20 minutes

Uranus and Neptune are extremely cold.

The seventh and eighth planets from the Sun are Uranus and Neptune. These planets are similar in size—both have diameters roughly one-third that of Jupiter. Unlike Jupiter and Saturn, Uranus and Neptune are only about 15 percent hydrogen and helium. Most of the mass of each planet is made up of heavier gases, such as methane, ammonia, and water. As a result, Uranus and Neptune are more dense than Jupiter.

Uranus looks blue-green, and Neptune appears deep blue. The color comes from methane gas, which absorbs certain colors of light. Each planet has methane gas above a layer of white clouds. Sunlight passes through the gas, reflects off the clouds, then passes through the gas again on its way out. The gas absorbs the red, orange, and yellow parts of sunlight, so each planet's bluish color comes from the remaining green, blue, and violet light that passes back out of the atmosphere.

Uranus is a smooth blue-green in visible light. The small infrared image shows that the pole facing the Sun is warmer than the equator.

rings

pole

Uranus

Uranus is about twice Saturn's distance from the Sun. The farther a planet is from the Sun, the more slowly it moves along its orbit. The greater distance also results in a larger orbit, so it takes Uranus 84 Earth years to travel around the Sun.

Like the other gas giants, Uranus has a system of rings and moons around its equator. The ring particles and moons orbit Uranus in the same direction as the planet's spin. Unlike the other planets, Uranus has an axis of rotation that is almost in the plane of its orbit. As a result, Uranus seems to spin on its side. During a solstice, one pole of Uranus points almost straight toward the Sun.

Some scientists think that there was a large collision early in Uranus's history. The result left the planet and its system spinning at an unusual angle.

Uranus

Each pole of Uranus experiences more than 40 years of sunlight and then more than 40 years of darkness as the planet orbits the Sun.

Mass 15 Earth masses   **Orbits in** 84 Earth years

Diameter 4 Earth diameters   **Rotates in** 17 hours

Average distance from Sun 19 AU

Neptune

Neptune orbits about 10 AU farther from the Sun than Uranus, so you would expect it to be colder. However, Neptune has about the same outside temperature as Uranus because it is hotter inside.

Uranus is usually one smooth color, but light and dark areas often appear on Neptune. Clouds of methane ice crystals can form high enough in the atmosphere of Neptune to look white.

Storm systems can appear in darker shades of blue than the rest of the planet. One storm, seen during the flyby of the *Voyager 2* spacecraft in 1989, was named the Great Dark Spot. Unlike the huge storm on Jupiter, the Great Dark Spot did not stay at the same latitude. It moved toward Neptune's equator. The winds there may have broken up the storm. Images of Neptune obtained a few years later with the Hubble Space Telescope showed no sign of the Great Dark Spot.

CHECK YOUR READING What are the white patches often seen on Neptune?

Neptune

Neptune has a large moon that orbits in a direction opposite to Neptune's rotation. Scientists think a giant collision might have occurred in Neptune's past.

Mass 17 Earth masses
Diameter 4 Earth diameters
Average distance from Sun 30 AU
Orbits in 164 Earth years
Rotates in 16 hours

High clouds cast shadows on the layer below.

cloud

shadow

3.3 Review

KEY CONCEPTS

1. Which planet has a greater mass than all the other planets put together?
2. What do you see instead of a solid surface when you look at an image of a giant planet?
3. Which planets have rings?

CRITICAL THINKING

4. **Compare and Contrast** Why do Jupiter and Saturn show a lot of white, while Uranus and Neptune are more blue in color?
5. **Analyze** Most of Saturn is much less dense than most of Earth. Yet Saturn's mass is much greater than Earth's mass. How can this be so?

⚠ CHALLENGE

6. **Apply** If Uranus had areas of ice crystals high in its atmosphere, how would its appearance change?

KEY CONCEPT

Small objects are made of ice and rock.

BEFORE, you learned

- Smaller bodies formed with the Sun and planets
- Planets in the inner solar system consist of rock and metal
- The outer solar system is cold

NOW, you will learn

- About Pluto and the moons of the giant planets
- How asteroids and comets are similar and different
- What happens when tiny objects hit Earth's atmosphere

VOCABULARY

asteroid p. 103
comet p. 104
meteor p. 105
meteorite p. 105

THINK ABOUT

Do small space bodies experience erosion?

Very small bodies in space often have potato-like shapes. Some are covered with dust, boulders, and craters. Solar radiation can break down material directly or by heating and cooling a surface. Broken material can slide downhill, even on a small asteroid. What other processes do you think might act on small and medium-sized bodies in space?

Pluto and most objects in the outer solar system are made of ice and rock.

READING TIP

The name of Earth's satellite is the Moon, but the word *moon* is also used to refer to other satellites.

The materials in a space body depend on where it formed. The disk of material that became the solar system was cold around the outside and hottest in the center, where the Sun was forming. Far from the center, chemicals such as carbon dioxide, ammonia, and water were frozen solid. These ices became part of the material that formed bodies in the outer solar system. Bodies that formed near the center of the solar system are made mostly of rock and metal. Bodies that formed far from the center are mostly ice with some rock and a little metal.

Some of the bodies had enough mass to become rounded. Some even melted and formed cores, mantles, and crusts. Many of these bodies have mountains and valleys, volcanoes, and even winds and clouds. The processes at work on Earth also affect other space bodies.

CHECK YOUR READING What do the proportions of ice, rock, and metal show about a space object?

Pluto and Charon

Many space bodies of ice and rock orbit the Sun at the distance of Neptune and beyond. Since 1992, scientists have been using sophisticated equipment to find and study these bodies. However, one body has been known since 1930. Because Pluto was discovered decades before the other objects, it is considered one of the nine major planets.

Pluto is the smallest of the nine planets. It is smaller than the Moon. Pluto's mass is less than 0.3 percent of Earth's mass, so its gravitational pull is weak. However, Pluto is round and probably has a core, mantle, and crust. Pluto also has a thin atmosphere. No spacecraft has passed close to Pluto, so scientists do not have clear images of the planet's surface.

CHECK YOUR READING Why do scientists know less about Pluto than about other planets?

Pluto's moon, Charon, has a diameter half that of Pluto and a mass about 15 percent of Pluto's. Because Pluto and Charon orbit each other, they are sometimes called a double planet. Just as the Moon always has the same side facing Earth, Pluto and Charon always keep the same sides turned toward each other.

Pluto and Charon also move together around the Sun. Pluto's path around the Sun is not as round as the orbits of the rest of the planets, so its distance from the Sun changes a lot as it orbits. Pluto gets closer to the Sun than Neptune's distance of 30 AU. At the other side of its orbit, Pluto is about 50 AU from the Sun. Pluto's orbit is at an angle with respect to Neptune's, as you can see in the diagram below, so the two paths do not cross and the planets will not collide.

> **Pluto**
>
> This map of Pluto's surface shows only bright and dark areas because Pluto is very distant from Earth and no spacecraft has been close enough to see Pluto's surface in detail.
>
> **Mass** 0.2% Earth's mass
> **Diameter** 18% Earth's diameter
> **Average distance from Sun** 40 AU
> **Orbits in** 248 Earth years
> **Rotates in** 6 Earth days

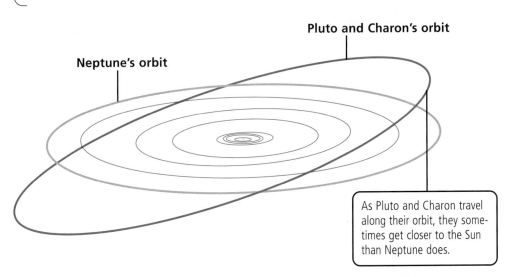

Neptune's orbit

Pluto and Charon's orbit

As Pluto and Charon travel along their orbit, they sometimes get closer to the Sun than Neptune does.

Moons of Gas Giants

RESOURCE CENTER
CLASSZONE.COM

Learn more about the different moons of giant planets.

Each giant planet has a system of moons. Six of the moons are larger than Pluto. Their features are formed by the same processes that shape the terrestrial planets. Saturn's largest moon, Titan, has a dense atmosphere of nitrogen, as Earth does, although a haze hides Titan's surface. Neptune's largest moon, Triton, has a thin atmosphere and ice volcanoes. Jupiter has four large moons—Io, Europa, Ganymede, and Callisto. Io (EYE-oh) is dotted with volcanoes, which continue to erupt, so Io has few impact craters. Europa (yu-ROH-puh) has long ridges where the crust has been pushed and pulled by the material beneath it. The outer two moons have craters over most of their surfaces.

The other moons of the gas giants are all smaller than Pluto, with diameters ranging from about 1600 kilometers (1000 mi) down to just a few kilometers. The smallest moons have irregular shapes, and some may be bodies that were captured into orbit.

CHECK YOUR READING What processes are at work on the largest moons?

Some Moons of Gas Giants

Moons in the outer solar system are shaped by the same processes that produce features on the terrestrial planets.

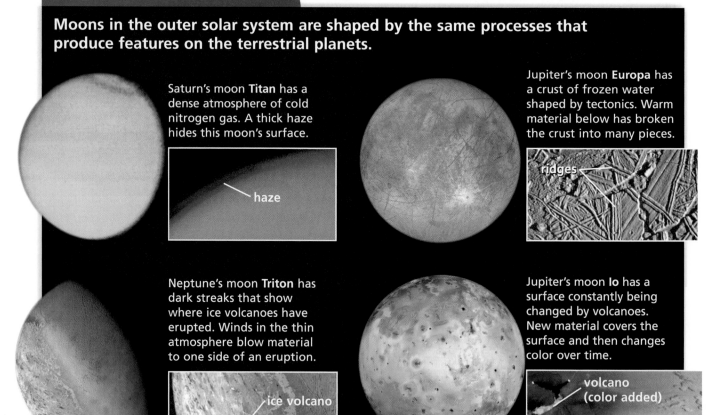

Saturn's moon **Titan** has a dense atmosphere of cold nitrogen gas. A thick haze hides this moon's surface.

haze

Jupiter's moon **Europa** has a crust of frozen water shaped by tectonics. Warm material below has broken the crust into many pieces.

ridges

Neptune's moon **Triton** has dark streaks that show where ice volcanoes have erupted. Winds in the thin atmosphere blow material to one side of an eruption.

ice volcano

streak

Jupiter's moon **Io** has a surface constantly being changed by volcanoes. New material covers the surface and then changes color over time.

volcano (color added)

READING VISUALS Which images show volcanoes?

Asteroids and comets orbit the Sun.

Objects called asteroids and comets formed along with the Sun, planets, and moons. These objects still orbit the Sun at different distances. Most of the objects are much smaller than planets and had too little mass to become round. The objects that formed far from the Sun are made mostly of ice, with some rock and metal. The objects that formed closer to the Sun, where it was warmer, have little or no ice.

MAIN IDEA AND DETAILS
Remember to take notes to help you study later.

Asteroids

Small, solid, rocky bodies that orbit close to the Sun are called **asteroids.** They range from almost 1000 kilometers (600 mi) in diameter down to a kilometer or less. Except for the largest, their gravity is too weak to pull them into round spheres. Therefore, most asteroids have irregular shapes. Some asteroids are the broken pieces of larger, rounded asteroids.

Most asteroids have paths that keep them between the orbits of Mars and Jupiter. This huge region is called the asteroid belt, and contains more than 10,000 asteroids. However, the asteroids are so far apart that spacecraft from Earth have passed completely through the belt without danger of collision. The mass of all the asteroids put together is estimated to be less than the mass of our Moon.

large crater

This asteroid is small compared with a planet, but it is large compared with a person. The large crater at the bottom is about the size of a small city.

The surfaces of asteroids are covered with craters, broken rock, and dust. Even though asteroids are far apart, smaller objects do hit them from time to time. Impacts from very long ago are still visible because most asteroids are not massive enough to have formed cores, mantles, and crusts. Therefore, they do not have volcanism or tectonics to erase the craters. Most asteroids do not have atmospheres, so their surfaces change only when impacts happen or when gravity pulls material downhill.

 CHECK YOUR READING Why do asteroids have craters?

Some asteroids have collided with Earth in the past. The collisions left impact craters, some of which can still be seen today. Scientists have found evidence that an asteroid 10 kilometers (6 mi) in diameter hit Earth 65 million years ago. A cloud of dust from the collision spread around the world and probably affected surface temperatures. Many forms of life, including dinosaurs, died off at about that time, and the impact may have been part or all of the reason. Today astronomers are working to study all asteroids larger than 1 kilometer (0.6 mi) in diameter to determine whether any could hit Earth.

Comets

Sometimes, a fuzzy spot appears in the night sky. It grows from night to night as it changes position against the background stars. The fuzzy spot is a cloud of material, called a coma (KOH-muh), around a small space object. An object that produces a coma is called a **comet.** A comet without its coma is a small, icy object that is difficult to see even with a powerful telescope. Scientists use the number of comets that have become visible to infer that vast numbers of comets exist.

Comets formed far from the Sun, so they are made of different ices as well as rock and some metal. Their orbits are usually more oval than the paths of planets. A comet's orbit may carry it from regions far beyond Pluto's orbit to the inner solar system.

When a comet gets close to the Sun, solar radiation warms the surface and turns some of the ice into gas. A coma forms as the gas moves outward, often carrying dust with it. High-speed particles and radiation from the Sun push this material into one or more tails that can stretch for millions of kilometers. A comet's tails point away from the Sun no matter which way the comet is moving. The coma and tails look bright because sunlight shines on them, even though they may be less dense than Earth's atmosphere.

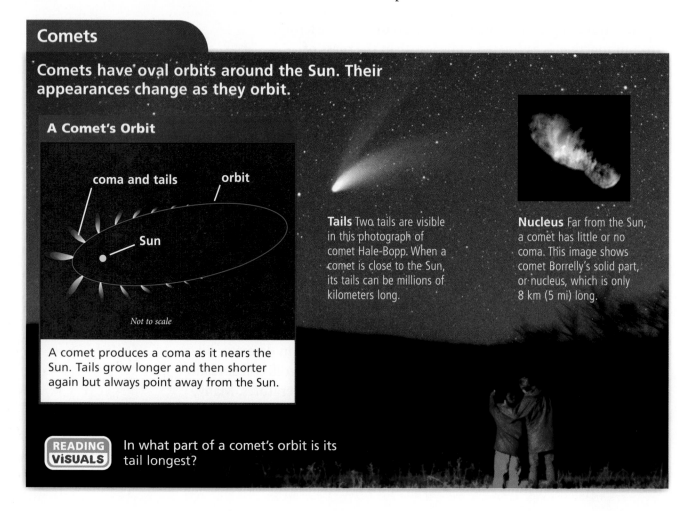

Comets

Comets have oval orbits around the Sun. Their appearances change as they orbit.

A Comet's Orbit

coma and tails   orbit

Sun

Not to scale

A comet produces a coma as it nears the Sun. Tails grow longer and then shorter again but always point away from the Sun.

Tails Two tails are visible in this photograph of comet Hale-Bopp. When a comet is close to the Sun, its tails can be millions of kilometers long.

Nucleus Far from the Sun, a comet has little or no coma. This image shows comet Borrelly's solid part, or nucleus, which is only 8 km (5 mi) long.

READING VISUALS In what part of a comet's orbit is its tail longest?

Most comets are too faint to be noticed easily from Earth. Many years can go by between appearances of bright comets, such as the one in the photograph on page 104.

 CHECK YOUR READING What makes a comet visible?

Meteors and Meteorites

Earth collides constantly with particles in space. Earth orbits the Sun at about 100,000 kilometers per hour (70,000 mi/h), so these particles enter Earth's thin upper atmosphere at very high speeds. The particles and the air around them become hot enough to glow, producing brief streaks of light called **meteors.** You may be able to see a few meteors per hour on a clear, dark night. Several times during the year, Earth passes through a stream of orbiting particles left by a comet. In the resulting meteor shower, you can see many meteors per hour.

A meteor produced by a particle from a comet may last less than a second. Bits of rock or metal from asteroids may produce brighter, longer-lasting meteors. Rarely, a very bright meteor, called a fireball, lights up the sky for several seconds.

An object with greater mass, perhaps 10 grams or more, may not be destroyed by Earth's atmosphere. A **meteorite** is a space object that reaches Earth's surface. The outside of a meteorite is usually smooth from melting, but the inside may still be frozen. Most meteorites come from the asteroid belt, but a few are rocky fragments that have been blasted into space from the Moon and Mars.

This piece of iron is part of a huge meteorite. The energy of the impact melted the metal and changed its shape.

 CHECK YOUR READING What is the difference between a meteor and a meteorite?

3.4 Review

KEY CONCEPTS

1. How are Pluto and most moons of the gas giant planets similar?

2. List two differences between asteroids and comets.

3. What causes meteors?

CRITICAL THINKING

4. **Apply** Of the four types of processes that shape terrestrial worlds, which also shape the surfaces of moons of giant planets?

5. **Compare and Contrast** How is a comet different from a meteor?

⬤ CHALLENGE

6. **Predict** What do you think Pluto would look like if its orbit brought it close to the Sun?

CHAPTER INVESTIGATION

Exploring Impact Craters

DESIGN
— YOUR OWN —
EXPERIMENT

OVERVIEW AND PURPOSE Nearly 50,000 years ago, an asteroid plummeted through Earth's atmosphere and exploded near what is now Winslow, Arizona. The photograph at left shows the resulting impact crater, which is about 1.2 kilometers (0.7 mi) wide. Most of the other craters on Earth have been erased. However, some planets and most moons in the solar system have surfaces that are covered with craters. In this investigation you will

- use solid objects to make craters in a flour surface
- determine how one variable affects the resulting crater

▶ Problem

Write It Up

How does one characteristic of an impact or a colliding object affect the resulting crater?

▶ Hypothesize

Write It Up

Complete steps 1–5 before writing your problem statement and hypothesis. Once you have identified a variable to test, write a hypothesis to explain how changing this variable will affect the crater. Your hypothesis should take the form of an "If . . . , then . . . , because . . ." statement.

MATERIALS
- newspapers
- container
- flour
- colored powder
- several objects
- meter stick
- ruler
- balance

▶ Procedure

1. Place the container on newspapers and add flour to a depth of 2–4 cm. Stir the flour to break up any lumps, and then smooth the surface with a ruler. Sprinkle the top with colored powder.

2. Drop an object into the flour from waist height, then carefully remove it without disturbing the flour. Use the diagram to identify the various parts of the impact crater you made.

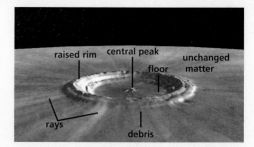

raised rim   central peak   unchanged matter

floor

rays   debris

3. To help you design your experiment, try several cratering methods. Make each new crater in a different location in the container. If your container becomes too full of craters, stir the flour, smooth it, and sprinkle on more colored powder.

4. Design an experiment to test the effects of a variable. Choose just one variable to change—the height, the size or mass of the object, or perhaps the fluffiness of the flour. Determine how much you need to change your variable in order to get results different enough to see.

5. Experiment to find some part of the crater that is affected by changing your variable, such as the depth, the size of the blanket of debris, or the number of rays. Design your experiment so that you measure the part of the crater that changes the most.

6. Write a specific problem statement by completing the question, How does _____ affect _____? Write a hypothesis to answer your problem statement.

7. Perform your experiment. Do not change any factors except your chosen variable.

8. Make several trials for each value of your variable, because there are some factors you cannot control.

9. Record measurements and other observations and make drawings as you go along.

▶ Observe and Analyze
Write It Up

1. **RECORD** Use a diagram to show how you measure the craters. Organize your data into a table. Include spaces for averages.

2. **IDENTIFY VARIABLES** List the variables and constants. The independent variable is the factor that you changed. The dependent variable is affected by this change. Use these definitions when you graph your results.

3. **CALCULATE** Determine averages by adding all of your measurements at each value of your independent variable, then dividing the sum by the number of measurements.

4. **GRAPH** Make a line graph of your average results. Place the independent variable on the horizontal axis and the dependent variable on the vertical axis. Why should you use a line graph instead of a bar graph for these data?

▶ Conclude
Write It Up

1. **ANALYZE** Answer your problem statement. Do your data support your hypothesis?

2. **EVALUATE** Did you identify a trend in your results? Is your experiment a failure if you did not identify a trend? Why or why not?

3. **IDENTIFY LIMITS** How would you modify the design of your experiment now that you have seen the results?

4. **APPLY** What do you think would happen if a colliding object hit water instead of land?

▶ INVESTIGATE Further

CHALLENGE How do the craters in this model differ from real impact craters? Design, but do not attempt, an experiment to simulate the cratering process more realistically.

Exploring Impact Craters
Problem How does _____ affect _____?
Hypothesize
Observe and Analyze
Table 1. Data and Averages

Conclude

the BIG idea

Planets and other objects form a system around our Sun.

CONTENT REVIEW
CLASSZONE.COM

KEY CONCEPTS SUMMARY

 Planets orbit the Sun at different distances.

The planets have different sizes and distances from the Sun. The solar system formed from a disk of dust and gas. Massive objects became round.

inner solar system
Mercury, Venus, Earth, Mars, asteroids

outer solar system
Jupiter, Saturn, Uranus, Neptune, Pluto, comets

VOCABULARY
astronomical unit (AU) p. 81
ellipse p. 81

3.2 The inner solar system has rocky planets.

- The terrestrial planets are round and have layers.
- Atmospheres came from volcanoes and impacts.
- Four processes produce surface features.

   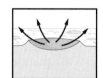

tectonics   volcanism   weathering and erosion   impact cratering

VOCABULARY
terrestrial planet p. 85
tectonics p. 86
volcanism p. 86

3.3 The outer solar system has four giant planets.

- The gas giants have very dense, deep atmospheres with layers of clouds.
- All four giant planets have ring systems.

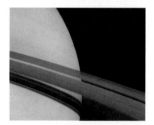

Close-up of Saturn's rings

VOCABULARY
gas giant p. 94
ring p. 97

3.4 Small objects are made of ice and rock.

- Objects in the inner solar system are rocky.
- Pluto and most other objects in the outer solar system are made of ice and rock.
- Rocky asteroids and icy comets orbit the Sun and produce tiny fragments that may become meteors.

The asteroid Eros

VOCABULARY
asteroid p. 103
comet p. 104
meteor p. 105
meteorite p. 105

Reviewing Vocabulary

Make a Venn diagram for each pair of terms. Put an important similarity in the overlapping part. Use the rest of the diagram to show an important difference.

Example:

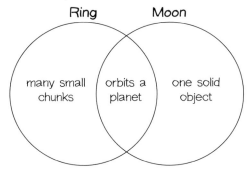

Ring — Moon

many small chunks | orbits a planet | one solid object

1. terrestrial planet, gas giant

2. volcanism, impact cratering

3. erosion, tectonics

4. asteroid, comet

5. meteor, meteorite

6. comet, meteor

Reviewing Key Concepts

Multiple Choice *Choose the letter of the best answer.*

7. Even though orbits are ellipses, what shape is a typical planet's orbit most like?
   a. a short rectangle
   b. an egg-shape with a pointy end
   c. a long, narrow oval
   d. a circle

8. How is a moon different from a planet?
   a. A moon is smaller than any planet.
   b. A moon is less massive than any planet.
   c. A moon is in orbit around a planet.
   d. A moon is unable to have an atmosphere.

9. Which of these appears in Earth's atmosphere?
   a. a moon   c. a meteor
   b. an asteroid   d. a comet

10. How did planets and other objects in the solar system form?
    a. After the Sun formed, it threw off hot pieces that spun and cooled.
    b. The Sun captured objects that formed in other places in the galaxy.
    c. Two stars collided, and the broken pieces went into orbit around the Sun.
    d. Material in a disk formed large clumps as the Sun formed in the center of the disk.

11. Which process occurs only when a small space object interacts with a larger space body?
    a. tectonics   c. erosion
    b. volcanism   d. impact cratering

12. Which processes occur because a planet or another space body is hot inside?
    a. tectonics and volcanism
    b. volcanism and erosion
    c. erosion and impact cratering
    d. impact cratering and tectonics

13. What do all four gas giants have that terrestrial planets do not have?
    a. atmospheres   c. moons
    b. solid surfaces   d. rings

14. What are the white stripes of Jupiter and the white spots of Neptune?
    a. clouds high in the atmosphere
    b. smoke from volcanoes
    c. continents and islands
    d. holes in the atmosphere

Short Answer *Write a short answer to each question.*

15. The solid part of a comet is small in comparison with a planet. However, sometimes a comet appears to be larger than the Sun. What makes it seem so large?

16. Why do all nine major planets orbit the Sun in the same direction?

Thinking Critically

Use the image of Jupiter's moon Ganymede to answer the next five questions.

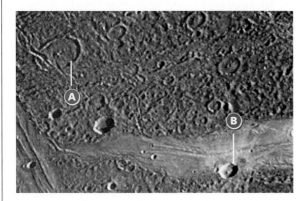

17. OBSERVE Which crater, A or B, is more eroded? Explain why you think so.

18. COMPARE AND CONTRAST Describe the differences between the surface in the upper half of the image and the long, triangular area near the bottom of the image.

19. INFER Explain which area of the surface, the smooth part or the heavily cratered part, is probably older.

20. APPLY The lighter area was produced by tectonic processes and may have been covered with molten material. What can you infer about the inside of this moon?

21. SEQUENCE A crack runs through part of crater A. Explain how you can tell whether the crack or the crater formed first. **Hint:** Think about what would have happened if the other feature had formed first.

22. PREDICT Suppose the Moon were hotter inside. How might its surface be different?

23. IDENTIFY CAUSE Mercury's surface is not as hot as Venus's, even though Mercury is closer to the Sun. In addition, the night side of Mercury gets very cold, while the night side of Venus is about as hot as the day side. Why are the temperature patterns on these two planets so different?

24. EVALUATE Would it be easier to design a lander mission for the surface of Venus or the surface of Mercury? Explain your reasoning.

25. INFER Some comets orbit in a direction opposite to that of the planets. Why might this make some scientists wonder if they formed with the rest of the solar system?

26. HYPOTHESIZE Scientists calculate the mass of a planet from the effects of its gravity on other objects, such as moons. However, Mercury and Venus have no moons. What other objects in space could have been used to determine the planets' masses?

27. COMPARE AND CONTRAST Images of Earth from space show white clouds above darker land and water. In what ways are they like and unlike images of Jupiter?

Earth   **Jupiter**

28. ANALYZE Scientists sometimes use round numbers to compare quantities. For example, a scientist might say that the Sun's diameter is about 100 times Earth's diameter, even though she knows that the precise value is 109 times. Why might she use such an approximation?

the BIG idea

29. APPLY Look back at pages 76–77. Think about the answer you gave to the question about the large image of a planet and moon. How would you answer this question differently now?

30. SYNTHESIZE Ice is generally less dense than rock, which is generally less dense than metal. Use what you know about materials in the solar system to estimate whether a moon of Mars, a moon of Uranus, or the planet Mercury should be the least dense.

UNIT PROJECTS

Check your schedule for your unit project. How are you doing? Be sure that you have placed data or notes from your research in your project folder.

Standardized Test Practice

For practice on your
state test, go to . . .
TEST PRACTICE
CLASSZONE.COM

Interpreting a Passage

Read the following passage. Then answer the questions that follow.

Life in Extreme Environments

Could living organisms survive in the crushing, hot atmosphere of Venus? Could they thrive on a waterless asteroid or get their energy from tides in the dark ocean that might be beneath the surface of Europa? Scientists are looking for answers to these questions right here on Earth. They study extremophiles, which are life forms that can survive in extreme environments—very high or low temperatures or other difficult conditions. These environments have conditions similar to those on other planets, and those on moons, asteroids, and comets.

Scientists have found tiny organisms that grow in the scalding water of hot vents on the ocean floor, deep inside rock, and in miniature ponds within glaciers. Scientists have also found organisms that were dormant because they were frozen solid for thousands of years but that were still capable of living and growing after warming up. By studying extremophiles, scientists learn more about the conditions needed to support life.

Choose from the following four environments to answer each of the next three questions.

- the dark ocean that might be underneath Europa's surface
- the flood channels on Mars, which have been dry and frozen for a long time
- the very hot, high-pressure environment of Venus
- the dry rock of an asteroid that alternately heats and cools

1. Some organisms survive deep underwater, where photosynthesis does not occur because little or no sunlight reaches those depths. Which environment can these organisms teach about?

a. under Europa's surface **c.** Venus
b. Martian flood channels **d.** an asteroid

2. Some organisms survive in very deep cracks in rocks, where they are protected from changing temperatures. Where else might scientists look for these types of organisms?

a. under Europa's surface **c.** Venus
b. Martian flood channels **d.** an asteroid

3. Where might scientists look for tiny organisms that are dormant but that might revive if given warmth and water?

a. under Europa's surface **c.** Venus
b. Martian flood channels **d.** an asteroid

4. Where, outside Earth, should scientists look for tiny ponds of water within solid ice?

a. the other terrestrial planets
b. the gas giants
c. small space objects in the inner solar system
d. small space objects in the outer solar system

Extended Response

Answer the two questions in detail.

5. A class was given a sample of ordinary dormant, dry yeast that had been exposed to an extreme environment. Describe ways the students might test the yeast to see if it remained undamaged, or even survived, the conditions.

6. Imagine that scientists have found extremophiles in clouds of frozen water crystals high in Earth's atmosphere. How might this discovery affect a search for organisms on the gas giants?

Stars, Galaxies, and the Universe

the **BIG** idea

Our Sun is one of billions of stars in one of billions of galaxies in the universe.

> **What could be present in the light and dark areas in this galaxy?**

Key Concepts

SECTION
4.1 **The Sun is our local star.** Learn how the Sun produces energy and about the Sun's layers and features.

SECTION
4.2 **Stars change over their life cycles.** Learn how stars form and change.

SECTION
4.3 **Galaxies have different sizes and shapes.** Learn how galaxies are classified.

SECTION
4.4 **The universe is expanding.** Learn about the formation and expansion of the universe.

Internet Preview

CLASSZONE.COM

Chapter 4 online resources: Visualization, Simulation, three Resource Centers, Math Tutorial, Test Practice

EXPLORE (the BIG idea)

How Can Stars Differ?

Look at the sky at night
and find three stars that
differ in appearance. Try to
identify the locations of
these stars, using the star
maps in the Appendix at
the back of this book.

Observe and Think
How did the characteristics
of the stars differ?

How Do Galaxies Move Apart?

Blow air into a balloon until
it is partially inflated. Use a
felt-tip pen to make 12 dots
on the round end. Then
stand in front of a mirror
and observe the dots as you
completely inflate the balloon.

Observe and Think What caused the dots to
move apart? What might cause galaxies to
move apart in the universe?

Internet Activity: Galaxy Shapes

Go to **ClassZone.com**
to explore the different
shapes of galaxies in
the universe.

Observe and Think
How do the types of
galaxies differ from
one another?

NSTA
scilinks.org

*SCi*LINKS

The Sun **Code: MDL060**

Getting Ready to Learn

◀ CONCEPT REVIEW

- Electromagnetic radiation carries information about space.
- Our solar system is in the Milky Way galaxy.
- A galaxy is a group of millions or billions of stars.

◀ VOCABULARY REVIEW

solar system p. 10

galaxy p. 10

universe p. 10

electromagnetic radiation p. 15

wavelength p. 16

CONTENT REVIEW
CLASSZONE.COM
Review concepts and vocabulary.

▶ TAKING NOTES

CHOOSE YOUR OWN STRATEGY

Take notes using one or more of the strategies from earlier chapters—**main idea web, combination notes,** or **main idea and details.** Feel free to mix and match the strategies, or use an entirely different note-taking strategy.

VOCABULARY STRATEGY

Place each vocabulary term at the center of a **description wheel** diagram. Write some words describing it on the spokes.

See the Note-Taking Handbook on pages R45–R51.

SCIENCE NOTEBOOK

Main Idea Web

Combination Notes

Main Idea and Details

very low density

seen only during eclipse

extends outward several million km

CORONA

outer layer of Sun's atmosphere

uneven shape

The Sun is our local star.

 BEFORE, you learned

- There are different wavelengths of electromagnetic radiation
- The Sun provides light in the solar system

▷ **NOW, you will learn**

- How the Sun produces energy
- How energy flows through the Sun's layers
- About solar features and solar wind

VOCABULARY

fusion p. 116
convection p. 116
corona p. 116
sunspot p. 118
solar wind p. 119

EXPLORE Solar Atmosphere

How can blocking light reveal dim features?

PROCEDURE

1. Unbend the paper clip and use it to make a tiny hole in the center of the card.

2. Turn on the lamp, and briefly try to read the writing on the bulb.

3. Close one eye, and hold the card in front of your other eye. Through the hole, try to read the writing on the bulb.

WHAT DO YOU THINK?

- How did looking through the hole affect your view of the writing?
- How might a solar eclipse affect your view of the Sun's dim outermost layer?

MATERIALS

- small paper clip
- index card
- lamp with 45-watt bulb

The Sun produces energy from hydrogen.

MAIN IDEA AND DETAILS
You could record information about the Sun by using a main idea and details table.

The Sun is the only star in our solar system. Astronomers have been able to study the Sun in more detail than other stars because it is much closer to Earth. As a result, they have learned a great deal about its size and composition and the way it produces energy.

The Sun is far larger than any of the planets. It contains 99.9 percent of the mass of the entire solar system. For comparison, imagine that Earth had the mass of a sparrow; then the Sun would have the mass of an elephant.

The Sun consists mostly of hydrogen gas. Energy is produced when hydrogen in the Sun's interior turns into helium. This energy is the source of light and warmth that make life possible on Earth.

Energy flows through the Sun's layers.

Although the Sun is made entirely of gas, it does have a structure. Energy produced in the center of the Sun flows out through the Sun's layers in different forms, including visible light.

The Sun's Interior

The Sun's interior generally becomes cooler and less dense as you move away from the center.

1 **Core** The center of the Sun, called the core, is made of very dense gas. Temperatures reach about 15 million degrees Celsius. Under these extreme conditions, some hydrogen particles collide and combine to form helium in a process called **fusion.** The process releases energy that travels through the core by radiation.

2 **Radiative Zone** Energy from the core moves by radiation through a thick layer called the radiative zone. Although this layer is very hot and dense, conditions in the radiative zone are not extreme enough for fusion to occur.

3 **Convection Zone** In the convection zone, energy moves mainly by convection. **Convection** is the transfer of energy from place to place by the motion of heated gas or liquid. Rising currents of hot gas in the convection zone carry energy toward the Sun's surface.

REMINDER

Remember that radiation is energy that travels across distances as electromagnetic waves.

CHECK YOUR READING Where does the Sun's energy come from?

The Sun's Atmosphere

SIMULATION
CLASSZONE.COM

View the Sun at different wavelengths.

The Sun's outer layers are called its atmosphere. These layers are much less dense than the interior. The atmosphere generally becomes hotter and less dense as you move outward.

4 **Photosphere** Visible light moves by radiation out into space from the photosphere. It takes about eight minutes for the light to reach Earth. Since the photosphere is the layer you see in photographs of the Sun, it is often called the Sun's surface. Convection currents beneath the photosphere cause it to have a bumpy texture.

5 **Chromosphere** The chromosphere is the thin middle layer of the Sun's atmosphere. It gives off a pinkish light.

6 **Corona** The Sun's outermost layer is called the **corona.** The corona, which varies in shape, extends outward several million kilometers. Both the chromosphere and the corona are much hotter than the photosphere. However, they have such low densities that you can see their light only during a total eclipse of the Sun, when the Moon blocks the much brighter light from the photosphere.

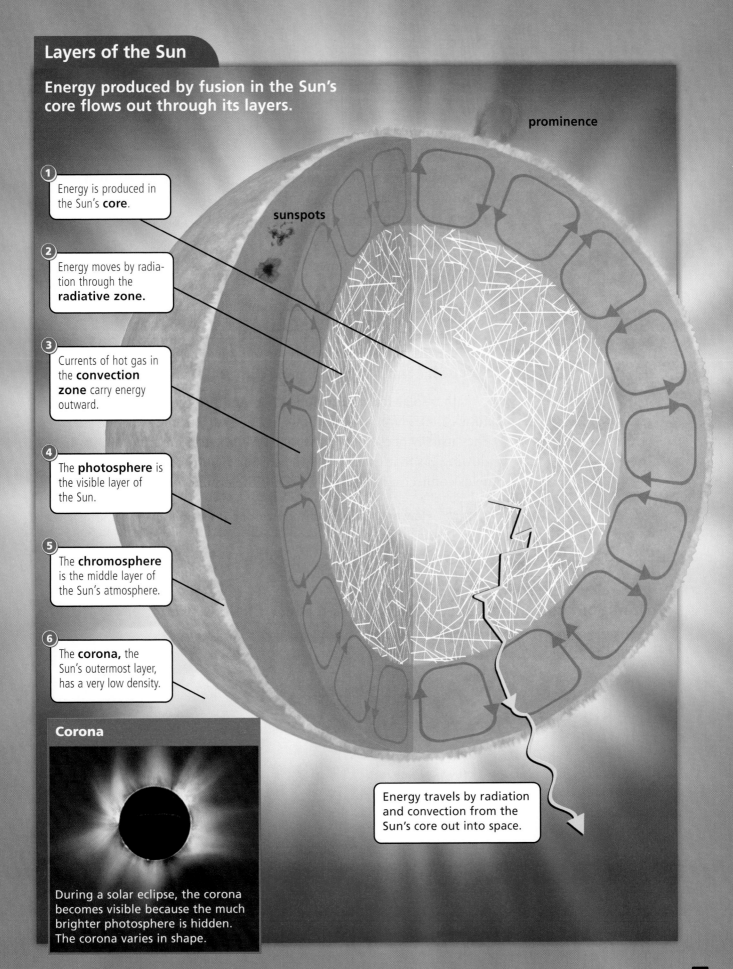

Layers of the Sun

Energy produced by fusion in the Sun's core flows out through its layers.

prominence

sunspots

1 Energy is produced in the Sun's **core**.

2 Energy moves by radiation through the **radiative zone.**

3 Currents of hot gas in the **convection zone** carry energy outward.

4 The **photosphere** is the visible layer of the Sun.

5 The **chromosphere** is the middle layer of the Sun's atmosphere.

6 The **corona,** the Sun's outermost layer, has a very low density.

Energy travels by radiation and convection from the Sun's core out into space.

Corona

During a solar eclipse, the corona becomes visible because the much brighter photosphere is hidden. The corona varies in shape.

Features on the Sun

Astronomers have observed features on the Sun that vary over time. Near the Sun's surface there are regions of magnetic force called magnetic fields. These magnetic fields get twisted into different positions as the Sun rotates. Features appear on the surface in areas where strong magnetic fields are located.

Sunspots are spots on the photosphere that are cooler than surrounding areas. Although they appear dark, sunspots are actually bright. They only seem dim because the rest of the photosphere is so much brighter.

Sunspot activity follows a pattern that lasts about 11 years. At the peak of the cycle, dozens of sunspots may appear. During periods of low activity, there may not be any sunspots.

Sunspots move across the Sun's surface as it rotates. Astronomers first realized that the Sun rotates when they noticed this movement. Because the Sun is not solid, some parts rotate faster than others.

Other solar features include flares and prominences (PRAHM-uh-nuhn-sihz). Flares are eruptions of hot gas from the Sun's surface. They usually occur near sunspots. Prominences are huge loops of glowing gas that extend into the corona. They occur where magnetic fields connecting sunspots soar into the outer atmosphere.

CHECK YOUR READING How are sunspots different from other areas of the photosphere?

Solar Features

Features on the Sun appear in areas where a magnetic field is strong.

Sunspots

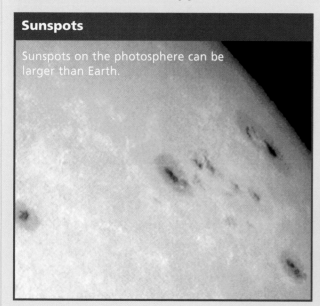

Sunspots on the photosphere can be larger than Earth.

Prominences

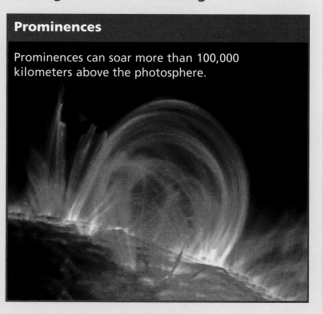

Prominences can soar more than 100,000 kilometers above the photosphere.

Solar Wind

Material in the Sun's corona is continually streaming out into space. The electrically charged particles that flow out in all directions from the corona are called the **solar wind.** The solar wind extends throughout our solar system.

This circular green aurora occurred over Alaska when particles from the solar wind entered the atmosphere.

Most of the solar wind flowing toward Earth is safely guided around the planet by Earth's magnetic field. When solar-wind particles do enter the upper atmosphere, they release energy, which can produce beautiful patterns of glowing light in the sky. Such displays of light are called auroras (uh-RAWR-uhz), or the northern and southern lights. Auroras often occur near the poles.

Earth's atmosphere usually prevents charged particles from reaching the surface. However, during the peak of the sunspot cycle, flares and other kinds of solar activity release strong bursts of charged particles into the solar wind. These bursts, called magnetic storms, can disrupt electric-power delivery across large regions by causing surges in power lines. They can also interfere with radio communication.

Magnetic storms are much more harmful above the protective layers of Earth's atmosphere. Bursts of particles in the solar wind can damage or destroy orbiting satellites. The solar wind also poses a danger to astronauts during space flights.

 What causes auroras to form?

4.1 Review

KEY CONCEPTS

1. How does the Sun produce energy?
2. How does energy move from the Sun's core to the photosphere?
3. How does the solar wind normally affect Earth?

CRITICAL THINKING

4. **Analyze** Why is the core the only layer of the Sun where energy is produced?
5. **Compare and Contrast** Make a diagram comparing sunspots, flares, and prominences.

⬥ CHALLENGE

6. **Infer** A communications satellite stops working while in orbit, and a surge in an electric power line causes blackouts in cities across a large region. What probably happened in the Sun's atmosphere shortly before these events?

CHAPTER INVESTIGATION

Temperature, Brightness, and Color

OVERVIEW AND PURPOSE Think of the metal heating surface on a hot plate. How can you tell whether the hot plate is fully heated? Is the metal surface brighter or dimmer than when it is just starting to get warm? Does the color of the surface change as the hot plate gets hotter? You may already have an idea of how temperature, brightness, and color are related—at least when it comes to heated metal. Do the same relationships apply to electric lights? to stars? This investigation is designed to help you find out. You will

- construct a wax photometer to compare the brightnesses and colors of different light sources
- determine how the temperature of a light source affects its brightness and color

MATERIALS

- 2 paraffin blocks
- aluminum foil
- 2 rubber bands
- 2 light-bulb holders
- 2 miniature light bulbs
- 3 AA batteries
- 4 pieces of uninsulated copper wire 15 cm long
- masking tape
for Challenge:
- incandescent lamp
- dimmer switch

▶ Problem

How are brightness and color related to temperature?

▶ Hypothesize

Write a hypothesis to explain how brightness and color are related to temperature. Your hypothesis should take the form of an "If . . . , then . . . , because . . ." statement.

▶ Procedure

1. An instrument called a photometer makes it easier to compare the brightnesses and colors of different light sources. Assemble the wax photometer as shown on page 121. The aluminum foil between the wax blocks should be folded so that the shiny side faces out on both sides.

2. Hold the photometer so that you can see both blocks. Bring it to different locations in the classroom, and observe how the brightnesses and colors of the blocks change as the two sides of the photometer are exposed to different light conditions.

3. Tape a piece of copper wire to each end of a battery, and connect the wires to a light-bulb holder. The battery will provide electricity to heat up the wire inside a light bulb.

step 3

4. Tape the negative terminal, or flat end, of one battery to the positive terminal of another battery. Tape a piece of copper wire to each end, and connect the wires to a light-bulb holder. Because two batteries will provide electricity to the bulb in this holder, the wire in the bulb will be hotter than the wire in the bulb powered by one battery.

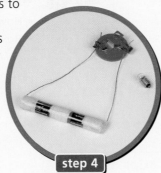

step 4

5. With the room darkened, insert a bulb into each light-bulb holder. If the bulb connected to two batteries does not light up, you may need to press the two batteries together with your fingers.

6. Place the photometer halfway between the two light bulbs. Compare the brightnesses of the two light sources. Record your observations in your **Science Notebook.**

7. Move the photometer closer to the cooler bulb until both sides of the photometer are equally bright. Compare the colors of the two light sources. Record your observations in your **Science Notebook**. To avoid draining the batteries, remove the bulbs from the holders when you have completed this step.

Observe and Analyze
Write It Up

1. **RECORD OBSERVATIONS** Draw the setup of your photometer and light sources. Be sure your data table is complete with descriptions of brightness and color.

2. **IDENTIFY** Identify the variables in this experiment. List them in your **Science Notebook.**

Conclude
Write It Up

1. **INTERPRET** Answer the question in the problem. Compare your results with your hypothesis.

2. **ANALYZE** How does distance affect your perception of the brightness of an object?

3. **APPLY** Judging by the results of the investigation, would you expect a red star or a yellow star to be hotter? Explain why.

INVESTIGATE Further

CHALLENGE Connect an incandescent lamp to a dimmer switch. Write a procedure to show how you would use a photometer to show the relationship between the color and the temperature of the bulb as it fades from brightest to dimmest. Then carry out your procedure.

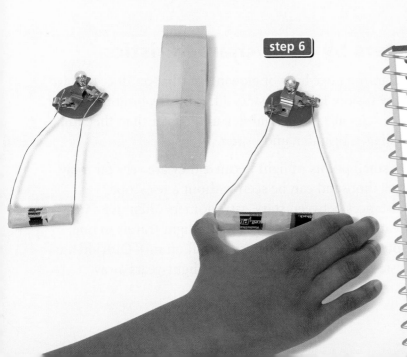

step 6

Temperature, Brightness, and Color

Observe and Analyze

Table 1. Properties of Light from Two Sources

	Cooler Bulb (one battery)	Warmer Bulb (two batteries)
Brightness		
Color		

Stars change over their life cycles.

◀ BEFORE, you learned	▶ NOW, you will learn
• The Sun is our local star	• How stars are classified
• The other stars are outside our solar system	• How stars form and change
• There are huge distances between objects in the universe	

VOCABULARY

light-year p. 122
parallax p. 123
nebula p. 125
main sequence p. 126
neutron star p. 126
black hole p. 126

EXPLORE Characteristics of Stars

How does distance affect brightness?

PROCEDURE

① In a darkened room, shine a flashlight onto a dark surface from 30 cm away while your partner shines a flashlight onto the surface from the same distance. Observe the two spots of light.

② Move one of the flashlights back 15 cm and then another 15 cm. Compare the two spots of light each time you move the flashlight.

MATERIALS
• 2 flashlights
• meter stick
• dark surface

WHAT DO YOU THINK?
• How did distance affect the brightness of the light on the dark surface?
• How does the distance of a star from Earth affect our view of it?

MAIN IDEA WEB
A main idea web would be a good choice for taking notes about the characteristics of stars.

We classify stars by their characteristics.

Like our Sun, all stars are huge balls of glowing gas that produce or have produced energy by fusion. However, stars differ in size, brightness, and temperature. Some stars are smaller, fainter, and cooler than the Sun. Others are much bigger, brighter, and hotter.

Stars look like small points of light because they are very far away. At most, only a few thousand can be seen without a telescope. To describe the distances between stars, astronomers often use a unit called the light-year. A **light-year** is the distance light travels in one year, which is about 9.5 trillion kilometers (6 trillion mi). Outside the solar system, the star closest to Earth is about 4 light-years away.

Brightness and Distance

If you look at stars, you will probably notice that some appear to be brighter than others. The amount of light a star gives off and its distance from Earth determine how bright it appears to an observer. A star that gives off a huge amount of light can appear faint if it is far away. On the other hand, a star that gives off much less light can appear bright if it is closer to Earth. Therefore, to determine the true brightness of a star, astronomers must measure its distance from Earth.

One way astronomers measure distance is by using **parallax,** which is the apparent shift in the position of an object when viewed from different locations. Look at an object with your right eye closed. Now quickly open it and close your left eye. The object will seem to move slightly because you are viewing it from a different angle. The same kind of shift occurs when astronomers view stars from different locations.

To measure the parallax of a star, astronomers plot the star's position in the sky from opposite sides of Earth's orbit around the Sun. They then use the apparent shift in position and the diameter of Earth's orbit to calculate the star's distance.

 CHECK YOUR READING What factors affect how bright a star appears from Earth?

INVESTIGATE Parallax

How does the distance of an object affect parallax?

PROCEDURE

1. Stand 1 m away from a classmate. Have the classmate hold up a meter stick at eye level.

2. With your left eye closed, hold a capped pen up close to your face. Look at the pen with your right eye, and line it up with the zero mark on the meter stick. Then open your left eye and quickly close your right eye. Observe how many centimeters the pen seems to move. Record your observation.

3. Repeat step 2 with the pen held at arm's length and then with the pen held at half your arm's length. Record your observation each time.

WHAT DO YOU THINK?

• How many centimeters did the pen appear to move each time you observed it?

• How is parallax affected when you change the distance of the pen from you?

CHALLENGE How could you use this method to estimate distances that you cannot measure directly?

SKILL FOCUS
Measuring

MATERIALS
• meter stick
• capped pen

TIME
10 minutes

Size

It is hard to get a sense of how large stars are from viewing them in the sky. Even the Sun, which is much closer than any other star, is far larger than its appearance suggests. The diameter of the Sun is about 100 times greater than that of Earth. A jet plane flying 800 kilometers per hour (500 mi/h) would travel around Earth's equator in about two days. If you could travel around the Sun's equator at the same speed, the trip would take more than seven months.

Some stars are much larger than the Sun. Giant and supergiant stars range from ten to hundreds of times larger. A supergiant called Betelgeuse (BEET-uhl-JOOZ) is more than 600 times greater in diameter than the Sun. If Betelgeuse replaced the Sun, it would fill space in our solar system well beyond Earth's orbit. Because giant and supergiant stars have such huge surface areas to give off light, they are very bright. Betelgeuse is one of the brightest stars in the sky, even though it is 522 light-years away.

There are also stars much smaller than the Sun. Stars called white dwarfs are about 100 times smaller in diameter than the Sun, or roughly the size of Earth. White dwarfs cannot be seen without a telescope.

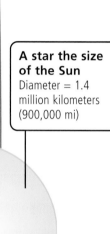

A star the size of the Sun
Diameter = 1.4 million kilometers (900,000 mi)

White dwarf
1/100 the Sun's diameter

Giant star
10–100 times the Sun's diameter

Supergiant star
100–1000 times the Sun's diameter

Color and Temperature

If you observe stars closely, you may notice that they vary slightly in color. Most stars look white. However, a few appear slightly blue or red. The differences in color are due to differences in temperature.

You can see how temperature affects color by heating up metal. For example, if you turn on a toaster, the metal coils inside will start to glow a dull red. As they get hotter, the coils will turn a brighter orange. The illustration on page 125 shows changes in the color of a metal bar as it heats up.

Like the color of heated metal, the color of a star indicates its temperature. Astronomers group stars into classes by color and surface temperature. The chart on page 125 lists the color and temperature range of each class of star. The coolest stars are red. The hottest stars are blue-white. Our Sun—a yellow, G-class star—has a surface temperature of about 6000°C.

Stars of every class give off light that is made up of a range of colors. Astronomers can spread a star's light into a spectrum to learn about the star's composition. The colors and lines in a spectrum reveal which gases are present in the star's outer layers.

CHECK YOUR READING How does a star's temperature affect its appearance?

Color and Temperature

Objects that radiate light change color as they heat up.

Classification of Stars		
Class	**Color**	**Surface Temperature (°C)**
O	blue-white	above 25,000
B	blue-white	10,000–25,000
A	white	7500–10,000
F	yellow-white	6000–7500
G	yellow	5000–6000
K	orange	3500–5000
M	red	below 3500

Stars are classified according to their colors and temperatures. The Sun is a G-class star.

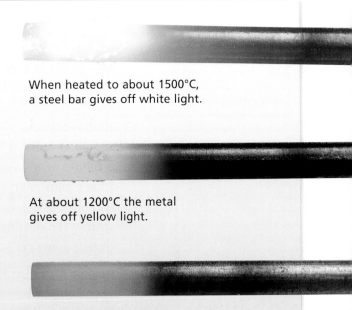

When heated to about 1500°C, a steel bar gives off white light.

At about 1200°C the metal gives off yellow light.

A steel bar glows red when heated to about 600°C.

Stars have life cycles.

Although stars last for very long periods, they are not permanent. Like living organisms, stars go through cycles of birth, maturity, and death. The life cycle of a star varies, depending on the mass of the star. Higher-mass stars develop more quickly than lower-mass stars. Toward the end of their life cycles, higher-mass stars also behave differently from lower-mass stars.

Stars form inside a cloud of gas and dust called a **nebula** (NEHB-yuh-luh). Gravity pulls gas and dust closer together in some regions of a nebula. As the matter contracts, it forms a hot, dense sphere. The sphere becomes a star if its center grows hot and dense enough for fusion to occur.

When a star dies, its matter does not disappear. Some of it may form a nebula or move into an existing one. There, the matter may eventually become part of new stars.

CHECK YOUR READING How is gravity involved in the formation of stars?

Colors have been added to this photograph of the Omega Nebula in order to bring out details.

Stages in the Life Cycles of Stars

The diagram on page 127 shows the stages that stars go through in their life cycles. Notice that the length of a cycle and the way a star changes depend on the mass of the star at its formation.

RESOURCE CENTER
CLASSZONE.COM

Learn more about life cycles of stars.

Lower-Mass Stars The stage in which stars produce energy through the fusion of hydrogen into helium is called the **main sequence.** Because they use their fuel slowly, lower-mass stars can remain in the main-sequence stage for billions of years. The Sun has been a main-sequence star for 4.6 billion years and will remain one for about another 5 billion years. When a lower-mass star runs out of hydrogen, it expands into a giant star, in which helium fuses into carbon. Over time a giant star sheds its outer layers and becomes a white dwarf. A white dwarf is simply the dead core of a giant star. Although no fusion occurs in white dwarfs, they remain hot for billions of years.

Higher-Mass Stars Stars more than eight times as massive as our Sun spend much less time in the main-sequence stage because they use their fuel rapidly. After millions of years, a higher-mass star expands to become a supergiant star. In the core of a supergiant, fusion produces heavier and heavier elements. When an iron core forms, fusion stops and gravity causes the core to collapse. Then part of the core bounces outward, and the star erupts in an explosion called a supernova.

For a brief period, a supernova can give off as much light as a galaxy. The outer layers of the exploded star shoot out into space, carrying with them heavy elements that formed inside the star. Eventually this matter may become part of new stars and planets.

Neutron Stars and Black Holes

The collapsed core of a supergiant star may form an extremely dense body called a **neutron star.** Neutron stars measure only about 20 kilometers (12 mi) in diameter, but their masses are one to three times that of the Sun.

Neutron stars emit little visible light. However, they strongly emit other forms of radiation, such as x-rays. Some neutron stars emit beams of radio waves as they spin. These stars are called pulsars because they seem to pulse as the beams rotate.

Sometimes a supernova leaves behind a core with a mass more than three times that of the Sun. In such a case, the core does not end up as a neutron star. Instead, it collapses even further, forming an invisible object called a **black hole.** The gravity of a black hole is so strong that no form of radiation can escape from it.

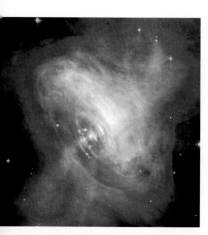

A pulsar emits beams of radio waves as it spins rapidly. The pulsar seems to pulse as the beams rotate toward and away from Earth.

 CHECK YOUR READING How do lower-mass stars differ from higher-mass stars after the main-sequence stage?

Life Cycles of Stars

A star forms inside a cloud of gas and dust called a nebula.
The life cycle of a star depends on its mass.

Lower-Mass Stars

A lower-mass star can fuse hydrogen into helium for billions of years. This stage is called the **main sequence.**

After the main-sequence stage, the star expands into a **giant star.**

When a giant star sheds its outer layers, it leaves behind a dead core called a **white dwarf.**

Higher-Mass Stars

A higher-mass star remains in the **main-sequence** stage for millions of years.

After the main-sequence stage, the star expands into a **supergiant.**

When fusion can no longer occur in the supergiant, it undergoes an explosion called a **supernova.**

A high-mass star leaves behind a densely packed core called a **neutron star.**

A star with an extremely high mass leaves behind an invisible **black hole.** Astronomers can sometimes detect matter and energy around a black hole.

READING VISUALS How do the stars shown in this illustration differ in the main-sequence stage of their life cycles?

Star Systems

Unlike our Sun, most stars do not exist alone. Instead, they are grouped with one or more companion stars. The stars are held together by the force of gravity between them. A binary star system consists of two stars that orbit each other. A multiple star system consists of more than two stars.

In many star systems, the stars are too close together to be seen individually. However, astronomers have developed ways of detecting such systems. For example, in a binary star system, one of the stars may orbit in front of the other when viewed from Earth. The star that orbits in front will briefly block some of the other star's light, providing a clue that more than one star is present. The illustration at right shows a binary star system that can be detected this way. Sometimes astronomers can also figure out whether a star is really a star system by studying its spectrum.

Star systems are an important source of information about star masses. Astronomers cannot measure the mass of a star directly. However, they can figure out a star's mass by observing the effect of the star's gravity on a companion star.

Binary Star System

Some binary star systems appear to dim briefly when one star orbits in front of the other and blocks some of its light.

When neither star is in front of the other, the star system appears to give off more light.

CHECK YOUR READING Why are star systems important to astronomers?

Review

KEY CONCEPTS

1. Why must astronomers figure out a star's distance to calculate its actual brightness?
2. How are color and temperature related in stars?
3. How does a star's mass affect its life cycle?

CRITICAL THINKING

4. **Analyze** Some of the brightest stars are red supergiants. How can stars with cooler red surfaces be so bright?
5. **Infer** Will the Sun eventually become a black hole? Why or why not?

○ CHALLENGE

6. **Infer** At what stage in the life cycle of the Sun will it be impossible for life to exist on Earth? Explain.

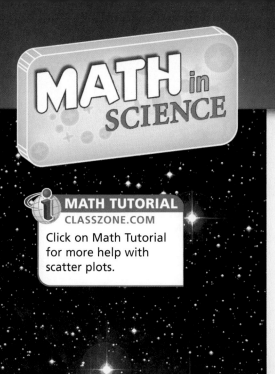

Brightness and Temperature of Stars

A star's brightness, or luminosity, depends on the star's surface temperature and size. If two stars have the same surface temperature, the larger star will be more luminous. The Hertzsprung-Russell (H-R) diagram below is a scatter plot that shows the relative temperatures and luminosities of various stars.

Example

Describe the surface temperature and luminosity of Spica.

(1) Surface temperature: Without drawing on the graph, imagine a line extending from Spica down to the temperature axis. Spica is one of the hottest stars.

(2) Luminosity: Imagine a line extending from Spica across to the luminosity axis. Spica has a high luminosity.

ANSWER Spica is one of the hottest and most luminous stars.

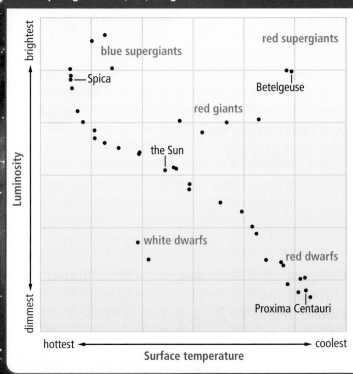

Hertzsprung-Russell (H-R) Diagram

Use the diagram to answer the questions.

1. Describe the surface temperature and luminosity of Proxima Centauri.

2. Compare the surface temperature and luminosity of the Sun with the surface temperature and luminosity of Betelgeuse.

3. Compare the surface temperature and luminosity of the red dwarfs with the surface temperature and luminosity of the blue supergiants.

CHALLENGE When an old red giant star loses its outer atmosphere, all that remains is the very hot core of the star. Because the core is small, it does not give off much light. What kind of star does the red giant star become after it loses its outer atmosphere? How can you tell from the diagram?

KEY CONCEPT

4.3 Galaxies have different sizes and shapes.

BEFORE, you learned

- Our solar system is part of a galaxy called the Milky Way
- Stars change over their life cycles

NOW, you will learn

- About the size and shape of the Milky Way
- How galaxies are classified
- About the centers of galaxies

VOCABULARY

quasar p. 133

EXPLORE The Milky Way

Why does the Milky Way look hazy?

PROCEDURE

1. Use a white gel pen to make 50 small dots close together on a piece of black paper.

2. Tape the paper to a wall, and move slowly away from it until you have difficulty seeing the individual dots.

WHAT DO YOU THINK?

- At what distance did the dots become hazy?
- Why might some of the stars in the Milky Way appear hazy from Earth?

MATERIALS
- white gel pen
- black paper
- tape

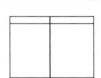

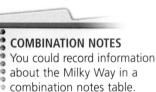

COMBINATION NOTES
You could record information about the Milky Way in a combination notes table.

Our solar system lies within the Milky Way galaxy.

The Sun lies within a galaxy called the Milky Way. Remember that a galaxy is a huge grouping of stars, gas, and dust held together by gravity. Without a telescope, you can only see nearby stars clearly. Those stars are a tiny fraction of the several hundred billion in the Milky Way.

The Milky Way is shaped like a disk with a bulge in the center. Because Earth is inside the disk, you have an edge-on view of part of the galaxy. On a dark night, the galaxy appears as a band of blended starlight. The Milky Way got its name from the hazy, or milky, appearance of this band of stars. You cannot see the center of the galaxy because it is hidden by dust.

 Why can't we see all of the Milky Way from Earth?

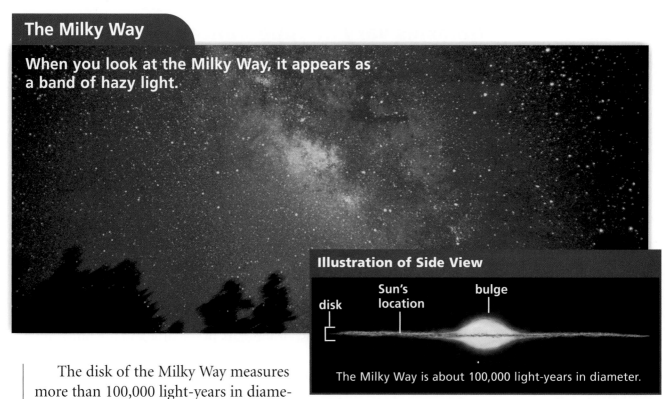

The Milky Way

When you look at the Milky Way, it appears as a band of hazy light.

Illustration of Side View

disk | Sun's location | bulge

The Milky Way is about 100,000 light-years in diameter.

The disk of the Milky Way measures more than 100,000 light-years in diameter. The bulge of densely packed stars at the center is located about 26,000 light-years from the Sun. A large but very faint layer of stars surrounds the disk and bulge. In addition to stars, the Milky Way contains clouds of gas and dust called nebulae.

The stars and nebulae in the Milky Way orbit the galaxy's center at very high speeds. However, the galaxy is so large that the Sun takes about 250 million years to complete one orbit.

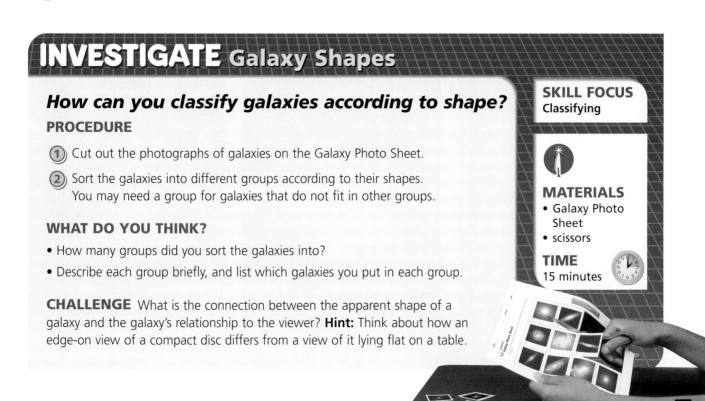

INVESTIGATE Galaxy Shapes

How can you classify galaxies according to shape?

PROCEDURE

1. Cut out the photographs of galaxies on the Galaxy Photo Sheet.

2. Sort the galaxies into different groups according to their shapes. You may need a group for galaxies that do not fit in other groups.

WHAT DO YOU THINK?

• How many groups did you sort the galaxies into?

• Describe each group briefly, and list which galaxies you put in each group.

CHALLENGE What is the connection between the apparent shape of a galaxy and the galaxy's relationship to the viewer? **Hint:** Think about how an edge-on view of a compact disc differs from a view of it lying flat on a table.

SKILL FOCUS
Classifying

MATERIALS
• Galaxy Photo Sheet
• scissors

TIME
15 minutes

Galaxies vary in appearance.

 **RESOURCE CENTER**
CLASSZONE.COM

Learn more about galaxies.

Galaxies differ greatly in size. Some contain as few as a hundred million stars, but the biggest have more than a trillion stars. Galaxies also vary in shape. Astronomers have classified galaxies into three main types based on their shape.

 CHECK YOUR READING What are two ways in which galaxies can differ from one another?

Types of Galaxies

VOCABULARY
Make a description wheel for each type of galaxy in your notebook.

The three main types of galaxies are spiral, elliptical, and irregular. Most galaxies are either spiral or elliptical.

Spiral galaxies have arms of stars, gas, and dust that curve away from the center of the galaxy in a spiral pattern. The Milky Way is a spiral galaxy. Like the Milky Way, other spiral galaxies are disk-shaped and have a central bulge. Most of the stars in the disk and the bulge are old stars. However, the dense spiral arms within the disk contain many young, bright stars.

Elliptical galaxies are shaped like spheres or eggs. Unlike spiral galaxies, elliptical galaxies have almost no dust or gas between stars, and all of their stars are old.

Irregular galaxies are faint galaxies without a definite shape. They are smaller than the other types of galaxies and have many fewer stars.

Galaxies sometimes collide with other galaxies. These collisions can cause changes in their shapes. The Extreme Science feature on page 134 describes such collisions.

Spiral Galaxy

Elliptical Galaxy

Irregular Galaxy

Centers of Galaxies

Most large galaxies seem to have supermassive black holes at their centers. The mass of a supermassive black hole can be millions or even billions of times greater than that of the Sun. At the center of the Milky Way, for example, is a black hole with a mass about three million times that of the Sun.

Like all black holes, a supermassive black hole is invisible. Astronomers can identify the presence of a black hole by the behavior of matter around it. The gravity of a supermassive black hole is so strong that it draws in a huge whirlpool of gas from nearby stars. As gases are pulled toward the black hole, they become compressed and extremely hot, so they give off very bright light. The motions of stars orbiting the black hole can also reveal its presence.

If the center of a galaxy is very bright, it may look like a star from a great distance. The very bright centers of some distant galaxies are called **quasars.** *Quasar* is a shortened form of *quasi-stellar,* which means "seeming like a star." The galaxy surrounding a quasar is often hard to see because the quasar is so much brighter than it.

Evidence of a Supermassive Black Hole

disk of gas swirling around the black hole

gas being drawn into the black hole

 How can astronomers detect the presence of a supermassive black hole at the center of a galaxy?

4.3 Review

KEY CONCEPTS

1. What is the shape of the Milky Way?
2. Why does the Milky Way look like a hazy band of stars in the sky?
3. What keeps the stars in galaxies from moving apart?

CRITICAL THINKING

4. **Compare and Contrast** Make a diagram showing similarities and differences among the three main types of galaxies.
5. **Infer** How might our view of the Milky Way be different if the Sun were located inside the central bulge?

CHALLENGE

6. **Predict** If two spiral galaxies collide, what might eventually happen to the supermassive black holes at their centers?

When Galaxies Collide

A small galaxy is moving through our galaxy, the Milky Way, right now!

- The small galaxy may be destroyed by the collision, but the Milky Way is not in danger.
- The same galaxy seems to have moved through the Milky Way ten times before.
- Other galaxies may also be moving through the Milky Way.

Not to Worry!

Galaxies containing many billions of stars are colliding all the time. What are the chances that their stars will crash into one another? The chances are very small, because there is so much empty space between stars.

Galactic Cannibals

When galaxies collide, a larger galaxy can "eat up" a smaller one.

- The stars of the smaller galaxy become part of the larger one.
- The collision of two spiral galaxies may form a new elliptical galaxy.

Bent Out of Shape

Sometimes galaxies pass very close to each other without actually colliding. In these near misses, gravity can produce some interesting new shapes. For example, the Tadpole Galaxy (left) has a long tail of dust and gas pulled out by the gravity of a passing galaxy.

Model Galaxies

Astronomers use computer simulations to predict how the stars and gas in galaxies are affected by a collision. To understand galaxy collisions better, they then compare the simulations with images of actual galaxies.

EXPLORE

1. **PREDICT** Draw the shape of the new galaxy that the two in the photograph on the left might form.

2. **CHALLENGE** Look at online images and simulations of galaxy collisions. Make a chart showing how these collisions can differ.

RESOURCE CENTER
CLASSZONE.COM
Find out more about galaxy collisions.

Come back in a few billion years and you may see that these two spiral galaxies have become one elliptical galaxy.

KEY CONCEPT

4.4 The universe is expanding.

◀ BEFORE, you learned

- Galaxies contain millions or billions of stars
- Electromagnetic radiation carries information about space

▶ NOW, you will learn

- How galaxies are moving apart in the universe
- What scientists are discovering about the development of the universe

VOCABULARY

Doppler effect p. 136
big bang p. 138

EXPLORE Large Numbers

How much is a billion?

PROCEDURE

① Guess how thick a billion-page book would be. Write down your guess.

② Count how many sheets of paper in a book add up to a millimeter in thickness. Multiply by 2 to calculate the number of pages.

③ Then divide 1 billion (1,000,000,000) by that number to determine how many millimeters thick the book would be. Divide your result by 1,000,000 to convert to kilometers.

WHAT DO YOU THINK?

- How thick would a billion-page book be?
- How close was your guess?

MATERIALS
- book
- ruler
- calculator

COMBINATION NOTES
You could record information about the expansion of the universe in a combination notes table.

Galaxies are moving farther apart in the universe.

The universe is unbelievably huge. It consists of all space, energy, and matter. The Milky Way is just one of about 100 billion galaxies. These galaxies occur in groups that together form superclusters. Between the superclusters are huge areas of nearly empty space.

Because the universe is so huge, you might think that the most distant regions of the universe are very different from space near Earth. However, by looking at the spectra of light from stars and galaxies, astronomers have determined that the same elements are found throughout the universe. Scientific observations also indicate that the same physical forces and processes operate everywhere.

Looking Back in Time

When we look far out into space, we see galaxies by the light they gave off long ago. This light has traveled millions or even billions of

years before reaching telescopes on Earth. The Andromeda Galaxy, for example, is the closest large galaxy. The light of its stars takes over 2 million years to reach Earth. When we view this galaxy through a telescope, we are seeing what happened in it 2 million years ago. To see what is happening there now, we would have to wait 2 million years for the light to arrive.

As astronomers look at galaxies farther and farther away, they see how the universe looked at different times in the past. These views are like photographs in an album that show someone at various stages of life. Astronomers can see how the universe has developed over billions of years.

Light from the Andromeda Galaxy takes 2 million years to reach Earth.

CHECK YOUR READING Why can astronomers learn about the past by looking at distant galaxies?

The Motion of Galaxies

Have you ever noticed that the sound of an ambulance siren changes as it travels toward and then away from you? The pitch of the siren seems to be higher as the ambulance approaches. As the ambulance passes you and starts moving away, the pitch of the siren seems to get lower. The shifting pitch of the siren is an example of the **Doppler effect,** which is a change in the observed wavelength or frequency of a wave that occurs when the source of the wave or the observer is moving.

The Doppler effect occurs with light as well as sound. If a galaxy is moving toward Earth, the light we receive will seem compressed to shorter wavelengths. This change is called a blue shift because the light shifts toward the blue end of the spectrum. If a galaxy is moving away from Earth, the light we receive will seem stretched to longer wave-lengths. This change is called a red shift because the light shifts toward the red end of the spectrum.

In the early 1900s, astronomers discovered that light from distant galaxies is stretched to longer wavelengths. This fact indicates that the galaxies are moving apart. By analyzing the spectra of galaxies, astronomers also discovered that the galaxies are moving apart faster the farther away they are. These observations led astronomers to conclude that the universe has been expanding throughout its history.

Evidence of an Expanding Universe

The Doppler effect can show how galaxies are moving in relation to Earth.

moving away

moving toward

Earth

Light from a galaxy moving away from Earth will seem stretched to longer wavelengths.

Light from a galaxy moving toward Earth will seem compressed to shorter wavelengths.

READING VISUALS What do the arrows on the light waves indicate?

The illustration of raisin-bread dough rising will help you imagine this expansion. Suppose you were a raisin. You would observe that all the other raisins are moving away from you as the dough expands. The raisins are being moved apart by the expanding dough. Furthermore, you would observe that distant raisins are moving away faster than nearby raisins. They move away faster because there is more dough expanding between you and those raisins.

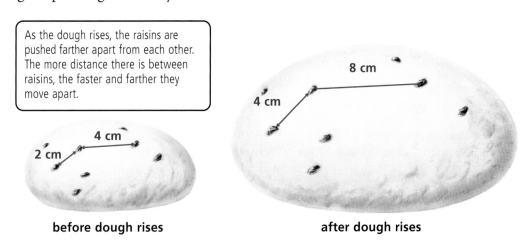

As the dough rises, the raisins are pushed farther apart from each other. The more distance there is between raisins, the faster and farther they move apart.

2 cm   4 cm

4 cm   8 cm

before dough rises

after dough rises

Like the dough that expands and moves raisins apart, space in the universe is expanding and moving galaxies apart. The universe does not expand into anything, since there is nothing outside the universe. Rather, the universe itself is expanding.

CHECK YOUR READING How are galaxies moving in relation to each other?

INVESTIGATE Galaxies

How does the universe expand?

PROCEDURE

① Spread the cut rubber band against the ruler without stretching it. Mark off every centimeter for 6 centimeters.

② Align the first mark on the rubber band with the 1-centimeter mark on the ruler and hold it in place tightly. Stretch the rubber band so that the second mark is next to the 3-centimeter mark on the ruler.

③ Observe how many centimeters each mark has moved from its original location against the ruler.

WHAT DO YOU THINK?

• How far did each mark on the rubber band move from its original location?

• What does this activity demonstrate about the expansion of the universe?

CHALLENGE How could you calculate the rates at which the marks moved when you stretched the rubber band?

SKILL FOCUS
Measuring

MATERIALS
• thick rubber band cut open
• ballpoint pen
• ruler

TIME
20 minutes

Scientists are investigating the origin of the universe.

After astronomers learned that galaxies are moving apart, they developed new ideas about the origin of the universe. They concluded that all matter was once merged together and then the universe suddenly began to expand. The evidence for this scientific theory is so strong that almost all astronomers now accept it.

The **big bang** is the moment in time when the universe started to expand out of an extremely hot, dense state. Astronomers have calculated that this event happened about 14 billion years ago. The expansion was very rapid. In a tiny fraction of a second, the universe may have expanded from a size much smaller than a speck of dust to the size of our solar system.

VOCABULARY
Add a description wheel for *big bang* in your notebook.

Evidence of the Big Bang

Evidence for the big bang comes from various sources. One important source of evidence is microwave radiation. Astronomers predicted in 1948 that the universe would still be filled with microwaves emitted shortly after the big bang. In 1965 researchers detected this kind of radiation streaming through space in all directions.

Besides the presence of microwave radiation and the motions of galaxies, scientists have found other evidence of the big bang by observing space. For example, images of very distant galaxies provide information about the universe's development. Additional evidence of the big bang has come from experiments and computer models.

Development of the Universe

Immediately after the big bang, the universe was incredibly dense and hot—much hotter than the core of the Sun. Matter and energy behaved very differently than they do under present conditions. As the universe rapidly expanded, it went through a series of changes.

Scientists do not fully understand what conditions were like in the early universe. However, they are gaining a clearer picture of how the universe developed. One way that scientists are learning about this development is by performing experiments in particle accelerators. These huge machines expose matter to extreme conditions.

Scientists have found that the earliest stages in the universe's development occurred in a tiny fraction of a second. However, it took about 300,000 years for the first elements to form. Stars, planets, and galaxies began to appear within the next billion years. Some evidence suggests that the first stars formed only a few hundred million years after the big bang.

This Hubble telescope image of very distant galaxies has helped scientists learn what the universe was like about 13 billion years ago.

 **CHECK YOUR READING** What happened to the universe shortly after the big bang?

4.4 Review

KEY CONCEPTS

1. How are distant regions of the universe similar to space near Earth?

2. What does the Doppler effect indicate about the motion of galaxies?

3. How do scientists explain the origin of the universe?

CRITICAL THINKING

4. **Apply** If a star 100 light-years from Earth is beginning to expand into a giant star, how long will it take for astronomers to observe this development? Explain.

5. **Analyze** Why do scientists need to perform experiments to learn about the earliest stages of the universe?

○ CHALLENGE

6. **Infer** Galaxy A and galaxy B both give off light that appears stretched to longer wavelengths. The light from galaxy B is stretched to even longer wavelengths than the light from galaxy A. What can you infer from these data?

Chapter Review

the BIG idea

Our Sun is one of billions of stars in one of billions of galaxies in the universe.

◀ KEY CONCEPTS SUMMARY

4.1 ## The Sun is our local star.

The Sun produces energy from hydrogen. Energy flows through the Sun's layers. Features appear on the Sun's surface.

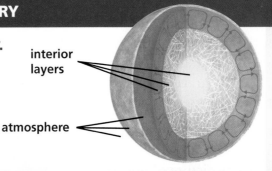

interior layers

atmosphere

VOCABULARY
fusion p. 116
convection p. 116
corona p. 116
sunspot p. 118
solar wind p. 119

4.2 ## Stars change over their life cycles.

Stars vary in brightness, size, color, and temperature. The development of a star depends on the mass of the star. Most stars are grouped with one or more companion stars.

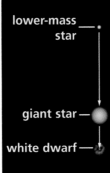

lower-mass star

giant star

white dwarf

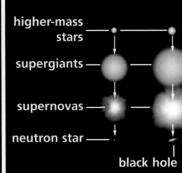

higher-mass stars

supergiants

supernovas

neutron star

black hole

VOCABULARY
light-year p. 122
parallax p. 123
nebula p. 125
main sequence p. 126
neutron star p. 126
black hole p. 126

4.3 ## Galaxies have different sizes and shapes.

Our galaxy, the Milky Way, is a spiral galaxy. Galaxies can also be elliptical or irregular. Irregular galaxies have no definite shape.

Spiral Galaxy   Elliptical Galaxy   Irregular Galaxy

VOCABULARY
quasar p. 133

4.4 ## The universe is expanding.

Galaxies are moving farther apart in the universe. Scientists are investigating the origin and development of the universe.

VOCABULARY
Doppler effect p. 136
big bang p. 138

Reviewing Vocabulary

Make a frame for each of the vocabulary words listed below. Write the word in the center. Decide what information to frame it with. Use definitions, examples, descriptions, parts, or pictures. An example is shown below.

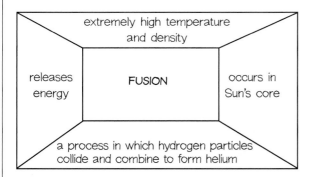

extremely high temperature and density

releases energy

FUSION

occurs in Sun's core

a process in which hydrogen particles collide and combine to form helium

1. convection
2. corona
3. sunspot
4. solar wind
5. nebula
6. black hole
7. Doppler effect
8. big bang

Reviewing Key Concepts

Multiple Choice *Choose the letter of the best answer.*

9. Which layer do you usually see in photographs of the Sun?
   a. convection zone
   b. photosphere
   c. chromosphere
   d. corona

10. Which statement is true of sunspots?
    a. They are permanent features on the Sun's surface.
    b. They are caused by solar wind.
    c. They are where fusion occurs.
    d. They are cooler than surrounding areas.

11. Which unit is usually used to describe the distances of stars?
    a. astronomical units
    b. light-years
    c. kilometers
    d. miles

12. Which example best shows the relationship between color and temperature?
    a. A rainbow forms when sunlight strikes raindrops.
    b. A flashlight beam looks red when passed through a red plastic filter.
    c. A chemical light-stick glows a yellow-green color.
    d. A metal rod in a fireplace changes in color from red to orange.

13. How do lower-mass stars differ from higher-mass stars?
    a. They develop more quickly.
    b. They develop more slowly.
    c. They end up as black holes.
    d. They have too little mass to produce energy.

14. Which term describes the Milky Way?
    a. spiral galaxy
    b. elliptical galaxy
    c. irregular galaxy
    d. quasar

15. The Doppler effect is used to determine
    a. the number of stars in a galaxy
    b. the number of galaxies in the universe
    c. the size of the universe
    d. whether a galaxy is moving toward or away from Earth

16. What is the big bang?
    a. the collision of galaxies
    b. the formation of the solar system
    c. the beginning of the universe's expansion
    d. the time when stars began to form

Short Answer *Write a short answer to each question.*

17. Why can't we see the Sun's corona under normal conditions?

18. How do astronomers use parallax to calculate a star's distance?

19. Where do heavy elements, such as iron, come from?

20. How can astronomers tell whether a black hole exists in the center of a galaxy?

The table below shows the distances of some galaxies and the speeds at which they are moving away from the Milky Way. Use the table to answer the next three questions.

Galaxy	Distance (million light-years)	Speed (kilometers per second)
NGC 7793	14	241
NGC 6946	22	336
NGC 2903	31	472
NGC 6744	42	663

21. COMPARE AND CONTRAST How do the speed and distance of NGC 7793 compare with the speed and distance of NGC 2903?

22. ANALYZE What general pattern do you see in these data?

23. APPLY What would you estimate to be the speed of a galaxy located 60 million light-years away? **Hint:** Notice the pattern between the first and third rows and the second and fourth rows in the chart.

24. INFER Why might the solar wind have a stronger effect on inner planets than on outer planets in the solar system?

25. PREDICT The core of a particular star consists almost entirely of helium. What will soon happen to this star?

26. ANALYZE Planets shine by reflected light. Why do some planets in our solar system appear brighter than stars, even though the stars give off their own light?

27. IDENTIFY CAUSE A star dims for a brief period every three days. What could be causing it to dim?

28. COMPARE AND CONTRAST Describe the similarities and differences between the life cycles of lower-mass stars and higher-mass stars.

29. EVALUATE If you wanted to study a neutron star, would you use a visible-light telescope or an x-ray telescope? Explain why.

30. INFER Suppose that astronomers find evidence of iron and other heavy elements in a galaxy. On the basis of this evidence, what can you assume has already occurred in that galaxy?

31. ANALYZE Why did the discovery that galaxies are moving farther apart help scientists conclude that all matter was once merged together?

32. PREDICT What changes do you predict will happen in the universe over the next 10 billion years?

33. COMPARE AND CONTRAST The photographs above show a spiral galaxy and an elliptical galaxy. What similarities and differences do you see in these two types of galaxies?

the BIG idea

34. INFER Look again at the photograph on pages 112–113. Now that you have finished the chapter, how would you change your response to the question on the photograph? What else might be present?

35. SYNTHESIZE Think of a question that you still have about the universe. What information would you need to answer the question? How might you obtain this information?

UNIT PROJECTS

Evaluate all the data, results, and information in your project folder. Prepare to present your project.

Analyzing a Chart

Use the chart and diagram to answer the next six questions.

Classification of Stars

Class	Color	Surface Temperature (°C)
O	blue-white	above 25,000
B	blue-white	10,000–25,000
A	white	7500–10,000
F	yellow-white	6000–7500
G	yellow	5000–6000
K	orange	3500–5000
M	red	below 3500

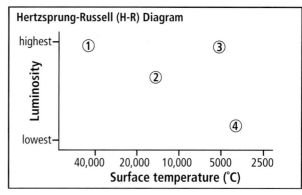

1. Which class of star has the lowest surface temperature?

  a. O   **c.** G

  b. B   **d.** M

2. Which class of star has the highest surface temperature?

  a. O   **c.** G

  b. B   **d.** M

3. What would be the color of a star with a surface temperature of 8000°C?

  a. blue-white   **c.** orange

  b. white   **d.** red

4. Toward the end of their life cycles, very massive stars expand in size, and their surface temperature becomes lower. Which of the following is an example of this change?

  a. A white star becomes a blue-white star.

  b. A blue-white star becomes a red star.

  c. A red star becomes a blue-white star.

  d. A yellow star becomes a yellow-white star.

5. The H-R diagram above shows the surface temperatures and luminosities, or true brightnesses, of four stars. Which of the stars is a type O?

  a. 1   **c.** 3

  b. 2   **d.** 4

6. Which two stars on the H-R diagram have the most similar surface temperatures?

  a. 1 and 2   **c.** 2 and 3

  b. 1 and 3   **d.** 3 and 4

Extended Response

Answer the two questions below in detail.

7. Why is looking at a star in the night sky like seeing back into time?

8. How could you use two flashlights to demonstrate the concept that the apparent brightness of a star is affected by its distance from Earth? You can include a diagram as part of your answer.

Student Resource Handbooks

Scientific Thinking Handbook

SCIENTIFIC THINKING HANDBOOK

Making Observations

An **observation** is an act of noting and recording an event, character-istic, behavior, or anything else detected with an instrument or with the senses.

Observations allow you to make informed hypotheses and to gather data for experiments. Careful observations often lead to ideas for new experiments. There are two categories of observations:

- **Quantitative observations** can be expressed in numbers and include records of time, temperature, mass, distance, and volume.

- **Qualitative observations** include descriptions of sights, sounds, smells, and textures.

EXAMPLE

A student dissolved 30 grams of Epsom salts in water, poured the solution into a dish, and let the dish sit out uncovered overnight. The next day, she made the following observations of the Epsom salt crystals that grew in the dish.

Table 1. Observations of Epsom Salt Crystals

Quantitative Observations	Qualitative Observations
• mass = 30 g • mean crystal length = 0.5 cm • longest crystal length = 2 cm	• Crystals are clear. • Crystals are long, thin, and rectangular. • White crust has formed around edge of dish.

To determine the mass, the student found the mass of the dish before and after growing the crystals and then used subtraction to find the difference.

The student measured several crystals and calculated the mean length. (To learn how to calculate the mean of a data set, see page R36.)

Photographs or sketches are useful for recording qualitative observations.

Epsom salt crystals

MORE ABOUT OBSERVING

- Make quantitative observations whenever possible. That way, others will know exactly what you observed and be able to compare their results with yours.

- It is always a good idea to make qualitative observations too. You never know when you might observe something unexpected.

Predicting and Hypothesizing

A **prediction** is an expectation of what will be observed or what will happen. A **hypothesis** is a tentative explanation for an observation or scientific problem that can be tested by further investigation.

EXAMPLE

Suppose you have made two paper airplanes and you wonder why one of them tends to glide farther than the other one.

1. Start by asking a question.

2. Make an educated guess. After examination, you notice that the wings of the airplane that flies farther are slightly larger than the wings of the other airplane.

3. Write a prediction based upon your educated guess, in the form of an "If . . . , then . . ." statement. Write the independent variable after the word *if*, and the dependent variable after the word *then*.

4. To make a hypothesis, explain why you think what you predicted will occur. Write the explanation after the word *because*.

---

1. Why does one of the paper airplanes glide farther than the other?

2. The size of an airplane's wings may affect how far the airplane will glide.

3. Prediction: If I make a paper airplane with larger wings, then the airplane will glide farther.

To read about independent and dependent variables, see page R30.

4. Hypothesis: If I make a paper airplane with larger wings, then the airplane will glide farther, because the additional surface area of the wing will produce more lift.

Notice that the part of the hypothesis after *because* adds an explanation of why the airplane will glide farther.

MORE ABOUT HYPOTHESES

- The results of an experiment cannot prove that a hypothesis is correct. Rather, the results either support or do not support the hypothesis.

- Valuable information is gained even when your hypothesis is not supported by your results. For example, it would be an important discovery to find that wing size is not related to how far an airplane glides.

- In science, a hypothesis is supported only after many scientists have conducted many experiments and produced consistent results.

Inferring

An **inference** is a logical conclusion drawn from the available evidence and prior knowledge. Inferences are often made from observations.

EXAMPLE

A student observing a set of acorns noticed something unexpected about one of them. He noticed a white, soft-bodied insect eating its way out of the acorn.

The student recorded these observations.

Here are some inferences that can be made on the basis of the observations.

Observations
- There is a hole in the acorn, about 0.5 cm in diameter, where the insect crawled out.
- There is a second hole, which is about the size of a pinhole, on the other side of the acorn.
- The inside of the acorn is hollow.

Inferences
- The insect formed from the material inside the acorn, grew to its present size, and ate its way out of the acorn.
- The insect crawled through the smaller hole, ate the inside of the acorn, grew to its present size, and ate its way out of the acorn.
- An egg was laid in the acorn through the smaller hole. The egg hatched into a larva that ate the inside of the acorn, grew to its present size, and ate its way out of the acorn.

When you make inferences, be sure to look at all of the evidence available and combine it with what you already know.

MORE ABOUT INFERENCES

Inferences depend both on observations and on the knowledge of the people making the inferences. Ancient people who did not know that organisms are produced only by similar organisms might have made an inference like the first one. A student today might look at the same observations and make the second inference. A third student might have knowledge about this particular insect and know that it is never small enough to fit through the smaller hole, leading her to the third inference.

Identifying Cause and Effect

In a **cause-and-effect relationship,** one event or characteristic is the result of another. Usually an effect follows its cause in time.

There are many examples of cause-and-effect relationships in everyday life.

Cause	Effect
Turn off a light.	Room gets dark.
Drop a glass.	Glass breaks.
Blow a whistle.	Sound is heard.

Scientists must be careful not to infer a cause-and-effect relationship just because one event happens after another event. When one event occurs after another, you cannot infer a cause-and-effect relationship on the basis of that information alone. You also cannot conclude that one event caused another if there are alternative ways to explain the second event. A scientist must demonstrate through experimentation or continued observation that an event was truly caused by another event.

EXAMPLE

Make an Observation

Suppose you have a few plants growing outside. When the weather starts getting colder, you bring one of the plants indoors. You notice that the plant you brought indoors is growing faster than the others are growing. You cannot conclude from your observation that the change in temperature was the cause of the increased plant growth, because there are alternative explanations for the observation. Some possible explanations are given below.

- The humidity indoors caused the plant to grow faster.

- The level of sunlight indoors caused the plant to grow faster.

- The indoor plant's being noticed more often and watered more often than the outdoor plants caused it to grow faster.

- The plant that was brought indoors was healthier than the other plants to begin with.

To determine which of these factors, if any, caused the indoor plant to grow faster than the outdoor plants, you would need to design and conduct an experiment.

See pages R28–R35 for information about designing experiments.

Recognizing Bias

Television, newspapers, and the Internet are full of experts claiming to have scientific evidence to back up their claims. How do you know whether the claims are really backed up by good science?

Bias is a slanted point of view, or personal prejudice. The goal of scientists is to be as objective as possible and to base their findings on facts instead of opinions. However, bias often affects the conclusions of researchers, and it is important to learn to recognize bias.

When scientific results are reported, you should consider the source of the information as well as the information itself. It is important to critically analyze the information that you see and read.

SOURCES OF BIAS

There are several ways in which a report of scientific information may be biased. Here are some questions that you can ask yourself:

1. **Who is sponsoring the research?**

   Sometimes, the results of an investigation are biased because an organization paying for the research is looking for a specific answer. This type of bias can affect how data are gathered and interpreted.

2. **Is the research sample large enough?**

   Sometimes research does not include enough data. The larger the sample size, the more likely that the results are accurate, assuming a truly random sample.

3. **In a survey, who is answering the questions?**

   The results of a survey or poll can be biased. The people taking part in the survey may have been specifically chosen because of how they would answer. They may have the same ideas or lifestyles. A survey or poll should make use of a random sample of people.

4. **Are the people who take part in a survey biased?**

   People who take part in surveys sometimes try to answer the questions the way they think the researcher wants them to answer. Also, in surveys or polls that ask for personal information, people may be unwilling to answer questions truthfully.

SCIENTIFIC BIAS

It is also important to realize that scientists have their own biases because of the types of research they do and because of their scientific viewpoints. Two scientists may look at the same set of data and come to completely different conclusions because of these biases. However, such disagreements are not necessarily bad. In fact, a critical analysis of disagreements is often responsible for moving science forward.

Identifying Faulty Reasoning

Faulty reasoning is wrong or incorrect thinking. It leads to mistakes and to wrong conclusions. Scientists are careful not to draw unreasonable conclusions from experimental data. Without such caution, the results of scientific investigations may be misleading.

EXAMPLE

Scientists try to make generalizations based on their data to explain as much about nature as possible. If only a small sample of data is looked at, however, a conclusion may be faulty. Suppose a scientist has studied the effects of the El Niño and La Niña weather patterns on flood damage in California from 1989 to 1995. The scientist organized the data in the bar graph below.

The scientist drew the following conclusions:

1. The La Niña weather pattern has no effect on flooding in California.

2. When neither weather pattern occurs, there is almost no flood damage.

3. A weak or moderate El Niño produces a small or moderate amount of flooding.

4. A strong El Niño produces a lot of flooding.

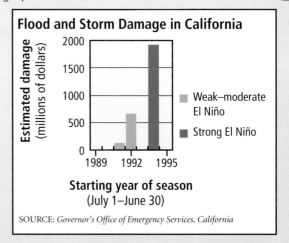

For the six-year period of the scientist's investigation, these conclusions may seem to be reasonable. However, a six-year study of weather patterns may be too small of a sample for the conclusions to be supported. Consider the following graph, which shows information that was gathered from 1949 to 1997.

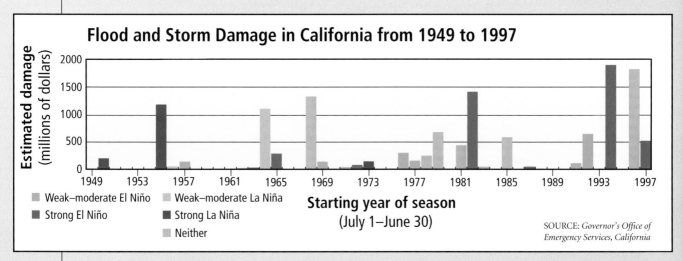

The only one of the conclusions that all of this information supports is number 3: a weak or moderate El Niño produces a small or moderate amount of flooding. By collecting more data, scientists can be more certain of their conclusions and can avoid faulty reasoning.

Analyzing Statements

To **analyze** a statement is to examine its parts carefully. Scientific findings are often reported through media such as television or the Internet. A report that is made public often focuses on only a small part of research. As a result, it is important to question the sources of information.

Evaluate Media Claims

To **evaluate** a statement is to judge it on the basis of criteria you've established. Sometimes evaluating means deciding whether a statement is true.

Reports of scientific research and findings in the media may be misleading or incomplete. When you are exposed to this information, you should ask yourself some questions so that you can make informed judgments about the information.

1. **Does the information come from a credible source?**

   Suppose you learn about a new product and it is stated that scientific evidence proves that the product works. A report from a respected news source may be more believable than an advertisement paid for by the product's manufacturer.

2. **How much evidence supports the claim?**

   Often, it may seem that there is new evidence every day of something in the world that either causes or cures an illness. However, information that is the result of several years of work by several different scientists is more credible than an advertisement that does not even cite the subjects of the experiment.

3. **How much information is being presented?**

   Science cannot solve all questions, and scientific experiments often have flaws. A report that discusses problems in a scientific study may be more believable than a report that addresses only positive experimental findings.

4. **Is scientific evidence being presented by a specific source?**

   Sometimes scientific findings are reported by people who are called experts or leaders in a scientific field. But if their names are not given or their scientific credentials are not reported, their statements may be less credible than those of recognized experts.

Differentiate Between Fact and Opinion

Sometimes information is presented as a fact when it may be an opinion. When scientific conclusions are reported, it is important to recognize whether they are based on solid evidence. Again, you may find it helpful to ask yourself some questions.

1. **What is the difference between a fact and an opinion?**

   A **fact** is a piece of information that can be strictly defined and proved true. An **opinion** is a statement that expresses a belief, value, or feeling. An opinion cannot be proved true or false. For example, a person's age is a fact, but if someone is asked how old they feel, it is impossible to prove the person's answer to be true or false.

2. **Can opinions be measured?**

   Yes, opinions can be measured. In fact, surveys often ask for people's opinions on a topic. But there is no way to know whether or not an opinion is the truth.

HOW TO DIFFERENTIATE FACT FROM OPINION

Human Activities and the Environment

Unfortunately, human use of fossil fuels is one of the most significant developments of the past few centuries. Humans rely on fossil fuels, a non-renewable energy resource, for more than 90 percent of their energy needs.

This careless misuse of our planet's resources has resulted in pollution, global warming, and the destruction of fragile ecosystems. For example, oil pipelines carry more than one million barrels of oil each day across tundra regions. Transporting oil across such areas can only result in oil spills that poison the land for decades.

Opinions
Notice words or phrases that express beliefs or feelings. The words *unfortunately* and *careless* show that opinions are being expressed.

Opinion
Look for statements that speculate about events. These statements are opinions, because they cannot be proved.

Facts
Statements that contain statistics tend to be facts. Writers often use facts to support their opinions.

Lab Handbook

Safety Rules

Before you work in the laboratory, read these safety rules twice. Ask your teacher to explain any rules that you do not completely understand. Refer to these rules later on if you have questions about safety in the science classroom.

Directions

- Read all directions and make sure that you understand them before starting an investigation or lab activity. If you do not understand how to do a procedure or how to use a piece of equipment, ask your teacher.
- Do not begin any investigation or touch any equipment until your teacher has told you to start.
- Never experiment on your own. If you want to try a procedure that the directions do not call for, ask your teacher for permission first.
- If you are hurt or injured in any way, tell your teacher immediately.

Dress Code

goggles

apron

gloves

- Wear goggles when
  — using glassware, sharp objects, or chemicals
  — heating an object
  — working with anything that can easily fly up into the air and hurt someone's eye
- Tie back long hair or hair that hangs in front of your eyes.
- Remove any article of clothing—such as a loose sweater or a scarf—that hangs down and may touch a flame, chemical, or piece of equipment.
- Observe all safety icons calling for the wearing of eye protection, gloves, and aprons.

Heating and Fire Safety

fire
safety

heating
safety

- Keep your work area neat, clean, and free of extra materials.
- Never reach over a flame or heat source.
- Point objects being heated away from you and others.
- Never heat a substance or an object in a closed container.
- Never touch an object that has been heated. If you are unsure whether something is hot, treat it as though it is. Use oven mitts, clamps, tongs, or a test-tube holder.
- Know where the fire extinguisher and fire blanket are kept in your classroom.
- Do not throw hot substances into the trash. Wait for them to cool or use the container your teacher puts out for disposal.

Electrical Safety

electrical safety

- Never use lamps or other electrical equipment with frayed cords.
- Make sure no cord is lying on the floor where someone can trip over it.
- Do not let a cord hang over the side of a counter or table so that the equipment can easily be pulled or knocked to the floor.
- Never let cords hang into sinks or other places where water can be found.
- Never try to fix electrical problems. Inform your teacher of any problems immediately.
- Unplug an electrical cord by pulling on the plug, not the cord.

Chemical Safety

chemical safety

poison

fumes

- If you spill a chemical or get one on your skin or in your eyes, tell your teacher right away.
- Never touch, taste, or sniff any chemicals in the lab. If you need to determine odor, waft. Wafting consists of holding the chemical in its container 15 centimeters (6 in.) away from your nose, and using your fingers to bring fumes from the container to your nose.
- Keep lids on all chemicals you are not using.
- Never put unused chemicals back into the original containers. Throw away extra chemicals where your teacher tells you to.
- Pour chemicals over a sink or your work area, not over the floor.
- If you get a chemical in your eye, use the eyewash right away.
- Always wash your hands after handling chemicals, plants, or soil.

Wafting

Glassware and Sharp-Object Safety

sharp objects

- If you break glassware, tell your teacher right away.
- Do not use broken or chipped glassware. Give these to your teacher.
- Use knives and other cutting instruments carefully. Always wear eye protection and cut away from you.

Animal Safety

- Never hurt an animal.
- Touch animals only when necessary. Follow your teacher's instructions for handling animals.
- Always wash your hands after working with animals.

Cleanup

disposal

- Follow your teacher's instructions for throwing away or putting away supplies.
- Clean your work area and pick up anything that has dropped to the floor.
- Wash your hands.

Using Lab Equipment

Different experiments require different types of equipment. But even though experiments differ, the ways in which the equipment is used are the same.

LAB HANDBOOK

Beakers

- Use beakers for holding and pouring liquids.
- Do not use a beaker to measure the volume of a liquid. Use a graduated cylinder instead. (See page R16.)
- Use a beaker that holds about twice as much liquid as you need. For example, if you need 100 milliliters of water, you should use a 200- or 250-milliliter beaker.

Test Tubes

- Use test tubes to hold small amounts of substances.
- Do not use a test tube to measure the volume of a liquid.
- Use a test tube when heating a substance over a flame. Aim the mouth of the tube away from yourself and other people.
- Liquids easily spill or splash from test tubes, so it is important to use only small amounts of liquids.

Test-Tube Holder

- Use a test-tube holder when heating a substance in a test tube.
- Use a test-tube holder if the substance in a test tube is dangerous to touch.
- Make sure the test-tube holder tightly grips the test tube so that the test tube will not slide out of the holder.
- Make sure that the test-tube holder is above the surface of the substance in the test tube so that you can observe the substance.

Test-Tube Rack

- Use a test-tube rack to organize test tubes before, during, and after an experiment.

- Use a test-tube rack to keep test tubes upright so that they do not fall over and spill their contents.

- Use a test-tube rack that is the correct size for the test tubes that you are using. If the rack is too small, a test tube may become stuck. If the rack is too large, a test tube may lean over, and some of its contents may spill or splash.

Forceps

- Use forceps when you need to pick up or hold a very small object that should not be touched with your hands.

- Do not use forceps to hold anything over a flame, because forceps are not long enough to keep your hand safely away from the flame. Plastic forceps will melt, and metal forceps will conduct heat and burn your hand.

Hot Plate

- Use a hot plate when a substance needs to be kept warmer than room temperature for a long period of time.

- Use a hot plate instead of a Bunsen burner or a candle when you need to carefully control temperature.

- Do not use a hot plate when a substance needs to be burned in an experiment.

- Always use "hot hands" safety mitts or oven mitts when handling anything that has been heated on a hot plate.

Microscope

Scientists use microscopes to see very small objects that cannot easily be seen with the eye alone. A microscope magnifies the image of an object so that small details may be observed. A microscope that you may use can magnify an object 400 times—the object will appear 400 times larger than its actual size.

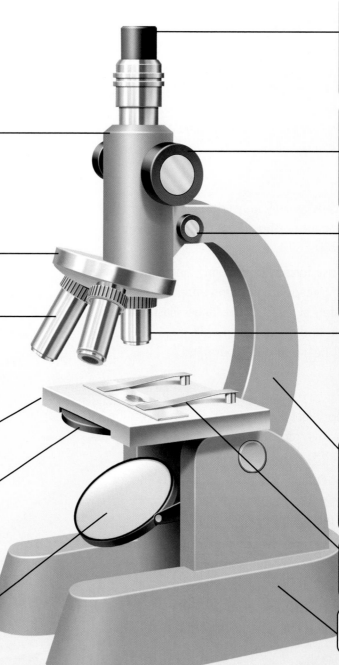

Body The body separates the lens in the eyepiece from the objective lenses below.

Nosepiece The nosepiece holds the objective lenses above the stage and rotates so that all lenses may be used.

High-Power Objective Lens This is the largest lens on the nosepiece. It magnifies an image approximately 40 times.

Stage The stage supports the object being viewed.

Diaphragm The diaphragm is used to adjust the amount of light passing through the slide and into an objective lens.

Mirror or Light Source Some microscopes use light that is reflected through the stage by a mirror. Other microscopes have their own light sources.

Eyepiece Objects are viewed through the eyepiece. The eyepiece contains a lens that commonly magnifies an image 10 times.

Coarse Adjustment This knob is used to focus the image of an object when it is viewed through the low-power lens.

Fine Adjustment This knob is used to focus the image of an object when it is viewed through the high-power lens.

Low-Power Objective Lens This is the smallest lens on the nosepiece. It magnifies an image approximately 10 times.

Arm The arm supports the body above the stage. Always carry a microscope by the arm and base.

Stage Clip The stage clip holds a slide in place on the stage.

Base The base supports the microscope.

VIEWING AN OBJECT

1. Use the coarse adjustment knob to raise the body tube.

2. Adjust the diaphragm so that you can see a bright circle of light through the eyepiece.

3. Place the object or slide on the stage. Be sure that it is centered over the hole in the stage.

4. Turn the nosepiece to click the low-power lens into place.

5. Using the coarse adjustment knob, slowly lower the lens and focus on the specimen being viewed. Be sure not to touch the slide or object with the lens.

6. When switching from the low-power lens to the high-power lens, first raise the body tube with the coarse adjustment knob so that the high-power lens will not hit the slide.

7. Turn the nosepiece to click the high-power lens into place.

8. Use the fine adjustment knob to focus on the specimen being viewed. Again, be sure not to touch the slide or object with the lens.

MAKING A SLIDE, OR WET MOUNT

1 Place the specimen in the center of a clean slide.

2 Place a drop of water on the specimen.

3 Place a cover slip on the slide. Put one edge of the cover slip into the drop of water and slowly lower it over the specimen.

4 Remove any air bubbles from under the cover slip by gently tapping the cover slip.

5 Dry any excess water before placing the slide on the microscope stage for viewing.

Spring Scale (Force Meter)

- Use a spring scale to measure a force pulling on the scale.

- Use a spring scale to measure the force of gravity exerted on an object by Earth.

- To measure a force accurately, a spring scale must be zeroed before it is used. The scale is zeroed when no weight is attached and the indicator is positioned at zero.

- Do not attach a weight that is either too heavy or too light to a spring scale. A weight that is too heavy could break the scale or exert too great a force for the scale to measure. A weight that is too light may not exert enough force to be measured accurately.

Graduated Cylinder

- Use a graduated cylinder to measure the volume of a liquid.

- Be sure that the graduated cylinder is on a flat surface so that your measurement will be accurate.

- When reading the scale on a graduated cylinder, be sure to have your eyes at the level of the surface of the liquid.

- The surface of the liquid will be curved in the graduated cylinder. Read the volume of the liquid at the bottom of the curve, or meniscus (muh-NIHS-kuhs).

- You can use a graduated cylinder to find the volume of a solid object by measuring the increase in a liquid's level after you add the object to the cylinder.

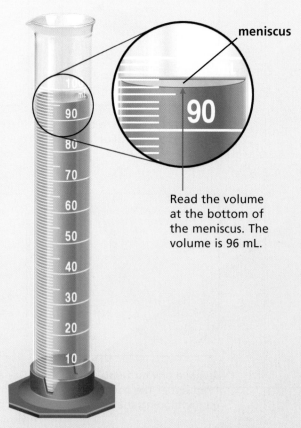

meniscus

Read the volume at the bottom of the meniscus. The volume is 96 mL.

Metric Rulers

- Use metric rulers or meter sticks to measure objects' lengths.

- Do not measure an object from the end of a metric ruler or meter stick, because the end is often imperfect. Instead, measure from the 1-centimeter mark, but remember to subtract a centimeter from the apparent measurement.

- Estimate any lengths that extend between marked units. For example, if a meter stick shows centimeters but not millimeters, you can estimate the length that an object extends between centimeter marks to measure it to the nearest millimeter.

- **Controlling Variables** If you are taking repeated measurements, always measure from the same point each time. For example, if you're measuring how high two different balls bounce when dropped from the same height, measure both bounces at the same point on the balls—either the top or the bottom. Do not measure at the top of one ball and the bottom of the other.

EXAMPLE

How to Measure a Leaf

1. Lay a ruler flat on top of the leaf so that the 1-centimeter mark lines up with one end. Make sure the ruler and the leaf do not move between the time you line them up and the time you take the measurement.

2. Look straight down on the ruler so that you can see exactly how the marks line up with the other end of the leaf.

3. Estimate the length by which the leaf extends beyond a marking. For example, the leaf below extends about halfway between the 4.2-centimeter and 4.3-centimeter marks, so the apparent measurement is about 4.25 centimeters.

4. Remember to subtract 1 centimeter from your apparent measurement, since you started at the 1-centimeter mark on the ruler and not at the end. The leaf is about 3.25 centimeters long (4.25 cm − 1 cm = 3.25 cm).

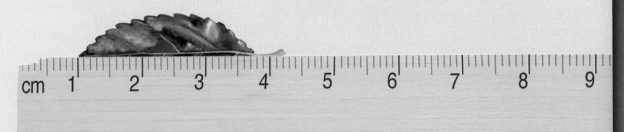

Triple-Beam Balance

This balance has a pan and three beams with sliding masses, called riders. At one end of the beams is a pointer that indicates whether the mass on the pan is equal to the masses shown on the beams.

1. Make sure the balance is zeroed before measuring the mass of an object. The balance is zeroed if the pointer is at zero when nothing is on the pan and the riders are at their zero points. Use the adjustment knob at the base of the balance to zero it.

2. Place the object to be measured on the pan.

3. Move the riders one notch at a time away from the pan. Begin with the largest rider. If moving the largest rider one notch brings the pointer below zero, begin measuring the mass of the object with the next smaller rider.

4. Change the positions of the riders until they balance the mass on the pan and the pointer is at zero. Then add the readings from the three beams to determine the mass of the object.

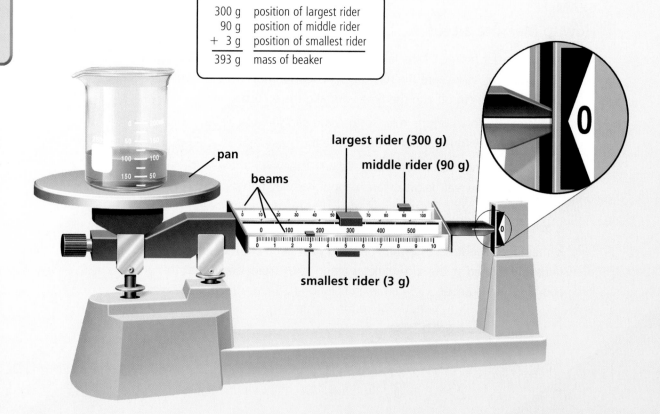

300 g	position of largest rider
90 g	position of middle rider
+ 3 g	position of smallest rider
393 g	mass of beaker

pan

beams

largest rider (300 g)

middle rider (90 g)

smallest rider (3 g)

Double-Pan Balance

This type of balance has two pans. Between the pans is a pointer that indicates whether the masses on the pans are equal.

1. Make sure the balance is zeroed before measuring the mass of an object. The balance is zeroed if the pointer is at zero when there is nothing on either of the pans. Many double-pan balances have sliding knobs that can be used to zero them.

2. Place the object to be measured on one of the pans.

3. Begin adding standard masses to the other pan. Begin with the largest standard mass. If this adds too much mass to the balance, begin measuring the mass of the object with the next smaller standard mass.

4. Add standard masses until the masses on both pans are balanced and the pointer is at zero. Then add the standard masses together to determine the mass of the object being measured.

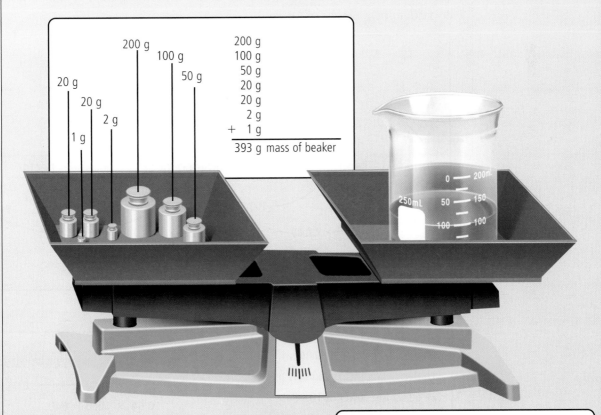

200 g
100 g
50 g
20 g
20 g
+ 2 g
   1 g
_____
393 g mass of beaker

Never place chemicals or liquids directly on a pan. Instead, use the following procedure:

1. Determine the mass of an empty container, such as a beaker.

2. Pour the substance into the container, and measure the total mass of the substance and the container.

3. Subtract the mass of the empty container from the total mass to find the mass of the substance.

The Metric System and SI Units

Scientists use International System (SI) units for measurements of distance, volume, mass, and temperature. The International System is based on multiples of ten and the metric system of measurement.

Basic SI Units		
Property	Name	Symbol
length	meter	m
volume	liter	L
mass	kilogram	kg
temperature	kelvin	K

SI Prefixes		
Prefix	Symbol	Multiple of 10
kilo-	k	1000
hecto-	h	100
deca-	da	10
deci-	d	$0.1 \left(\frac{1}{10}\right)$
centi-	c	$0.01 \left(\frac{1}{100}\right)$
milli-	m	$0.001 \left(\frac{1}{1000}\right)$

Changing Metric Units

You can change from one unit to another in the metric system by multiplying or dividing by a power of 10.

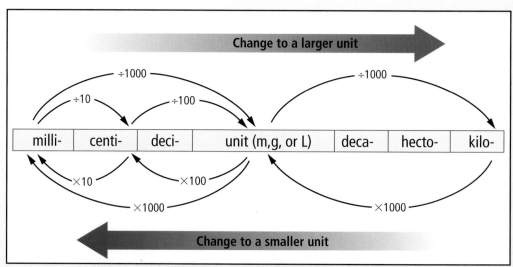

Example

Change 0.64 liters to milliliters.

(1) Decide whether to multiply or divide.

(2) Select the power of 10.

ANSWER 0.64 L = 640 mL

Change to a smaller unit by multiplying.

mL ◀——— × 1000 ——— L

0.64 × 1000 = **640.**

Example

Change 23.6 grams to kilograms.

(1) Decide whether to multiply or divide.

(2) Select the power of 10.

ANSWER 23.6 g = 0.0236 kg

Change to a larger unit by dividing.

g ——— ÷ 1000 ——▶ kg

23.6 ÷ 1000 = **0.0236**

Temperature Conversions

Even though the kelvin is the SI base unit of temperature, the degree Celsius will be the unit you use most often in your science studies. The formulas below show the relationships between temperatures in degrees Fahrenheit (°F), degrees Celsius (°C), and kelvins (K).

$$°C = \frac{5}{9} (°F - 32)$$

$$°F = \frac{9}{5} °C + 32$$

$$K = °C + 273$$

See page R42 for help with using formulas.

Examples of Temperature Conversions		
Condition	Degrees Celsius	Degrees Fahrenheit
Freezing point of water	0	32
Cool day	10	50
Mild day	20	68
Warm day	30	86
Normal body temperature	37	98.6
Very hot day	40	104
Boiling point of water	100	212

Converting Between SI and U.S. Customary Units

Use the chart below when you need to convert between SI units and U.S. customary units.

SI Unit	From SI to U.S. Customary			From U.S. Customary to SI		
Length	When you know	multiply by	to find	When you know	multiply by	to find
kilometer (km) = 1000 m	kilometers	0.62	miles	miles	1.61	kilometers
meter (m) = 100 cm	meters	3.28	feet	feet	0.3048	meters
centimeter (cm) = 10 mm	centimeters	0.39	inches	inches	2.54	centimeters
millimeter (mm) = 0.1 cm	millimeters	0.04	inches	inches	25.4	millimeters
Area	When you know	multiply by	to find	When you know	multiply by	to find
square kilometer (km²)	square kilometers	0.39	square miles	square miles	2.59	square kilometers
square meter (m²)	square meters	1.2	square yards	square yards	0.84	square meters
square centimeter (cm²)	square centimeters	0.155	square inches	square inches	6.45	square centimeters
Volume	When you know	multiply by	to find	When you know	multiply by	to find
liter (L) = 1000 mL	liters	1.06	quarts	quarts	0.95	liters
	liters	0.26	gallons	gallons	3.79	liters
	liters	4.23	cups	cups	0.24	liters
	liters	2.12	pints	pints	0.47	liters
milliliter (mL) = 0.001 L	milliliters	0.20	teaspoons	teaspoons	4.93	milliliters
	milliliters	0.07	tablespoons	tablespoons	14.79	milliliters
	milliliters	0.03	fluid ounces	fluid ounces	29.57	milliliters
Mass	When you know	multiply by	to find	When you know	multiply by	to find
kilogram (kg) = 1000 g	kilograms	2.2	pounds	pounds	0.45	kilograms
gram (g) = 1000 mg	grams	0.035	ounces	ounces	28.35	grams

Precision and Accuracy

When you do an experiment, it is important that your methods, observations, and data be both precise and accurate.

low precision

precision,
but not accuracy

precision and
accuracy

LAB HANDBOOK

Precision

In science, **precision** is the exactness and consistency of measurements. For example, measurements made with a ruler that has both centimeter and millimeter markings would be more precise than measurements made with a ruler that has only centimeter markings. Another indicator of precision is the care taken to make sure that methods and observations are as exact and consistent as possible. Every time a particular experiment is done, the same procedure should be used. Precision is necessary because experiments are repeated several times and if the procedure changes, the results will change.

EXAMPLE

Suppose you are measuring temperatures over a two-week period. Your precision will be greater if you measure each temperature at the same place, at the same time of day, and with the same thermometer than if you change any of these factors from one day to the next.

Accuracy

In science, it is possible to be precise but not accurate. **Accuracy** depends on the difference between a measurement and an actual value. The smaller the difference, the more accurate the measurement.

EXAMPLE

Suppose you look at a stream and estimate that it is about 1 meter wide at a particular place. You decide to check your estimate by measuring the stream with a meter stick, and you determine that the stream is 1.32 meters wide. However, because it is hard to measure the width of a stream with a meter stick, it turns out that you didn't do a very good job. The stream is actually 1.14 meters wide. Therefore, even though your estimate was less precise than your measurement, your estimate was actually more accurate.

Making Data Tables and Graphs

Data tables and graphs are useful tools for both recording and communicating scientific data.

Making Data Tables

You can use a **data table** to organize and record the measurements that you make. Some examples of information that might be recorded in data tables are frequencies, times, and amounts.

EXAMPLE

Suppose you are investigating photosynthesis in two elodea plants. One sits in direct sunlight, and the other sits in a dimly lit room. You measure the rate of photosynthesis by counting the number of bubbles in the jar every ten minutes.

1. Title and number your data table.

2. Decide how you will organize the table into columns and rows.

3. Any units, such as seconds or degrees, should be included in column headings, not in the individual cells.

Table 1. Number of Bubbles from Elodea

Time (min)	Sunlight	Dim Light
0	0	0
10	15	5
20	25	8
30	32	7
40	41	10
50	47	9
60	42	9

Always number and title data tables.

The data in the table above could also be organized in a different way.

Table 1. Number of Bubbles from Elodea

Light Condition	Time (min)						
	0	10	20	30	40	50	60
Sunlight	0	15	25	32	41	47	42
Dim light	0	5	8	7	10	9	9

Put units in column heading.

Making Line Graphs

You can use a **line graph** to show a relationship between variables. Line graphs are particularly useful for showing changes in variables over time.

EXAMPLE

Suppose you are interested in graphing temperature data that you collected over the course of a day.

Table 1. Outside Temperature During the Day on March 7

	Time of Day						
	7:00 A.M.	9:00 A.M.	11:00 A.M.	1:00 P.M.	3:00 P.M.	5:00 P.M.	7:00 P.M.
Temp (°C)	8	9	11	14	12	10	6

1. Use the vertical axis of your line graph for the variable that you are measuring—temperature.

2. Choose scales for both the horizontal axis and the vertical axis of the graph. You should have two points more than you need on the vertical axis, and the horizontal axis should be long enough for all of the data points to fit.

3. Draw and label each axis.

4. Graph each value. First find the appropriate point on the scale of the horizontal axis. Imagine a line that rises vertically from that place on the scale. Then find the corresponding value on the vertical axis, and imagine a line that moves horizontally from that value. The point where these two imaginary lines intersect is where the value should be plotted.

5. Connect the points with straight lines.

Be sure to add a number and a title to your graph. ▶

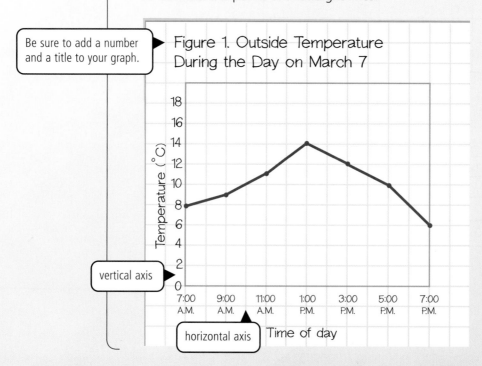

Figure 1. Outside Temperature During the Day on March 7

vertical axis

horizontal axis

Making Circle Graphs

You can use a **circle graph,** sometimes called a pie chart, to represent data as parts of a circle. Circle graphs are used only when the data can be expressed as percentages of a whole. The entire circle shown in a circle graph is equal to 100 percent of the data.

EXAMPLE

Suppose you identified the species of each mature tree growing in a small wooded area. You organized your data in a table, but you also want to show the data in a circle graph.

1. To begin, find the total number of mature trees.

    $$56 + 34 + 22 + 10 + 28 = 150$$

2. To find the degree measure for each sector of the circle, write a fraction comparing the number of each tree species with the total number of trees. Then multiply the fraction by 360°.

    Oak: $\frac{56}{150} \times 360° = 134.4°$

3. Draw a circle. Use a protractor to draw the angle for each sector of the graph.

4. Color and label each sector of the graph.

5. Give the graph a number and title.

Table 1. Tree Species in Wooded Area

Species	Number of Specimens
Oak	56
Maple	34
Birch	22
Willow	10
Pine	28

Figure 1. Tree Species in Wooded Area

Willow 10
Birch 22
Oak 56
Pine 28
Maple 34

Instead of labeling each sector, you could make a color key.

Oak 56
Maple 34
Pine 28
Birch 22
Willow 10

Bar Graph

A **bar graph** is a type of graph in which the lengths of the bars are used to represent and compare data. A numerical scale is used to determine the lengths of the bars.

EXAMPLE

To determine the effect of water on seed sprouting, three cups were filled with sand, and ten seeds were planted in each. Different amounts of water were added to each cup over a three-day period.

Table 1. Effect of Water on Seed Sprouting

Daily Amount of Water (mL)	Number of Seeds That Sprouted After 3 Days in Sand
0	1
10	4
20	8

1. Choose a numerical scale. The greatest value is 8, so the end of the scale should have a value greater than 8, such as 10. Use equal increments along the scale, such as increments of 2.

2. Draw and label the axes. Mark intervals on the vertical axis according to the scale you chose.

3. Draw a bar for each data value. Use the scale to decide how long to make each bar.

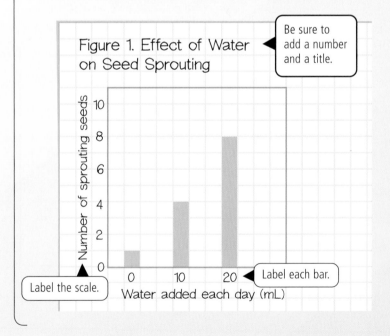

Figure 1. Effect of Water on Seed Sprouting

Be sure to add a number and a title.

Label the scale.

Label each bar.

Double Bar Graph

A **double bar graph** is a bar graph that shows two sets of data. The two bars for each measurement are drawn next to each other.

EXAMPLE

The seed-sprouting experiment was done using both sand and potting soil. The data for sand and potting soil can be plotted on one graph.

1. Draw one set of bars, using the data for sand, as shown below.

2. Draw bars for the potting-soil data next to the bars for the sand data. Shade them a different color. Add a key.

Table 2. Effect of Water and Soil on Seed Sprouting

Daily Amount of Water (mL)	Number of Seeds That Sprouted After 3 Days in Sand	Number of Seeds That Sprouted After 3 Days in Potting Soil
0	1	2
10	4	5
20	8	9

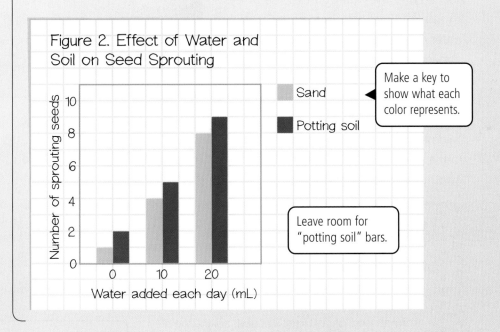

Figure 2. Effect of Water and Soil on Seed Sprouting

Make a key to show what each color represents.

Leave room for "potting soil" bars.

Designing an Experiment

Use this section when designing or conducting an experiment.

Determining a Purpose

You can find a purpose for an experiment by doing research, by examining the results of a previous experiment, or by observing the world around you. An **experiment** is an organized procedure to study something under controlled conditions.

> Don't forget to learn as much as possible about your topic before you begin.

1. Write the purpose of your experiment as a question or problem that you want to investigate.

2. Write down research questions and begin searching for information that will help you design an experiment. Consult the library, the Internet, and other people as you conduct your research.

EXAMPLE

Middle school students observed an odor near the lake by their school. They also noticed that the water on the side of the lake near the school was greener than the water on the other side of the lake. The students did some research to learn more about their observations. They discovered that the odor and green color in the lake

came from algae. They also discovered that a new fertilizer was being used on a field nearby. The students inferred that the use of the fertilizer might be related to the presence of the algae and designed a controlled experiment to find out whether they were right.

Problem
How does fertilizer affect the presence of algae in a lake?

Research Questions
- Have other experiments been done on this problem? If so, what did those experiments show?
- What kind of fertilizer is used on the field? How much?
- How do algae grow?
- How do people measure algae?
- Can fertilizer and algae be used safely in a lab? How?

> **Research**
> As you research, you may find a topic that is more interesting to you than your original topic, or learn that a procedure you wanted to use is not practical or safe. It is OK to change your purpose as you research.

Writing a Hypothesis

A **hypothesis** is a tentative explanation for an observation or scientific problem that can be tested by further investigation. You can write your hypothesis in the form of an "If . . . , then . . . , because . . ." statement.

Hypothesis

If the amount of fertilizer in lake water is increased, then the amount of algae will also increase, because fertilizers provide nutrients that algae need to grow.

Hypotheses
For help with hypotheses, refer to page R3.

Determining Materials

Make a list of all the materials you will need to do your experiment. Be specific, especially if someone else is helping you obtain the materials. Try to think of everything you will need.

Materials

- 1 large jar or container
- 4 identical smaller containers
- rubber gloves that also cover the arms
- sample of fertilizer-and-water solution
- eyedropper
- clear plastic wrap
- scissors
- masking tape
- marker
- ruler

Determining Variables and Constants

EXPERIMENTAL GROUP AND CONTROL GROUP

An experiment to determine how two factors are related always has two groups—a control group and an experimental group.

1. Design an experimental group. Include as many trials as possible in the experimental group in order to obtain reliable results.

2. Design a control group that is the same as the experimental group in every way possible, except for the factor you wish to test.

Experimental Group: two containers of lake water with one drop of fertilizer solution added to each

Control Group: two containers of lake water with no fertilizer solution added

> Go back to your materials list and make sure you have enough items listed to cover both your experimental group and your control group.

VARIABLES AND CONSTANTS

Identify the variables and constants in your experiment. In a controlled experiment, a **variable** is any factor that can change. **Constants** are all of the factors that are the same in both the experimental group and the control group.

1. Read your hypothesis. The **independent variable** is the factor that you wish to test and that is manipulated or changed so that it can be tested. The independent variable is expressed in your hypothesis after the word *if*. Identify the independent variable in your laboratory report.

2. The **dependent variable** is the factor that you measure to gather results. It is expressed in your hypothesis after the word *then*. Identify the dependent variable in your laboratory report.

> **Hypothesis**
> If the amount of fertilizer in lake water is increased, then the amount of algae will also increase, because fertilizers provide nutrients that algae need to grow.

Table 1. Variables and Constants in Algae Experiment

Independent Variable	Dependent Variable	Constants
Amount of fertilizer in lake water	Amount of algae that grow	• Where the lake water is obtained • Type of container used • Light and temperature conditions where water will be stored

> Set up your experiment so that you will test only one variable.

MEASURING THE DEPENDENT VARIABLE

Before starting your experiment, you need to define how you will measure the dependent variable. An **operational definition** is a description of the one particular way in which you will measure the dependent variable.

Your operational definition is important for several reasons. First, in any experiment there are several ways in which a dependent variable can be measured. Second, the procedure of the experiment depends on how you decide to measure the dependent variable. Third, your operational definition makes it possible for other people to evaluate and build on your experiment.

EXAMPLE 1

An operational definition of a dependent variable can be qualitative. That is, your measurement of the dependent variable can simply be an observation of whether a change occurs as a result of a change in the independent variable. This type of operational definition can be thought of as a "yes or no" measurement.

Table 2. Qualitative Operational Definition of Algae Growth

Independent Variable	Dependent Variable	Operational Definition
Amount of fertilizer in lake water	Amount of algae that grow	Algae grow in lake water

A qualitative measurement of a dependent variable is often easy to make and record. However, this type of information does not provide a great deal of detail in your experimental results.

EXAMPLE 2

An operational definition of a dependent variable can be quantitative. That is, your measurement of the dependent variable can be a number that shows how much change occurs as a result of a change in the independent variable.

Table 3. Quantitative Operational Definition of Algae Growth

Independent Variable	Dependent Variable	Operational Definition
Amount of fertilizer in lake water	Amount of algae that grow	Diameter of largest algal growth (in mm)

A quantitative measurement of a dependent variable can be more difficult to make and analyze than a qualitative measurement. However, this type of data provides much more information about your experiment and is often more useful.

Writing a Procedure

Write each step of your procedure. Start each step with a verb, or action word, and keep the steps short. Your procedure should be clear enough for someone else to use as instructions for repeating your experiment.

If necessary, go back to your materials list and add any materials that you left out.

Procedure

1. Put on your gloves. Use the large container to obtain a sample of lake water.

2. Divide the sample of lake water equally among the four smaller containers.

Controlling Variables
The same amount of fertilizer solution must be added to two of the four containers.

3. Use the eyedropper to add one drop of fertilizer solution to two of the containers.

4. Use the masking tape and the marker to label the containers with your initials, the date, and the identifiers "Jar 1 with Fertilizer," "Jar 2 with Fertilizer," "Jar 1 without Fertilizer," and "Jar 2 without Fertilizer."

5. Cover the containers with clear plastic wrap. Use the scissors to punch ten holes in each of the covers.

Controlling Variables
All four containers must receive the same amount of light.

6. Place all four containers on a window ledge. Make sure that they all receive the same amount of light.

7. Observe the containers every day for one week.

8. Use the ruler to measure the diameter of the largest clump of algae in each container, and record your measurements daily.

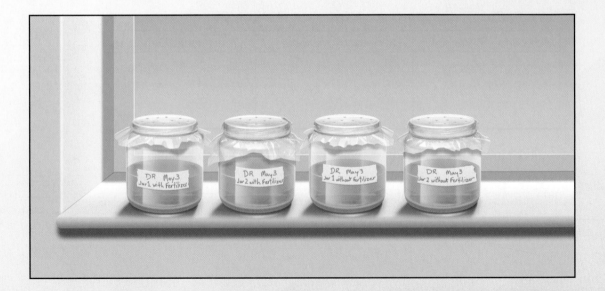

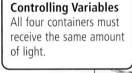

LAB HANDBOOK

Recording Observations

Once you have obtained all of your materials and your procedure has been approved, you can begin making experimental observations. Gather both quantitative and qualitative data. If something goes wrong during your procedure, make sure you record that too.

Observations
For help with making qualitative and quantitative observations, refer to page R2.

For more examples of data tables, see page R23.

Table 4. Fertilizer and Algae Growth

Date and Time	Experimental Group		Control Group		
	Jar 1 with Fertilizer (diameter of algae in mm)	Jar 2 with Fertilizer (diameter of algae in mm)	Jar 1 without Fertilizer (diameter of algae in mm)	Jar 2 without Fertilizer (diameter of algae in mm)	Observations
5/3 4:00 P.M.	0	0	0	0	condensation in all containers
5/4 4:00 P.M.	0	3	0	0	tiny green blobs in jar 2 with fertilizer
5/5 4:15 P.M.	4	5	0	3	green blobs in jars 1 and 2 with fertilizer and jar 2 without fertilizer
5/6 4:00 P.M.	5	6	0	4	water light green in jar 2 with fertilizer
5/7 4:00 P.M.	8	10	0	6	water light green in jars 1 and 2 with fertilizer and in jar 2 without fertilizer
5/8 3:30 P.M.	10	18	0	6	cover off jar 2 with fertilizer
5/9 3:30 P.M.	14	23	0	8	drew sketches of each container

Notice that on the sixth day, the observer found that the cover was off one of the containers. It is important to record observations of unintended factors because they might affect the results of the experiment.

Use technology, such as a microscope, to help you make observations when possible.

Drawings of Samples Viewed Under Microscope on 5/9 at 100x

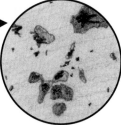
Jar 1
with Fertilizer

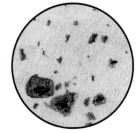
Jar 2
with Fertilizer

Jar 1
without Fertilizer

Jar 2
without Fertilizer

Summarizing Results

To summarize your data, look at all of your observations together. Look for meaningful ways to present your observations. For example, you might average your data or make a graph to look for patterns. When possible, use spreadsheet software to help you analyze and present your data. The two graphs below show the same data.

EXAMPLE 1

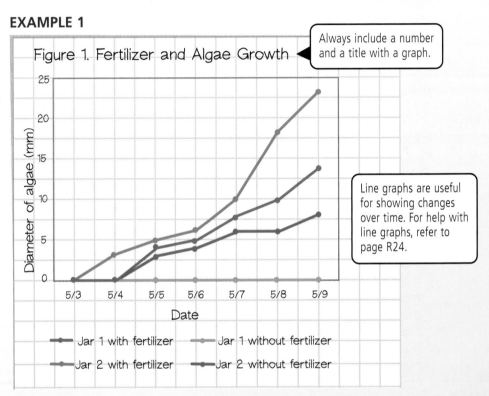

Always include a number and a title with a graph.

Line graphs are useful for showing changes over time. For help with line graphs, refer to page R24.

EXAMPLE 2

Bar graphs are useful for comparing different data sets. This bar graph has four bars for each day. Another way to present the data would be to calculate averages for the tests and the controls, and to show one test bar and one control bar for each day.

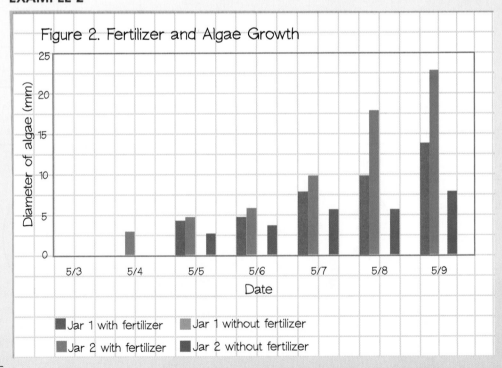

LAB HANDBOOK

Drawing Conclusions

RESULTS AND INFERENCES

To draw conclusions from your experiment, first write your results. Then compare your results with your hypothesis. Do your results support your hypothesis? Be careful not to make inferences about factors that you did not test.

> For help with making inferences, see page R4.

Results and Inferences

The results of my experiment show that more algae grew in lake water to which fertilizer had been added than in lake water to which no fertilizer had been added. My hypothesis was supported. I infer that it is possible that the growth of algae in the lake was caused by the fertilizer used on the field.

> Notice that you cannot conclude from this experiment that the presence of algae in the lake was due only to the fertilizer.

QUESTIONS FOR FURTHER RESEARCH

Write a list of questions for further research and investigation. Your ideas may lead you to new experiments and discoveries.

Questions for Further Research

- What is the connection between the amount of fertilizer and algae growth?
- How do different brands of fertilizer affect algae growth?
- How would algae growth in the lake be affected if no fertilizer were used on the field?
- How do algae affect the lake and the other life in and around it?
- How does fertilizer affect the lake and the life in and around it?
- If fertilizer is getting into the lake, how is it getting there?

Math Handbook

Describing a Set of Data

Means, medians, modes, and ranges are important math tools for describing data sets such as the following widths of fossilized clamshells.

13 mm   25 mm   14 mm   21 mm   16 mm   23 mm   14 mm

Mean

The **mean** of a data set is the sum of the values divided by the number of values.

Example

To find the mean of the clamshell data, add the values and then divide the sum by the number of values.

$$\frac{13 \text{ mm} + 25 \text{ mm} + 14 \text{ mm} + 21 \text{ mm} + 16 \text{ mm} + 23 \text{ mm} + 14 \text{ mm}}{7} = \frac{126 \text{ mm}}{7} = 18 \text{ mm}$$

ANSWER The mean is 18 mm.

Median

The **median** of a data set is the middle value when the values are written in numerical order. If a data set has an even number of values, the median is the mean of the two middle values.

Example

To find the median of the clamshell data, arrange the values in order from least to greatest. The median is the middle value.

13 mm   14 mm   14 mm   16 mm   21 mm   23 mm   25 mm

ANSWER The median is 16 mm.

Mode

The **mode** of a data set is the value that occurs most often.

Example

To find the mode of the clamshell data, arrange the values in order from least to greatest and determine the value that occurs most often.

13 mm   14 mm   14 mm   16 mm   21 mm   23 mm   25 mm

ANSWER The mode is 14 mm.

A data set can have more than one mode or no mode. For example, the following data set has modes of 2 mm and 4 mm:

2 mm   2 mm   3 mm   4 mm   4 mm

The data set below has no mode, because no value occurs more often than any other.

2 mm   3 mm   4 mm   5 mm

Range

The **range** of a data set is the difference between the greatest value and the least value.

Example

To find the range of the clamshell data, arrange the values in order from least to greatest.

13 mm   14 mm   14 mm   16 mm   21 mm   23 mm   25 mm

Subtract the least value from the greatest value.

13 mm is the least value.
25 mm is the greatest value.

25 mm − 13 mm = 12 mm

ANSWER The range is 12 mm.

Using Ratios, Rates, and Proportions

You can use ratios and rates to compare values in data sets. You can use proportions to find unknown values.

Ratios

A **ratio** uses division to compare two values. The ratio of a value a to a nonzero value b can be written as $\frac{a}{b}$.

Example

The height of one plant is 8 centimeters. The height of another plant is 6 centimeters. To find the ratio of the height of the first plant to the height of the second plant, write a fraction and simplify it.

$$\frac{8 \text{ cm}}{6 \text{ cm}} = \frac{4 \times \overset{1}{\cancel{2}}}{3 \times \underset{1}{\cancel{2}}} = \frac{4}{3}$$

ANSWER The ratio of the plant heights is $\frac{4}{3}$.

You can also write the ratio $\frac{a}{b}$ as "a to b" or as $a:b$. For example, you can write the ratio of the plant heights as "4 to 3" or as 4:3.

Rates

A **rate** is a ratio of two values expressed in different units. A unit rate is a rate with a denominator of 1 unit.

Example

A plant grew 6 centimeters in 2 days. The plant's rate of growth was $\frac{6 \text{ cm}}{2 \text{ days}}$. To describe the plant's growth in centimeters per day, write a unit rate.

Divide numerator and denominator by 2: $\quad \frac{6 \text{ cm}}{2 \text{ days}} = \frac{6 \text{ cm} \div 2}{2 \text{ days} \div 2}$

> You divide 2 days by 2 to get 1 day, so divide 6 cm by 2 also.

Simplify: $\quad = \frac{3 \text{ cm}}{1 \text{ day}}$

ANSWER The plant's rate of growth is 3 centimeters per day.

Proportions

A **proportion** is an equation stating that two ratios are equivalent. To solve for an unknown value in a proportion, you can use cross products.

Example

If a plant grew 6 centimeters in 2 days, how many centimeters would it grow in 3 days (if its rate of growth is constant)?

Write a proportion:	$\dfrac{6 \text{ cm}}{2 \text{ days}} = \dfrac{x}{3 \text{ days}}$
Set cross products:	$6 \text{ cm} \cdot 3 = 2x$
Multiply 6 and 3:	$18 \text{ cm} = 2x$
Divide each side by 2:	$\dfrac{18 \text{ cm}}{2} = \dfrac{2x}{2}$
Simplify:	$9 \text{ cm} = x$

ANSWER The plant would grow 9 centimeters in 3 days.

Using Decimals, Fractions, and Percents

Decimals, fractions, and percentages are all ways of recording and representing data.

Decimals

A **decimal** is a number that is written in the base-ten place value system, in which a decimal point separates the ones and tenths digits. The values of each place is ten times that of the place to its right.

Example

A caterpillar traveled from point *A* to point *C* along the path shown.

A   **36.9 cm**   **B**   **52.4 cm**   **C**

ADDING DECIMALS To find the total distance traveled by the caterpillar, add the distance from *A* to *B* and the distance from *B* to *C*. Begin by lining up the decimal points. Then add the figures as you would whole numbers and bring down the decimal point.

$$
\begin{array}{r}
36.9 \text{ cm} \\
+ \; 52.4 \text{ cm} \\
\hline
89.3 \text{ cm}
\end{array}
$$

ANSWER The caterpillar traveled a total distance of 89.3 centimeters.

Example *continued*

SUBTRACTING DECIMALS To find how much farther the caterpillar traveled on the second leg of the journey, subtract the distance from *A* to *B* from the distance from *B* to *C*.

$$\begin{array}{r} 52.4 \text{ cm} \\ - \ 36.9 \text{ cm} \\ \hline 15.5 \text{ cm} \end{array}$$

ANSWER The caterpillar traveled 15.5 centimeters farther on the second leg of the journey.

Example

A caterpillar is traveling from point *D* to point *F* along the path shown. The caterpillar travels at a speed of 9.6 centimeters per minute.

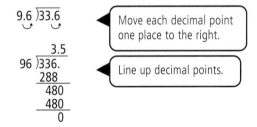

MULTIPLYING DECIMALS You can multiply decimals as you would whole numbers. The number of decimal places in the product is equal to the sum of the number of decimal places in the factors.

For instance, suppose it takes the caterpillar 1.5 minutes to go from *D* to *E*. To find the distance from *D* to *E*, multiply the caterpillar's speed by the time it took.

Align as shown.

$$\begin{array}{rl} 9.6 & \quad 1 \quad \text{decimal place} \\ \times \ 1.5 & \quad + \ 1 \quad \text{decimal place} \\ \hline 480 & \\ 96 \ \ & \\ \hline 14.40 & \quad 2 \quad \text{decimal places} \end{array}$$

ANSWER The distance from *D* to *E* is 14.4 centimeters.

DIVIDING DECIMALS When you divide by a decimal, move the decimal points the same number of places in the divisor and the dividend to make the divisor a whole number.

For instance, to find the time it will take the caterpillar to travel from *E* to *F*, divide the distance from *E* to *F* by the caterpillar's speed.

$$9.6\,\overline{)33.6}$$

Move each decimal point one place to the right.

$$\begin{array}{r} 3.5 \\ 96\,\overline{)336.} \\ \underline{288} \\ 480 \\ \underline{480} \\ 0 \end{array}$$

Line up decimal points.

ANSWER The caterpillar will travel from *E* to *F* in 3.5 minutes.

Fractions

A **fraction** is a number in the form $\frac{a}{b}$, where b is not equal to 0. A fraction is in **simplest form** if its numerator and denominator have a greatest common factor (GCF) of 1. To simplify a fraction, divide its numerator and denominator by their GCF.

Example

A caterpillar is 40 millimeters long. The head of the caterpillar is 6 millimeters long. To compare the length of the caterpillar's head with the caterpillar's total length, you can write and simplify a fraction that expresses the ratio of the two lengths.

$$\text{Write the ratio of the two lengths:} \quad \frac{\text{Length of head}}{\text{Total length}} = \frac{6 \text{ mm}}{40 \text{ mm}}$$

$$\text{Write numerator and denominator as products of numbers and the GCF:} \quad = \frac{3 \times 2}{20 \times 2}$$

$$\text{Divide numerator and denominator by the GCF:} \quad = \frac{3 \times \cancel{2}^{\,1}}{20 \times \cancel{2}_{\,1}}$$

$$\text{Simplify:} \quad = \frac{3}{20}$$

ANSWER In simplest form, the ratio of the lengths is $\frac{3}{20}$.

Percents

A **percent** is a ratio that compares a number to 100. The word *percent* means "per hundred" or "out of 100." The symbol for *percent* is %.

For instance, suppose 43 out of 100 caterpillars are female. You can represent this ratio as a percent, a decimal, or a fraction.

Percent	Decimal	Fraction
43%	0.43	$\frac{43}{100}$

Example

In the preceding example, the ratio of the length of the caterpillar's head to the caterpillar's total length is $\frac{3}{20}$. To write this ratio as a percent, write an equivalent fraction that has a denominator of 100.

$$\text{Multiply numerator and denominator by 5:} \quad \frac{3}{20} = \frac{3 \times 5}{20 \times 5}$$

$$= \frac{15}{100}$$

$$\text{Write as a percent:} \quad = 15\%$$

ANSWER The caterpillar's head represents 15 percent of its total length.

Using Formulas

A **formula** is an equation that shows the general relationship between two or more quantities.

The term *variable* is also used in science to refer to a factor that can change during an experiment.

In science, a formula often has a word form and a symbolic form. The formula below expresses Ohm's law.

Word Form

$$\text{Current} = \frac{\text{voltage}}{\text{resistance}}$$

Symbolic Form

$$I = \frac{V}{R}$$

In this formula, I, V, and R are variables. A mathematical **variable** is a symbol or letter that is used to represent one or more numbers.

Example

Suppose that you measure a voltage of 1.5 volts and a resistance of 15 ohms. You can use the formula for Ohm's law to find the current in amperes.

Write the formula for Ohm's law: $\quad I = \dfrac{V}{R}$

Substitute 1.5 volts for V and 15 ohms for R: $\quad I = \dfrac{1.5 \text{ volts}}{15 \text{ ohms}}$

Simplify: $\quad I = 0.1$ amp

ANSWER The current is 0.1 ampere.

If you know the values of all variables but one in a formula, you can solve for the value of the unknown variable. For instance, Ohm's law can be used to find a voltage if you know the current and the resistance.

Example

Suppose that you know that a current is 0.2 amperes and the resistance is 18 ohms. Use the formula for Ohm's law to find the voltage in volts.

Write the formula for Ohm's law: $\qquad I = \dfrac{V}{R}$

Substitute 0.2 amp for I and 18 ohms for R: $\qquad 0.2 \text{ amp} = \dfrac{V}{18 \text{ ohms}}$

Multiply both sides by 18 ohms: $\quad 0.2 \text{ amp} \cdot 18 \text{ ohms} = V$

Simplify: $\qquad 3.6 \text{ volts} = V$

ANSWER The voltage is 3.6 volts.

Finding Areas

The area of a figure is the amount of surface the figure covers.

Area is measured in square units, such as square meters (m^2) or square centimeters (cm^2). Formulas for the areas of three common geometric figures are shown below.

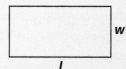

Area = (side length)^2
$A = s^2$

Area = length $\times$ width
$A = lw$

Area = $\frac{1}{2} \times$ base $\times$ height
$A = \frac{1}{2} bh$

Example

Each face of a halite crystal is a square like the one shown. You can find the area of the square by using the steps below.

Write the formula for the area of a square:	$A = s^2$
Substitute 3 mm for s:	$= (3 \text{ mm})^2$
Simplify:	$= 9 \text{ mm}^2$

3 mm

3 mm

ANSWER The area of the square is 9 square millimeters.

Finding Volumes

The volume of a solid is the amount of space contained by the solid.

Volume is measured in cubic units, such as cubic meters (m^3) or cubic centimeters (cm^3). The volume of a rectangular prism is given by the formula shown below.

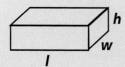

Volume = length $\times$ width $\times$ height
$V = lwh$

Example

A topaz crystal is a rectangular prism like the one shown. You can find the volume of the prism by using the steps below.

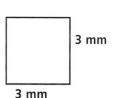

10 mm

12 mm

20 mm

Write the formula for the volume of a rectangular prism:	$V = lwh$
Substitute dimensions:	$= 20 \text{ mm} \times 12 \text{ mm} \times 10 \text{ mm}$
Simplify:	$= 2400 \text{ mm}^3$

ANSWER The volume of the rectangular prism is 2400 cubic millimeters.

Using Significant Figures

The **significant figures** in a decimal are the digits that are warranted by the accuracy of a measuring device.

When you perform a calculation with measurements, the number of significant figures to include in the result depends in part on the number of significant figures in the measurements. When you multiply or divide measurements, your answer should have only as many significant figures as the measurement with the fewest significant figures.

Example

Using a balance and a graduated cylinder filled with water, you determined that a marble has a mass of 8.0 grams and a volume of 3.5 cubic centimeters. To calculate the density of the marble, divide the mass by the volume.

Write the formula for density: $\quad \text{Density} = \dfrac{\text{mass}}{\text{Volume}}$

Substitute measurements: $\quad\quad\quad\quad = \dfrac{8.0 \text{ g}}{3.5 \text{ cm}^3}$

Use a calculator to divide: $\quad\quad\quad \approx 2.285714286 \text{ g/cm}^3$

ANSWER Because the mass and the volume have two significant figures each, give the density to two significant figures. The marble has a density of 2.3 grams per cubic centimeter.

Using Scientific Notation

Scientific notation is a shorthand way to write very large or very small numbers. For example, 73,500,000,000,000,000,000,000 kg is the mass of the Moon. In scientific notation, it is 7.35×10^{22} kg.

Example

You can convert from standard form to scientific notation.

Standard Form	Scientific Notation
720,000	7.2×10^5
5 decimal places left	Exponent is 5.
0.000291	2.91×10^{-4}
4 decimal places right	Exponent is −4.

You can convert from scientific notation to standard form.

Scientific Notation	Standard Form
4.63×10^7	46,300,000
Exponent is 7.	7 decimal places right
1.08×10^{-6}	0.00000108
Exponent is −6.	6 decimal places left

Note-Taking Handbook

Note-Taking Strategies

Taking notes as you read helps you understand the information. The notes you take can also be used as a study guide for later review. This handbook presents several ways to organize your notes.

Content Frame

1. Make a chart in which each column represents a category.
2. Give each column a heading.
3. Write details under the headings.

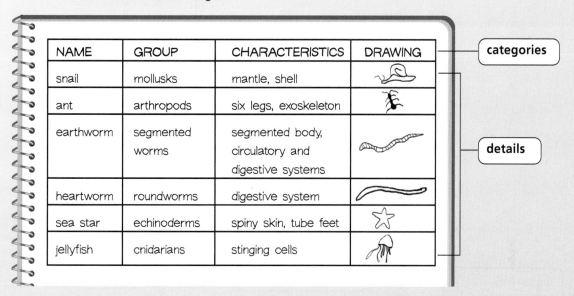

NAME	GROUP	CHARACTERISTICS	DRAWING
snail	mollusks	mantle, shell	
ant	arthropods	six legs, exoskeleton	
earthworm	segmented worms	segmented body, circulatory and digestive systems	
heartworm	roundworms	digestive system	
sea star	echinoderms	spiny skin, tube feet	
jellyfish	cnidarians	stinging cells	

categories

details

Combination Notes

1. For each new idea or concept, write an informal outline of the information.
2. Make a sketch to illustrate the concept, and label it.

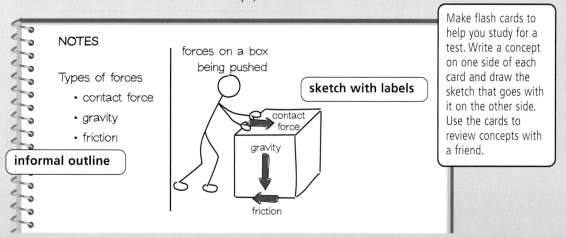

NOTES

Types of forces
- contact force
- gravity
- friction

informal outline

forces on a box being pushed

sketch with labels

contact force

gravity

friction

> Make flash cards to help you study for a test. Write a concept on one side of each card and draw the sketch that goes with it on the other side. Use the cards to review concepts with a friend.

Main Idea and Detail Notes

1. In the left-hand column of a two-column chart, list main ideas. The blue headings express main ideas throughout this textbook.

2. In the right-hand column, write details that expand on each main idea.

You can shorten the headings in your chart. Be sure to use the most important words.

When studying for tests, cover up the detail notes column with a sheet of paper. Then use each main idea to form a question—such as "How does latitude affect climate?" Answer the question, and then uncover the detail notes column to check your answer.

MAIN IDEAS	DETAIL NOTES
1. Latitude affects climate. *main idea 1*	1. Places close to the equator are usually warmer than places close to the poles. 1. Latitude has the same effect in both hemispheres.
2. Altitude affects climate. *main idea 2*	2. Temperature decreases with altitude. 2. Altitude can overcome the effect of latitude on temperature.

details about main idea 1

details about main idea 2

Main Idea Web

1. Write a main idea in a box.
2. Add boxes around it with related vocabulary terms and important details.

You can find definitions near highlighted terms.

definition of *work*
Work is the use of force to move an object.

formula
Work = force · distance

main idea
Force is necessary to do work.

The joule is the unit used to measure work.
definition of *joule*

Work depends on the size of a force.
important detail

Mind Map

1. Write a main idea in the center.

2. Add details that relate to one another and to the main idea.

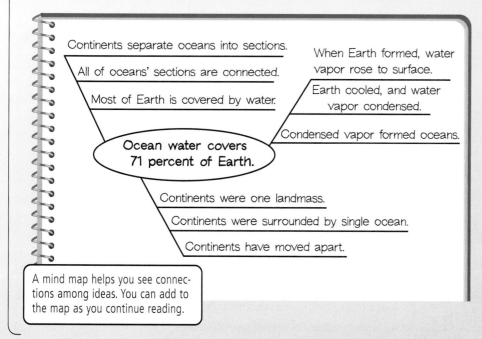

Continents separate oceans into sections.

All of oceans' sections are connected.

Most of Earth is covered by water.

When Earth formed, water vapor rose to surface.

Earth cooled, and water vapor condensed.

Condensed vapor formed oceans.

Ocean water covers 71 percent of Earth.

Continents were one landmass.

Continents were surrounded by single ocean.

Continents have moved apart.

A mind map helps you see connections among ideas. You can add to the map as you continue reading.

Supporting Main Ideas

1. Write a main idea in a box.

2. Add boxes underneath with information—such as reasons, explanations, and examples—that supports the main idea.

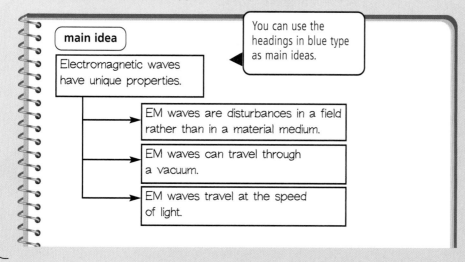

main idea

You can use the headings in blue type as main ideas.

Electromagnetic waves have unique properties.

EM waves are disturbances in a field rather than in a material medium.

EM waves can travel through a vacuum.

EM waves travel at the speed of light.

Outline

1. Copy the chapter title and headings from the book in the form of an outline.
2. Add notes that summarize in your own words what you read.

Cell Processes

1st key idea

I. Cells capture and release energy.

1st subpoint of I

  A. All cells need energy.

2nd subpoint of I

  B. Some cells capture light energy.

1st detail about B

    1. Process of photosynthesis

2nd detail about B

    2. Chloroplasts (site of photosynthesis)
    3. Carbon dioxide and water as raw materials
    4. Glucose and oxygen as products

  C. All cells release energy.
    1. Process of cellular respiration
    2. Fermentation of sugar to carbon dioxide
    3. Bacteria that carry out fermentation

II. Cells transport materials through membranes.
  A. Some materials move by diffusion.
    1. Particle movement from higher to lower concentrations
    2. Movement of water through membrane (osmosis)

  B. Some transport requires energy.
    1. Active transport
    2. Examples of active transport

Correct Outline Form
Include a title.

Arrange key ideas, subpoints, and details as shown.

Indent the divisions of the outline as shown.

Use the same grammatical form for items of the same rank. For example, if A is a sentence, B must also be a sentence.

You must have at least two main ideas or subpoints. That is, every A must be followed by a B, and every 1 must be followed by a 2.

NOTE-TAKING HANDBOOK

Concept Map

1. Write an important concept in a large oval.
2. Add details related to the concept in smaller ovals.
3. Write linking words on arrows that connect the ovals.

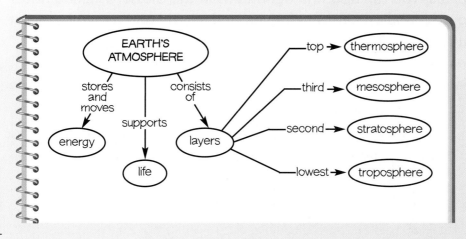

The main ideas or concepts can often be found in the blue headings. An example is "The atmosphere stores and moves energy." Use nouns from these concepts in the ovals, and use the verb or verbs on the lines.

Venn Diagram

1. Draw two overlapping circles, one for each item that you are comparing.
2. In the overlapping section, list the characteristics that are shared by both items.
3. In the outer sections, list the characteristics that are peculiar to each item.
4. Write a summary that describes the information in the Venn diagram.

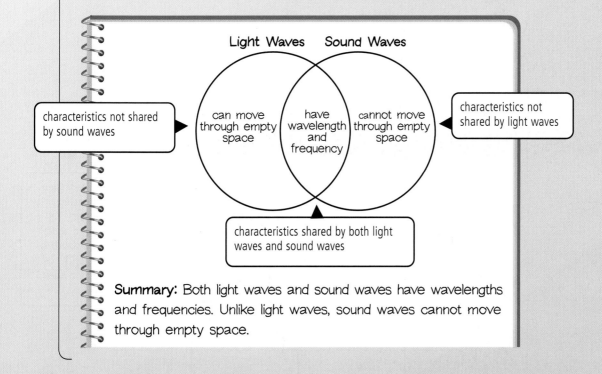

Summary: Both light waves and sound waves have wavelengths and frequencies. Unlike light waves, sound waves cannot move through empty space.

Vocabulary Strategies

Important terms are highlighted in this book. A definition of each term can be found in the sentence or paragraph where the term appears. You can also find definitions in the Glossary. Taking notes about vocabulary terms helps you understand and remember what you read.

Description Wheel

1. Write a term inside a circle.
2. Write words that describe the term on "spokes" attached to the circle.

When studying for a test with a friend, read the phrases on the spokes one at a time until your friend identifies the correct term.

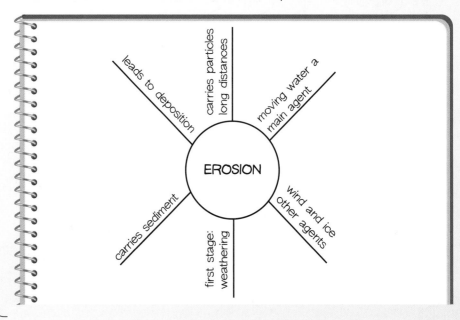

Four Square

1. Write a term in the center.
2. Write details in the four areas around the term.

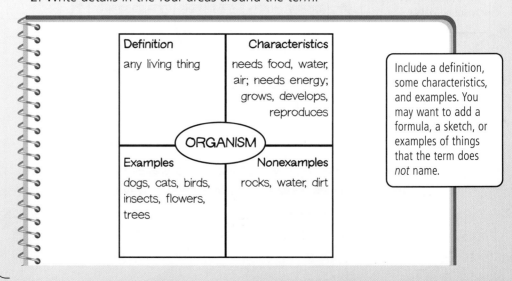

Include a definition, some characteristics, and examples. You may want to add a formula, a sketch, or examples of things that the term does *not* name.

Frame Game

1. Write a term in the center.

2. Frame the term with details.

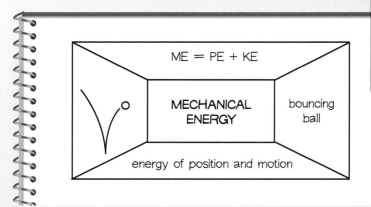

Include examples, descriptions, sketches, or sentences that use the term in context. Change the frame to fit each new term.

Magnet Word

1. Write a term on the magnet.

2. On the lines, add details related to the term.

You can also use phrases or sentences on the lines.

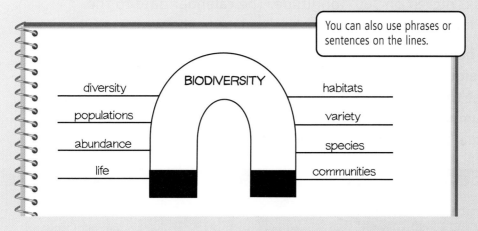

Word Triangle

1. Write a term and its definition in the bottom section.

2. In the middle section, write a sentence in which the term is used correctly.

3. In the top section, draw a small picture to illustrate the term.

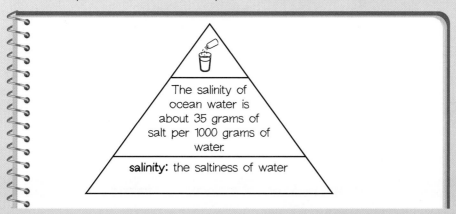

Appendix

Time Zones

Because Earth rotates, noon can occur in one location at the same moment that the Sun is setting in another location. To avoid confusion in transportation and communication, officials have divided Earth into 24 time zones. Within a time zone, clocks are set to the same time of day.

Time zones are centered on lines of longitude, but instead of running straight, their boundaries often follow political boundaries. The starting point for the times zones is centered on the prime meridian (0°). The time in this zone is generally called Greenwich Mean Time (GMT), but it is also called Universal Time (UT) by astronomers and Zulu Time (Z) by meteorologists. The International Date Line is centered on 180° longitude. The calendar date to the east of this line is one day earlier than the date to the west.

In the map below, each column of color represents one time zone. The color beige shows areas that do not match standard zones. The labels at the top show the times at noon GMT. Positive and negative numbers at the bottom show the difference between the local time in the zone and Greenwich Mean Time.

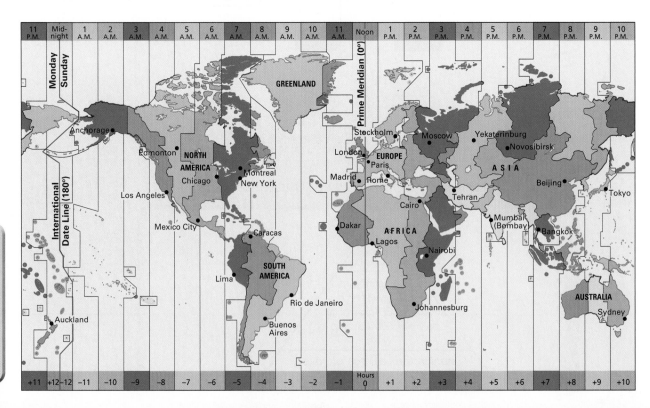

Characteristics of Planets

Some data about the planets and Earth's satellite, the Moon, are listed below. Some data, such as the tilt of Mercury and the mass of Pluto, are not known as well as other data. One astronomical unit (AU) is Earth's average distance from the Sun, or 149,597,870 kilometers. For comparison, Earth's mass is 5.97×10^{24} kilograms, and Earth's diameter is 12,756 kilometers.

Eccentricity is a measure of how flattened an ellipse is. An ellipse with an eccentricity of 0 is a circle. An ellipse with an eccentricity of 1 is completely flat.

Venus, Uranus, and Pluto rotate backward compared to Earth. If you use your left thumb as one of these planets' north pole, your fingers curve in the direction the planet turns.

Characteristics of Planets

Characteristic	Mercury	Venus	Earth	Mars	Jupiter	Saturn	Uranus	Neptune	Pluto	Moon
Mean distance from Sun (AU)	0.387	0.723	1.00	1.52	5.20	9.55	19.2	30.1	39.5	
Period of revolution (Earth years)	0.241 (88 Earth days)	0.615 (225 Earth days)	1.00	1.88	11.9	29.4	83.7	164	248	0.075 (27.3 Earth days)
Eccentricity of orbit	0.206	0.007	0.017	0.093	0.048	0.056	0.046	0.009	0.249	0.055
Diameter (Earth = 1)	0.382	0.949	1.00	0.532	11.21	9.45	4.01	3.88	0.180	0.272
Volume (Earth = 1)	0.06	0.86	1.00	0.15	1320	760	63	58	0.006	0.02
Period of rotation	58.6 Earth days	243 Earth days	23.9 hours	24.6 hours	9.93 hours	10.7 hours	17.2 hours	16.1 hours	6.39 Earth days	27.3 Earth days
Tilt of axis (°) (from perpendicular to orbit)	0.1 (approximate)	2.6	23.45	25.19	3.12	26.73	82.14	29.56	60.4	6.67
Mass (Earth = 1)	0.0553	0.815	1.00	0.107	318	95.2	14.5	17.1	0.002	0.0123
Mean density (g/cm³)	5.4	5.2	5.5	3.9	1.3	0.7	1.3	1.6	2	3.3

Seasonal Star Maps

Your view of the night sky changes as Earth orbits the Sun. Some constellations appear throughout the year, but others can be seen only during certain seasons. And over the course of one night, the constellations appear to move across the sky as Earth rotates.

When you go outside to view stars, give your eyes time to adjust to the darkness. Avoid looking at bright lights. If you need to look toward a bright light, preserve your night vision in one eye by keeping it closed.

The star maps on pages R55–R58 show parts of the night sky in different seasons. If you are using a flashlight to view the maps, you should attach a piece of red balloon over the lens. The balloon will dim the light and also give it a red color, which affects night vision less than other colors. The following steps will help you use the maps:

1. Stand facing north. To find this direction, use a compass or turn clockwise 90° from the location where the Sun set.

2. The top map for each season shows some constellations that appear over the northern horizon at 10 P.M. During the night, the constellations rotate in a circle around Polaris, the North Star.

3. Now turn so that you stand facing south. The bottom map for the season shows some constellations that appear over the southern horizon at 10 P.M.

WINTER SKY to the NORTH, *January 15*

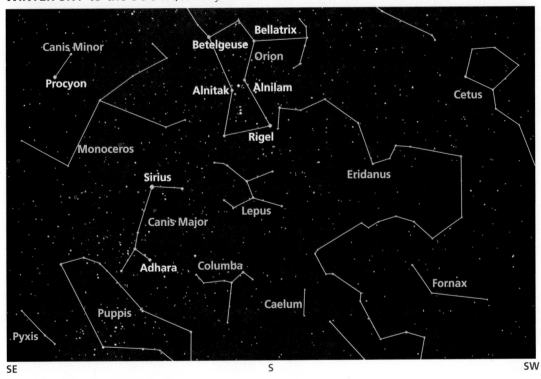

Cassiopeia

Polaris

Dubhe

Ursa Major

Cepheus

Ursa Minor

Kochab

Alioth

Mizar

Lacerta

Draco

Alkaid

Canes Venatici

Deneb

Cygnus

Eltanin

NW   N   NE

WINTER SKY to the SOUTH, *January 15*

Canis Minor

Bellatrix

Betelgeuse

Orion

Procyon

Cetus

Alnitak   Alnilam

Monoceros

Rigel

Sirius

Eridanus

Lepus

Canis Major

Adhara   Columba

Fornax

Puppis

Caelum

Pyxis

SE   S   SW

Seasonal Star Maps *continued*

SPRING SKY to the NORTH, *April 15*

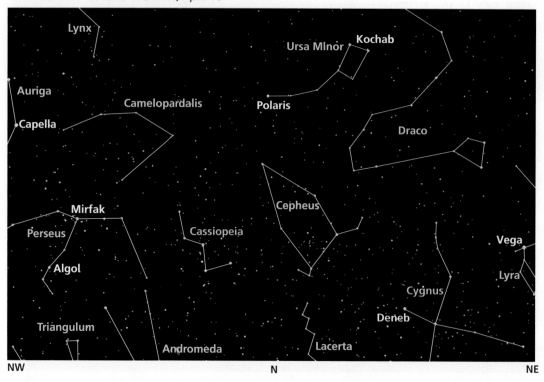

NW   N   NE

SPRING SKY to the SOUTH, *April 15*

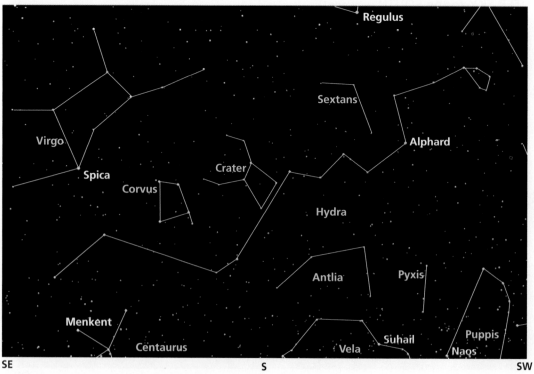

SE   S   SW

SUMMER SKY to the NORTH, *July 15*

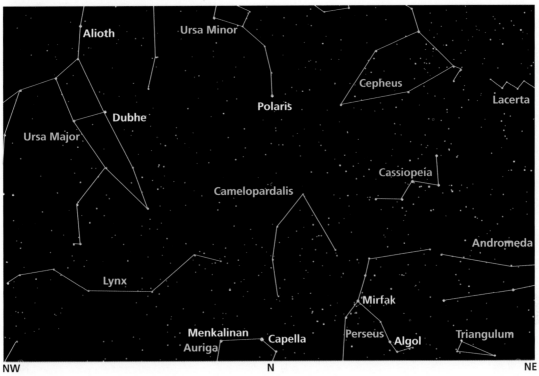

NW   N   NE

SUMMER SKY to the SOUTH, *July 15*

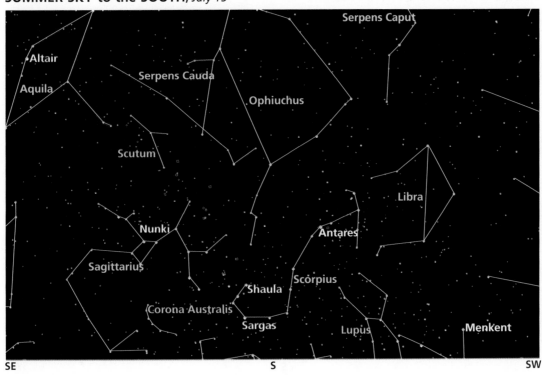

SE   S   SW

Seasonal Star Maps *continued*

AUTUMN SKY to the NORTH, *October 15*

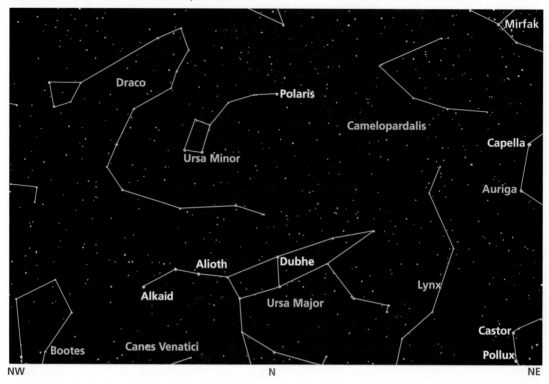

NW   N   NE

AUTUMN SKY to the SOUTH, *October 15*

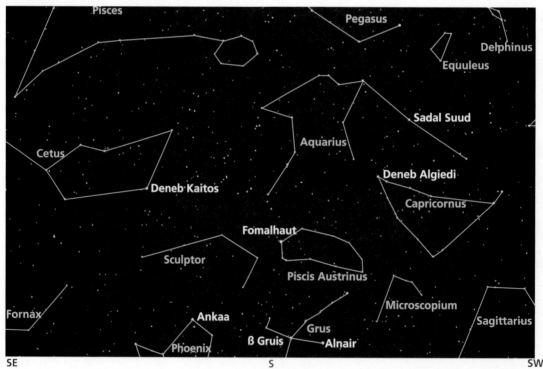

SE   S   SW

The Hertzsprung-Russell Diagram

The Hertzsprung-Russell (H-R) Diagram is a graph that shows stars plotted according to brightness and surface temperature. Most stars fall within a diagonal band called the main sequence. In the main-sequence stage of a star's life cycle, brightness is closely related to surface temperature. Red giant and red supergiant stars appear above the main sequence on the diagram. These stars are bright in relation to their surface temperatures because their huge surface areas give off a lot of light. Dim white dwarfs appear below the main sequence.

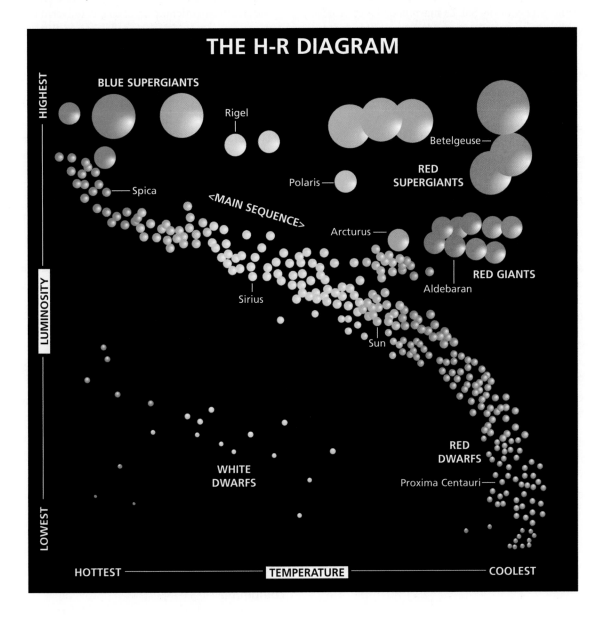

THE H-R DIAGRAM

BLUE SUPERGIANTS

Rigel

Betelgeuse

RED SUPERGIANTS

Polaris

Spica

MAIN SEQUENCE

Arcturus

Sirius

RED GIANTS

Aldebaran

Sun

HIGHEST

LUMINOSITY

LOWEST

WHITE DWARFS

RED DWARFS

Proxima Centauri

HOTTEST ——— TEMPERATURE ——— COOLEST

Glossary

A

asteroid
A small, solid, rocky body that orbits the Sun. Most asteroids orbit in a region between Mars and Jupiter called the asteroid belt. (p. 103)

asteroide Un pequeño cuerpo sólido y rocoso que orbita alrededor del Sol. La mayoría de los asteroides orbitan en una región entre Marte y Júpiter denominada cinturón de asteroides.

astronomical unit AU
Earth's average distance from the Sun, which is approximately 150 million kilometers (93 million mi). (p. 81)

unidad astronómica ua
La distancia promedio de la Tierra al Sol, la cual es de aproximadamente 150 millones de kilómetros (93 millones de millas).

atmosphere (AT-muh-SFEER)
The outer layer of gases of a large body in space, such as a planet or star; the mixture of gases that surrounds the solid Earth; one of the four parts of the Earth system. (p. xix)

atmósfera La capa externa de gases de un gran cuerpo que se encuentra en el espacio, como un planeta o una estrella; la mezcla de gases que rodea la Tierra sólida; una de las cuatro partes del sistema terrestre.

atom
The smallest particle of an element that has the chemical properties of that element. (p.xvii)

átomo La partícula más pequeña de un elemento que tiene las propiedades químicas de ese elemento.

axis of rotation
An imaginary line about which a turning body, such as Earth rotates. (p. 44)

eje de rotación Una línea imaginaria alrededor de la cual gira un cuerpo, como lo hace la Tierra.

B

big bang
The moment in time when the universe started to expand out of an extremely hot, dense state, according to scientific theory. (p. 138)

la gran explosión De acuerdo a la teoría científica, el momento en el tiempo en el cual el universo empezó a expandirse a partir de un estado extremadamente caliente y denso.

biosphere (BY-uh-SFEER)
All living organisms on Earth in the air, on the land, and in the waters; one of the four parts of the Earth system. (p. xix)

biosfera Todos los organismos vivos de la Tierra, en el aire, en la tierra y en las aguas; una de las cuatro partes del sistema de la Tierra.

black hole
The final stage of an extremely massive star, which is invisible because its gravity prevents any form of radiation from escaping. (p. 126)

hoyo negro La etapa final de una estrella de enorme masa, la cual es invisible porque su gravedad evita que cualquier tipo de radiación escape.

C

climate
The characteristic weather conditions in an area over a long period of time. (p. xxi)

clima Las condiciones meteorológicas características de un lugar durante un largo período de tiempo.

comet
A body that produces a coma of gas and dust; a small, icy body that orbits the Sun. (p. 104)

cometa Un cuerpo que produce una coma de gas y polvo; un cuerpo pequeño y helado que se mueve en órbita alrededor del Sol.

compound
A substance made up of two or more different types of atoms bonded together.

compuesto Una sustancia formada por dos o más diferentes tipos de átomos enlazados.

constellation

A group of stars that form a pattern in the sky. (p. 12)

constelación Un grupo de estrellas que forman un patrón en el cielo.

convection

The transfer of energy from place to place by the motion of heated gas or liquid; in Earth's mantle, convection is thought to transfer energy by the motion of solid rock, which when under great heat and pressure can move like a liquid. (p. 116)

convección La transferencia de energía de un lugar a otro por el movimiento de un líquido o gas calentado; se piensa que en el manto terrestre la convección transfiere energía mediante el movimiento de roca sólida, la cual puede moverse como un líquido cuando está muy caliente y bajo alta presión.

corona

The outer layer of the Sun's atmosphere. (p. 116)

corona La capa exterior de la atmósfera del Sol.

cycle

n. A series of events or actions that repeat themselves regularly; a physical and/or chemical process in which one material continually changes locations and/or forms. Examples include the water cycle, the carbon cycle, and the rock cycle.

v. To move through a repeating series of events or actions.

ciclo s. Una serie de eventos o acciones que se repiten regularmente; un proceso físico y/o químico en el cual un material cambia continuamente de lugar y/o forma. Ejemplos: el ciclo del agua, el ciclo del carbono y el ciclo de las rocas.

D

data

Information gathered by observation or experimentation that can be used in calculating or reasoning. *Data* is a plural word; the singular is *datum*.

datos Información reunida mediante observación o experimentación y que se puede usar para calcular o para razonar.

density

A property of matter representing the mass per unit volume.

densidad Una propiedad de la materia que representa la masa por unidad de volumen.

Doppler effect

A change in the observed frequency of a wave, occurring when the source of the wave or the observer is moving. Changes in the frequency of light are often measured by observing changes in wavelength, whereas changes in the frequency of sound are often detected as changes in pitch. (p. 136)

efecto Doppler Un cambio en la frecuencia observada de una onda que ocurre cuando la fuente de la onda o el observador están en movimiento. Los cambios en la frecuencia de la luz a menudo se miden observando los cambios en la longitud de onda, mientras que los cambios en la frecuencia del sonido a menudo se detectan como cambios en el tono.

E

eclipse

An event during which one object in space casts a shadow onto another. On Earth, a lunar eclipse occurs when the Moon moves through Earth's shadow, and a solar eclipse occurs when the Moon's shadow crosses Earth. (p. 63)

eclipse Un evento durante el cual un objeto en el espacio proyecta una sombra sobre otro. En la Tierra, un eclipse lunar ocurre cuando la Luna se mueve a través de la sombra de la Tierra, y un eclipse solar ocurre cuando la sombra de la Luna cruza la Tierra.

electromagnetic radiation

(ih-LEHK-troh-mag-NEHT-ihk)
Energy that travels across distances as certain types of waves. Types of electromagnetic radiation are radio waves, microwaves, infrared radiation, visible light, ultraviolet radiation, x-rays, and gamma rays. (p. 15)

radiación electromagnética Energía que viaja a través de las distancias en forma de ciertos tipos de ondas. Las ondas de radio, las microondas, la radiación infrarroja, la luz visible, la radiación ultravioleta, los rayos X y los rayos gama son tipos de radiación electromagnética.

element

A substance that cannot be broken down into a simpler substance by ordinary chemical changes. An element consists of atoms of only one type.

elemento Una sustancia que no puede descomponerse en otra sustancia más simple por medio de cambios químicos normales. Un elemento consta de átomos de un solo tipo.

ellipse

An oval or flattened circle. (p. 81)

elipse Un óvalo o círculo aplanado.

energy
The ability to do work or to cause a change. For example, the energy of a moving bowling ball knocks over pins; energy from food allows animals to move and to grow; and energy from the Sun heats Earth's surface and atmosphere, which causes air to move. (p. xv)

> **energía** La capacidad para trabajar o causar un cambio. Por ejemplo, la energía de una bola de boliche en movimiento tumba los pinos; la energía proveniente de su alimento permite a los animales moverse y crecer; la energía del Sol calienta la superficie y la atmósfera de la Tierra, lo que ocasiona que el aire se mueva.

equinox (EE-kwhu-NAHKS)
In an orbit, a position and time in which sunlight shines equally on the Northern Hemisphere and the Southern Hemisphere; a time of year when daylight and darkness are nearly equal for most of Earth. (p. 46)

> **equinoccio** En una órbita, la posición y el tiempo en los cuales la luz del Sol incide de la misma manera en el Hemisferio Norte y en el Hemisferio Sur; una época del año en la cual la luz del día y la oscuridad son casi iguales para la mayor parte de la Tierra.

evaporation
The process by which liquid changes into gas. (p. xv)

> **evaporación** El proceso por el cual un líquido se transforma en gas.

experiment
An organized procedure to study something under controlled conditions. (p. xxiv)

> **experimento** Un procedimiento organizado para estudiar algo bajo condiciones controladas.

F

force
A push or a pull; something that changes the motion of an object. (p. xvii)

> **fuerza** Un empuje o un jalón; algo que cambia el movimiento de un objeto.

fossil
A trace or the remains of a once-living thing from long ago. (p. xxi)

> **fósil** Un rastro o los restos de un organismo que vivió hace mucho tiempo.

friction
A force that resists the motion between two surfaces in contact. (p. xxi)

> **fricción** Una fuerza que resiste el movimiento entre dos superficies en contacto.

fusion
A process in which particles of an element collide and combine to form a heavier element, such as the fusion of hydrogen into helium that occurs in the Sun's core. (p. 116)

> **fusión** Un proceso en el cual las partículas de un elemento chocan y se combinan para formar un elemento más pesado, como la fusión de hidrógeno en helio que ocurre en el núcleo del Sol.

G

galaxy
Millions or billions of stars held together in a group by their own gravity. (p. 10)

> **galaxia** Millones o miles de millones de estrellas unidas en un grupo por su propia gravedad.

gas giant
A large planet that consists mostly of gases in a dense form. The four large planets in the outer solar system—Jupiter, Saturn, Uranus, and Neptune—are gas giants. (p. 94)

> **gigante de gas** Un planeta grande compuesto principalmente de gases en forma densa. Los cuatro planetas grandes en el sistema solar exterior—Júpiter, Saturno, Urano y Neptuno —son gigantes de gas.

geosphere (JEE-uh-SFEER)
All the features on Earth's surface—continents, islands, and seafloor—and everything below the surface—the inner and outer core and the mantle; one of the four parts of the Earth system. (p. xix)

> **geosfera** Todas las características de la superficie de la Tierra, es decir, continentes, islas y el fondo marino, y de todo bajo la superficie, es decir, el núcleo externo e interno y el manto; una de las cuatro partes del sistema de la Tierra.

gravity
The force that objects exert on each other because of their mass. (p. xvii)

> **gravedad** La fuerza que los objetos ejercen entre sí debido a su masa.

H

hydrosphere (HY-druh-SFEER)
All water on Earth—in the atmosphere and in the oceans, lakes, glaciers, rivers, streams, and underground reservoirs; one of the four parts of the Earth system. (p. xix)

> **hidrosfera** Toda el agua de la Tierra: en la atmósfera y en los océanos, lagos, glaciares, ríos, arroyos y depósitos subterráneos; una de las cuatro partes del sistema de la Tierra.

hypothesis
A tentative explanation for an observation or phenomenon. A hypothesis is used to make testable predictions. (p. xxiv)

> **hipótesis** Una explicación provisional de una observación o de un fenómeno. Una hipótesis se usa para hacer predicciones que se pueden probar.

I, J, K

impact crater
A round pit left behind on the surface of a planet or other body in space after a smaller object strikes the surface. (p. 32)

> **cráter de impacto** Un pozo circular en la superficie de un planeta u otro cuerpo en el espacio que se forma cuando un objeto más pequeño golpea la superficie.

L

lander
A craft designed to land on a planet's surface. (p. 28)

> **módulo de aterrizaje** Una nave diseñada para aterrizar en la superficie de un planeta.

law
In science, a rule or principle describing a physical relationship that always works in the same way under the same conditions. The law of conservation of energy is an example.

> **ley** En las ciencias, una regla o un principio que describe una relación física que siempre funciona de la misma manera bajo las mismas condiciones. La ley de la conservación de la energía es un ejemplo.

light-year
The distance light travels in one year, which is about 9.5 trillion kilometers (6 trillion mi). (p. 122)

> **año luz** La distancia que viaja la luz en un año, la cual es de casi 9.5 billones de kilómetros (6 billones de millas).

M

main sequence
The stage in which stars produce energy through the fusion of hydrogen into helium. (p. 126)

> **secuencia principal** La etapa en la cual las estrellas producen energía mediante la fusión de hidrógeno en helio.

mare (MAH-ray)
A large, dark plain of solidified lava on the Moon. The plural form of mare is maria (MAH-ree-uh). (p. 53)

> **mare** Una planicie grande y oscura de lava solidificada en la Luna. El plural de mare es maría.

mass
A measure of how much matter an object is made of.

> **masa** Una medida de la cantidad de materia de la que está compuesto un objeto.

matter
Anything that has mass and volume. Matter exists ordinarily as a solid, a liquid, or a gas. (p. xvii)

> **materia** Todo lo que tiene masa y volumen. Generalmente la materia existe como sólido, líquido o gas.

meteor
A brief streak of light produced by a small particle entering Earth's atmosphere at a high speed. (p. 105)

> **meteoro** Un breve rayo luminoso producido por una partícula pequeña que entra a la atmósfera de la Tierra a una alta velocidad.

meteorite
A small object from outer space that passes through Earth's atmosphere and reaches the surface. (p. 105)

> **meteorito** Un pequeño objeto del espacio exterior que pasa a través de la atmósfera de la Tierra y llega a la superficie.

molecule
A group of atoms that are held together by covalent bonds so that they move as a single unit.

> **molécula** Un grupo de átomos que están unidos mediante enlaces covalentes de tal manera que se mueven como una sola unidad.

N

nebula (NEHB-yuh-luh)
A cloud of gas and dust in space. Stars form in nebulae. (p. 125)

nebulosa Una nube de gas y polvo en el espacio. Las estrellas se forman en las nebulosas.

neutron star
A dense core that may be left behind after a higher-mass star explodes in a supernova. (p. 126)

estrella de neutrones Un núcleo denso que puede resultar después de que una estrella de mayor masa explota en una supernova.

O

orbit
n. The path of an object in space as it moves around another object due to gravity; for example, the Moon moves in an orbit around Earth. (p. 10)

v. To revolve around, or move in an orbit; for example, the Moon orbits Earth.

órbita s. La trayectoria de un objeto en el espacio a medida que se mueve alrededor de otro objeto debido a la gravedad; por ejemplo, la Luna se mueve en una órbita alrededor de la Tierra.

orbitar v. Girar alrededor de algo, o moverse en una órbita; por ejemplo, la Luna orbita la Tierra.

P

parallax
The apparent shift in the position of an object when viewed from different locations. (p. 123)

paralaje El cambio aparente en la posición de un objeto cuando se observa desde diferentes puntos.

penumbra
A region of lighter shadow that may surround an umbra; for example, the spreading cone of lighter shadow cast by a space object. (p. 63)

penumbra Una región de sombra más tenue que puede rodear a una umbra; por ejemplo, la sombra más tenue cónica proyectada por un objeto espacial.

probe
A spacecraft that is sent into a planet's atmosphere or onto a solid surface. (p. 29)

sonda espacial Una nave espacial enviada a la atmósfera de un planeta o a una superficie sólida.

Q

quasar
The very bright center of a distant galaxy. (p. 133)

quásar El centro muy brillante de una galaxia distante.

R

radiation (ray-dee-AY-shuhn)
Energy that travels across distances as certain types of waves. (p. xv)

radiación Energía que viaja a través de las distancias en forma de ciertos tipos de ondas.

revolution
The motion of one body around another, such as Earth in its orbit around the Sun; the time it takes an object to go around once. (p. 45)

revolución El movimiento de un cuerpo alrededor de otro, como la Tierra en su órbita alrededor del Sol; el tiempo que le toma a un objeto dar la vuelta una vez.

ring
In astronomy, a wide, flat zone of small particles that orbit around a planet's equator. (p. 97)

anillo En astronomía, una zona ancha y plana de pequeñas partículas que orbitan alrededor del ecuador de un planeta.

S

satellite
An object that orbits a more massive object. (p. 23)

satélite Un objeto que orbita un objeto de mayor masa.

season
One part of a pattern of temperature changes and other weather trends over the course of a year. Astronomical seasons are defined and caused by the position of Earth's axis relative to the direction of sunlight. (p. 46)

estación Una parte de un patrón de cambios de temperatura y otras tendencias meteorológicas en el curso de un año. Las estaciones astronómicas se definen y son causadas por la posición del eje de la Tierra en relación a la dirección de la luz del Sol.

solar system
The Sun and its family of orbiting planets, moons, and other objects. (p. 10)

sistema solar El Sol y su familia de planetas, lunas y otros objetos en órbita.

solar wind

A stream of electrically charged particles that flows out in all directions from the Sun's corona. (p. 119)

viento solar Una corriente de partículas eléctricamente cargadas que fluye hacia fuera de la corona del Sol en todas las direcciones.

solstice (SAHL-stihs)

In an orbit, a position and time during which one hemisphere gets its maximum area of sunlight, while the other hemisphere gets its minimum amount; the time of year when days are either longest or shortest, and the angle of sunlight reaches its maximum or minimum. (p. 46)

solsticio En una órbita, la posición y el tiempo durante los cuales un hemisferio obtiene su área máxima de luz del Sol, mientras que el otro hemisferio obtiene su cantidad mínima; la época del año en la cual los días son los más largos o los más cortos y el ángulo de la luz del Sol alcanza su máximo o su mínimo.

space station

A satellite in which people can live and work for long periods. (p. 24)

estación espacial Un satélite en el cual la gente puede vivir y trabajar durante períodos largos.

spectrum (SPEHK-truhm)

1. Radiation from a source separated into a range of wavelengths. 2. The range of colors that appears in a beam of visible light when it passes through a prism. See also electromagnetic radiation. (p. 16)

espectro 1. Radiación de una fuente separada en una gama de longitudes de onda. 2. La gama de colores que aparece en un haz de luz visible cuando éste pasa a través de un prisma. Ver también radiación electromagnética.

sunspot

A darker spot on the photosphere of the Sun. A sunspot appears dark because it is cooler than the surrounding area. (p. 118)

mancha solar Una mancha oscura en la fotosfera del Sol. Una mancha solar se ve oscura porque es más fría que el área que la rodea.

system

A group of objects or phenomena that interact. A system can be as simple as a rope, a pulley, and a mass. It also can be as complex as the interaction of energy and matter in the four spheres of the Earth system.

sistema Un grupo de objetos o fenómenos que interactúan. Un sistema puede ser algo tan sencillo como una cuerda, una polea y una masa. También puede ser algo tan complejo como la interacción de la energía y la materia en las cuatro esferas del sistema de la Tierra.

T

technology

The use of scientific knowledge to solve problems or engineer new products, tools, or processes.

tecnología El uso de conocimientos científicos para resolver problemas o para diseñar nuevos productos, herramientas o procesos.

tectonics

The processes in which the motion of hot material under a crust changes the crust of a space body. Earth has a specific type of tectonics called plate tectonics. (p. 86)

tectónica Los procesos en los cuales el movimiento del material caliente bajo una corteza cambia la corteza de un cuerpo espacial. La Tierra tiene un tipo específico de tectónica denominado tectónica de placas.

telescope

A device that gather visible light or another form of electromagnetic radiation. (p. 17)

telescopio Un aparato que reúne luz visible u otra forma de radiación electromagnética.

terrestrial planet

Earth or a planet similar to Earth that has a rocky surface. The four planets in the inner solar system—Mercury, Venus, Earth, and Mars—are terrestrial planets. (p. 85)

planeta terrestre La Tierra o un planeta parecido a la Tierra que tiene una superficie rocosa. Los cuatro planetas en el sistema solar interior — Mercurio, Venus, la Tierra y Marte — son planetas terrestres.

theory

In science, a set of widely accepted explanations of observations and phenomena. A theory is a well-tested explanation that is consistent with all available evidence.

teoría En las ciencias, un conjunto de explicaciones de observaciones y fenómenos que es ampliamente aceptado. Una teoría es una explicación bien probada que es consecuente con la evidencia disponible.

U

umbra

The dark, central region of a shadow, such as the cone of complete shadow cast by an object. (p. 63)

umbra La región central y oscura de una sombra, como la sombra completa cónica proyectada por un objeto.

universe
Space and all the matter and energy in it. (p. 10)

> **universo** El espacio y toda la materia y energía que hay dentro de él.

V

variable
Any factor that can change in a controlled experiment, observation, or model. (p. R30)

> **variable** Cualquier factor que puede cambiar en un experimento controlado, en una observación o en un modelo.

volcanism
The process of molten material moving from a space body's hot interior onto its surface. (p. 86)

> **vulcanismo** El proceso del movimiento de material fundido del interior caliente de un cuerpo espacial a su superficie.

volume
An amount of three-dimensional space, often used to describe the space that an object takes up.

> **volumen** Una cantidad de espacio tridimensional; a menudo se usa este término para describir el espacio que ocupa un objeto.

W, X, Y, Z

wavelength
The distance between one peak and the next peak on a wave. (p. 16)

> **longitud de onda** La distancia entre una cresta y la siguiente cresta en una onda.

Index

Page numbers for definitions are printed in **boldface** type.
Page numbers for illustrations, maps, and charts are printed in *italics*.

INDEX

INDEX

W

X, Y, Z

Acknowledgments

Photography

Cover © David Nunuk/Photo Researchers; **i** © David Nunuk/Photo Researchers; **iii** *left (top to bottom)* Photograph of James Trefil by Evan Cantwell; Photograph of Rita Ann Calvo by Joseph Calvo; Photograph of Linda Carnine by Amilcar Cifuentes; Photograph of Sam Miller by Samuel Miller; *right (top to bottom)* Photograph of Kenneth Cutler by Kenneth A. Cutler; Photograph of Donald Steely by Marni Stamm; Photograph of Vicky Vachon by Redfern Photographics; **vi** © Roger Ressmeyer/Corbis; **vii** Courtesy of NASA/JPL/Caltech; **ix** Photographs by Sharon Hoogstraten; **xiv–xv** Doug Scott/age fotostock; **xvi–xvii** © Aflo Foto Agency; **xviii–ix** © Tim Fitzharris/Masterfile; **xx–xxi** Ben Margot/AP/Wide World Photos; **xxii** © Vince Streano/Corbis; **xxiii** © Roger Ressmeyer/Corbis; **xxiv** *left* University of Florida Lightning Research Laboratory; *center* © Roger Ressmeyer/Corbis; **xxv** *center* © Mauro Fermariello/Science Researchers; *bottom* © Alfred Pasieka/Photo Researchers; **xxvi-xxvii** © Stocktrek/Corbis; *center* NOAA; **xxvii** *top* © Alan Schein Photography/Corbis; *right* Vaisala Oyj, Finland; **xxxii** © The Chedd-Angier Production Company; **2–3** © Charles O'Rear/Corbis; **3** *top right* © D. Nunuk/Photo Researchers; **4** © The Chedd-Angier Production Company; **4–5** © David Parker/Photo Researchers; **5** *top center* NASA/JPL; **6–7** NASA; **7, 9** Photographs by Sharon Hoogstraten; **11** Johnson Space Center/NASA; **12** Photograph by Sharon Hoogstraten; **13** *top* © Roger Ressmeyer/Corbis; *bottom* Photograph by Sharon Hoogstraten; **15** Photograph by Sharon Hoogstraten; **16** *center left* Kapteyn Laboratorium/Photo Researchers; *center* National Optical Astronomy Observatories/Photo Researchers; *center right* A. Wilson (UMD) et al., CXC/NASA; **18** © Roger Ressmeyer/Corbis; **19** *top left* NASA Johnson Space Center; *top right* © STScl/NASA/Photo Researchers; **20** *top left* © ImageState-Pictor/PictureQuest; **20–21, 22** Photographs by Sharon Hoogstraten; **23** *bottom, inset* NASA; **24** Courtesy of NASA/JSC; **25** *top* NASA; *bottom* Photograph by Sharon Hoogstraten; **27** Photograph by Bill Ingalls/NASA; **30** *left, inset* Chris Butler/Photo Researchers; **31** NASA; **32** Courtesy of V.R. Sharpton University of Alaska-Fairbanks and the Lunar and Planetary Institute; **33** Photograph by Sharon Hoogstraten; **34** NASA; **35** *background* © Jan Tove Johansson/Image State-Pictor/PictureQuest; *left inset* Andy Fyon, Ontariowildflower.com (Division of Professor Beaker's Learning Labs); *right inset* NASA; **36** *top* Photograph by Sharon Hoogstraten; *center* © Roger Ressmeyer/Corbis; *bottom* NASA; **40–41** © Roger Ressmeyer/Corbis; **41** *top right, center right* Photographs by Sharon Hoogstraten; *bottom right* NASA Goddard Space Flight Center; **43** *left* NASA; *right* Photograph by Sharon Hoogstraten; **44** *top* © 2003 The Living Earth Inc.; *bottom* Photograph by Sharon Hoogstraten; **45** Photograph by Sharon Hoogstraten; **47** NASA/JSC; **49** © Arnulf Husmo/Getty Images; **50** *top* © Christian Perret/jump; *bottom left, bottom right* Photograph by Sharon Hoogstraten; **51, 52** Photographs by Sharon Hoogstraten; **53** Courtesy of NASA and the Lunar and Planetary Institute; **54** USGS Flagstaff, Arizona; **55** *top right* Photograph by Sharon Hoogstraten; *bottom right* NASA; *right inset* NASA and the Lunar and Planetary Institute; **58** Photograph by Steve Irvine; **59** © DiMaggio/Kalish/Corbis; **61** *background* Lunar Horizon View/NASA; **62** Photograph by Sharon Hoogstraten; **63** *top* © Roger Ressmeyer/Corbis; *bottom* Photograph by Jean-Francois Guay; **64** *center* NASA/Getty Images; *bottom left* © Fred Espenak; **65** *top* © Jeff Greenberg/MRP/Photo Researchers; *bottom* © 1999 Ray Coleman/Photo Researchers; **67** *top left* © Peter Duke; *right inset* © David Parker/Photo Researchers; *bottom left* Public Domain; *bottom center* Barlow Aerial Photography, Ignacio, CO; **68** *top left* © 2003 The Living Earth, Inc.; *center left* Photograph courtesy of NASA and the Lunar and Planetary Institute; **70** *left* USGS Flagstaff, Arizona; *right* NASA Goddard Space Flight Center; **72** Courtesy of Adler Planetarium & Astronomy Museum, Chicago, Illinois; **73** *top left* © Stapleton/Corbis; *center* © Science Museum/Science & Society Picture Library; *right* Provided by Roger Bell, University of Maryland, and Michael Briley, University of Wisconsin, Oshkosh; *bottom* Courtesy of Adler Planetarium & Astronomy Museum, Chicago, Illinois; **74** *top left* © Harvard College Observatory/Photo Researchers; *top right* Robert Williams and the Hubble Deep Field Team (STScl) and NASA; *bottom* © Fermi National Accelerator Laboratory/Photo Researchers; **75** *top* Ann Feild (STScl); *bottom* © NASA/Photo Researchers; **76–77** Courtesy of NASA/JPL/University of Arizona;

未

77 *top right, center right* Photographs by Sharon Hoogstraten; **79, 82** Photographs by Sharon Hoogstraten; **83** *left* Photo © Calvin J. Hamilton; *right* Courtesy of NASA/JPL/Caltech; **84** NASA; **85** *top* Photograph by Sharon Hoogstraten; *bottom* Johnson Space Center NASA; **87** *background* Mark Robinson/Mariner 10/NASA; *top right* NASA; *top left* © Walt Anderson/Visuals Unlimited; *bottom left* NASA/ JPL/Malin Space Science Systems; **88** Photograph by Sharon Hoogstraten; **89** *top* USGS; *bottom* Courtesy of NASA/JPL/ Northwestern University; **90** *top, center, bottom* NASA; **91** NASA/JSC; **92** Courtesy of NASA/JPL/Caltech; **93** *left* Courtesy of NASA/JPL/Malin Space Science Systems; *right* MAP-A-Planet/NASA; *right inset* NASA/Goddard Space Flight Center Scientific Visualization Studio; **94, 95** Courtesy of NASA/JPL/Caltech; **96** *top* Courtesy of NASA/JPL/Caltech; *bottom* Photograph by Sharon Hoogstraten; **97** *top* NASA; *bottom* NASA and the Hubble Heritage Team (STScI/AURA); **98** *top* E. Karkoschka(LPL) and NASA; *bottom* © Calvin J. Hamilton; **99** *top* Courtesy of NASA/JPL/Caltech; *center* NASA; **100** near.jhuapl.edu; **101** Hubble Space Telescope, STScI-PR96-09a/NASA; **102** *top left, inset* NASA; *bottom left* Courtesy of NASA/JPL/Caltech; *bottom left inset* NASA; *top right* © NASA/ JPL/Photo Researchers; *top right inset, bottom right, bottom right inset* NASA; **103** Courtesy of NASA/JPL/Caltech; **104** *background* © 1997 Jerry Lodriguss; *right* Courtesy of NASA/JPL/ Caltech; **105** Fred R. Conrad/The New York Times; **106** *top left* © James L. Amos/Corbis; *bottom left* Photograph by Sharon Hoogstraten; **107** Photograph by Sharon Hoogstraten; **108** *top* NASA; *bottom* Courtesy of NASA/JPL/Caltech; **112–113** David Malin Images/Anglo-Australian Observatory; **113** *top left* © Jerry Schad/Photo Researchers; *center left* Photograph by Sharon Hoogstraten; **115** Photograph by Sharon Hoogstraten; **117** Photograph by Jay M. Paschoff, Bryce A. Babcock, Stephan Martin, Wendy Carlos, and Daniel B. Seaton © Williams College; **118** *left* © John Chumack/Photo Researchers; *right* © NASA/Photo Researchers; **119** © Patrick J. Endres/Alaskaphotographics.com; **120** *top* © Dave Robertson/Masterfile; *left bottom, right bottom* Photograph by Sharon Hoogstraten; **121, 122, 123** Photographs by Sharon Hoogstraten; **125** *top* © Dorling Kindersley; *bottom* ESA and J. Hester (ASU),NASA; **126** J. Hester et al./NASA/CXC/ASU; **127** Hubble Heritage Team/AURA/STScI/NASA; **129** © MPIA-HD, Birkle, Slawik/Photo Researchers; **130** Photograph by Sharon Hoogstraten; **131** *top* Allan Morton/Dennis Milon/Photo Researchers; *bottom* Photograph by Sharon Hoogstraten; **132** David Malin Images /Anglo-Australian Observatory; **133** Walter Jaffe/Leiden Observatory, Holland Ford/JHU/STScI, and NASA; **134** *left* NASA and Hubble Heritage Team (STScI); *center* NASA, H. Ford (JHU), G. Illingworth (UCSC/LO), M. Clampin (STScI), G. Hartig (STScI), the ACS Science Team, and ESA; **135** Photograph by Sharon Hoogstraten; **136** © Jason Ware; **138** Photograph by Sharon Hoogstraten; **139** N. Benitez (JHU), T. Broadhurst (The Hebrew University), H. Ford (JHU), M. Clampin (STScI), G. Hartig (STScI), G. Illingworth (UCO/Lick Observatory), the AGS Science Team and ESA/NASA; **140** *top* David Malin Images/Anglo-Australian Observatory; *bottom* N. Benitez (JHU), T. Broadhurst (The Hebrew University), H. Ford (JHU), M. Clampin (STScI), G. Hartig (STScI), G. Illingworth (UCO/Lick Observatory), the AGS Science Team and ESA/NASA; **142** *left* Hubble Heritage Team (AURA/STScI/NASA); *right* Anglo-Australian Observatory/David Malin Images; **R28** © Photodisc/Getty Images.

Illustrations and Maps

Accurate Art Inc. **106**
Julian Baum **57, 117, 127, 128, 131, 140**
Peter Bull/Wildlife Art Ltd. **26, 27, 47, 48, 68**
Bill Cigliano **67, 137**
Steve Cowden **48**
Stephen Durke **12, 14, 18**
David A. Hardy **11, 32, 80, 83, 95, 108**
Mapquest.com, Inc. **64**
Dan Maas/Maas Digital **28, 36**
Dan Stuckenschneider **17, 36, R11–R19, R22, R32**
Ron Wood/Wood Ronsaville Harlin **56, 68**